P9-CAA-820

# Polish
## Phrase Book
## &
## Dictionary

**Berlitz Publishing**
New York      Munich      Singapore

Contacting the Editors
Every effort has been made to provide accurate information in this publication, but changes are inevitable. The publisher cannot be responsible for any resulting loss, inconvenience or injury. We would appreciate it if readers would call our attention to any errors or outdated information. We also welcome your suggestions; if you come across a relevant expression not in our phrase book, please contact us: Berlitz Publishing, 193 Morris Avenue, Springfield, NJ 07081, USA. Email: comments@berlitzbooks.com

First Printing: December 2007
Printed in Singapore

Publishing Director: Sheryl Olinsky Borg
Senior Editor/Project Manager: Lorraine Sova
Translation: Quendi Language Services
Cover Design: Claudia Petrilli
Interior Design: Derrick Lim, Juergen Bartz
Production Manager: Elizabeth Gaynor
Cover Photo: © OJPHOTOS/Alamy
Interior Photos: p. 12 © Studio Fourteen/ Brand X Pictures/ AgeFotostock; p. 17 © Polish National Bank; p. 20 © Pixtal/ Agefotostock; p. 34-35 © Wikipedia Commons/GNU Free Documentation License; p. 40 © Corbis/fotosearch.com; p. 48 © Ryan McVay/Photodisc/ Agefotostock; p. 54, 69 © Quendi Language Services; p. 57 © Stockbyte Photography/2002-07 Veer Incorporated; p. 78 © Javier Larrea/Pixtal/Age Fotostock; p. 82 © Netfalls/2003-2007 Shutterstock, Inc.; p. 102 © Dariusz Zaród Photoagency.com.pl; p. 109 © image100/ Corbis; p. 112 © Dominik Dabrowski/2003-2007 Shutterstock, Inc.; p. 114, 117 © 2007 Jupiterimages Corporation; p. 124 © Roman Milert /2007 iStock International Inc.; p. 132 © 2007 Jupiterimages Corporation; p. 141 © Jupiterimages/Brand X/Corbis; p. 143 © Stockbyte/Fotosearch.com; p. 146 © Corbis/2006 JupiterImages Corporation; p. 150, 160, 170 © 2007 Jupiterimages Corporation

# *Contents*

## *Survival*

## Food

## People

# Fun

# Special Needs

## Resources

## Dictionary

# *Pronunciation*

This section is designed to familiarize you with the sounds of Polish using our simplified phonetic transcription. You'll find the pronunciation of the Polish letters and sounds explained below, together with their imitated equivalents. To use this system, found throughout the phrase book, simply read the pronunciation as if it were English, noting any special rules below.

Underlined letters indicate that the syllable should be stressed. In Polish, stress falls on the penultimate syllable: **au<u>to</u>bus**, **<u>szko</u>ła**. In some words of foreign origin (mostly Latin and Greek), stress is assigned to the third syllable from the end of the word: **uni<u>wer</u>sytet**

## Consonants/Consonant Clusters

| Letter | Approximate Pronunciation | Symbol | Example | Pronunciation |
|--------|---------------------------|--------|---------|---------------|
| c | like ts in fits | ts | cały | <u>tsah</u>-wyh |
| ć, ci | a soft, very short version of chee in cheese | ch' | cień | ch'yen'* |
| cz | like ch in church but harder | ch | czapka | <u>chahp</u>-kah |
| dz | like ds in beds | dz | dzwonek | <u>dzvoh</u>-nehk |
| drz, dż | like j in jam | dj | drzwi | djvee |
| dź, dzi | like ge in genius | dj' | dzień | dj'yen' |
| h, ch | hard, like the ch in Scottish loch | h | chleb | hlehp |
| j | like y in yes | y | jutro | <u>yuh</u>-troh |
| ł | like w in win | w | łóżko | <u>wuhzh</u>-koh |
| ń, ni | like ni in onion | n' | nie | n'yeh |

* The apostrophe (') in phonetics indicates a softening of the sound.

| r | rolled, distinct at the end of words | r | rower | <u>roh</u>-vehr |
| sz | like sh in shot but harder | sh | szkoła | <u>shkoh</u>-wah |
| ś, si | soft, very short version of shee in sheep | sh' | śmieci | <u>sh'myeh</u>-ch'ee |
| w | like v in very | v | woda | <u>voh</u>-dah |
| ź, zi | like s in pleasure but softer | zh' | źródło | <u>zh'ruhd</u>-woh |
| ż, rz | like s in pleasure but harder | zh | żaba | <u>zhah</u>-bah |

The letters b, d, f, k, l, m, n, p, s, t, z are pronounced approximately as in English.

## Vowels

| Letter | Approximate Pronunciation | Symbol | Example | Pronunciation |
|---|---|---|---|---|
| a | like a in father | ah | dach | dahh |
| e | like e in ten | eh | bez | behs |
| i | like ee in keen | ee | kino | <u>kee</u>-noh |
| o | like o in so | oh | okno | <u>ohk</u>-noh |
| u, ó | like u in put | uh | dół | duhw |
| y | like i in fit | yh | buty | <u>boo</u>-tyh |
| ą | 1. nasal, like an in fiancé, at the end of a word | 1. ohm | 1. są | 1. sohm |
| | 2. pronounced ohn before a consonant | 2. ohn | 2. kąt | 2. kohnt |

| | 3. pronounced ohm before b and p | 3. ohm | 3. ząb | 3. zohmb |
|---|---|---|---|---|
| ę | 1. ehn before a consonant | 1. ehn | 1. ręka | 1. <u>rehn</u>-kah |
| | 2. ehm before b and p | 2. ehm | 2. kępa | 2. <u>kehm</u>-pah |
| | 3. eh when final in a word | 3. eh | 3. tę | 3. teh |

Polish is a language with a long history. Like most other European languages, it has its origin in Sanskrit and is part of the Indo-European group. It is one of 14 Slavic languages.

Polish is a phonetic language—there is a good correlation of sound to spelling—and its pronunciation is much more systematic than that of English.

# *How to Use This Book*

These essential phrases can also be heard on the audio CD.

Sometimes you see two alternatives in italics, separated by a slash. Choose the one that's right for your situation.

## Essential

| | |
|---|---|
| I'm here on *vacation [holiday]/ business*. | **Przyjechałem♂/Przyjechałam♀ tutaj** *na wakacje/służbowo.* pshyh·yeh·<u>hah</u>·wehm♂/ pshyh·yeh·<u>hah</u>·wahm♀ <u>tuh</u>·tahy *nah vah·<u>kahts</u>·yeh/swuhzh·<u>boh</u>·voh* |
| I'm going to... | **Jadę do...** <u>yah</u>·deh doh... |
| I'm staying at the...Hotel. | **Zatrzymałem♂/Zatrzymałam♀ się w Hotelu...** zah·tshyh·<u>mah</u>·wehm♂/ zah·tshyh·<u>mah</u>·wahm♀ sh'yeh fhoh·<u>teh</u>·luh... |

## You May See...

| | |
|---|---|
| ŁODZIE RATUNKOWE | life boats |
| KAPOKI | life jackets |
| POKŁAD | deck |

## Ticketing

| | |
|---|---|
| When's...to Cracow? | **O której jest...do Krakowa?** oh <u>ktuh</u>·rehy yehst...doh kran·<u>koh</u>·vah |
| – the (first) bus | **– (pierwszy) autobus** (<u>pyehr</u>·shyh) ahw·<u>toh</u>·buhs |
| – the (next) flight | **– (następny) samolot** (nahs·<u>tehm</u>·pnyh) sah·<u>moh</u>·loht |
| – the (last) train | **– (ostatni) pociag** (ohs·<u>taht</u>·n'ee) <u>poh</u>·ch'yonk |

Words you may see are shown in *You May See* boxes.

Any of the words or phrases preceded by dashes can be plugged into the sentence above.

Polish phrases appear in red.

Read the simplified pronunciation as if it were English. For more on pronunciation, see page 7.

## ATM, Bank and Currency Exchange

| | |
|---|---|
| I'd like to change money. | **Chciałbym♂/Chciałabym♀ wymienić pieniądze.** hch'yahw·byhm♂/hch'yah·<u>wah</u>·byhm♀ vyh·<u>myeh</u>·n'eech' pyeh·<u>n'yohn</u>·dzeh |
| What's the exchange rate? | **Jaki jest kurs wymiany?** yah·kee vehst kurs vyh·<u>myah</u>·nyh |
| How much is the fee? | **Jaka jest prowizja?** |

▶ For numbers, see page 168.

When different gender forms apply, the masculine form is followed by ♂; feminine by ♀.

The arrow indicates a cross reference where you'll find related phrases.

Information boxes contain relevant country, culture and language tips.

*i*

When addressing a man in a formal situation, use **pan** (sir); when addressing a woman, use **pani** (ma'am or madam). Throughout this phrase book **pan** is used for the sake of simplicity. When speaking to a woman, be sure to substitute **pani** for **pan**.

## You May Hear...

*Bilet/Paszport*, **proszę.** <u>bee</u>·leht/<u>pahsh</u>·pohrt <u>proh</u>·sheh

Your *ticket/ passport*, please.

Expressions you may hear are shown in *You May Hear* boxes.

Color-coded side bars identify each section of the book.

11

# ▼ Survival

# Arrival and Departure

## Essential

| | |
|---|---|
| I'm here on *vacation [holiday]/business*. | **Przyjechałem♂/Przyjechałam♀ tutaj *na wakacje/służbowo*.** pshyh·yeh·<u>hah</u>·wehm♂/pshyh·yeh·<u>hah</u>·wahm♀ tuh·tahy nah vah·<u>kahts</u>·yeh/swuhzh·<u>boh</u>·voh |
| I'm going to... | **Jadę do...** <u>yah</u>·deh doh... |
| I'm staying at the...Hotel. | **Zatrzymałem♂/Zatrzymałam♀ się w Hotelu...** zah·tshyh·<u>mah</u>·wehm♂/zah·tshyh·<u>mah</u>·wahm♀ sh'yeh fhoh·<u>teh</u>·luh... |

## You May Hear...

| | |
|---|---|
| *Bilet/Paszport*, proszę. <u>bee</u>·leht/<u>pahsh</u>·pohrt <u>proh</u>·sheh | Your *ticket/passport*, please. |
| Jaki jest cel pana wizyty? <u>yah</u>·kee yehst tsehl <u>pah</u>·nah·vee·<u>zyh</u>·tyh | What's the purpose of your visit? |
| Gdzie pan się zatrzymał? gdj'yeh pahn sh'yeh zah·<u>tshyh</u>·mahw | Where are you staying? |
| Jak długo pan tu będzie? yahk <u>dwuh</u>·goh pahn tuh <u>behn</u>·dj'ye | How long are you staying? |
| Z kim pan tutaj jest? skeem pahn <u>tuh</u>·tahy yehst | Who are you here with? |

When addressing a man in a formal situation, use **pan** (sir); when addressing a woman, use **pani** (ma'am or madam). Throughout this phrase book **pan** is used for the sake of simplicity. When speaking to a woman, be sure to substitute **pani** for **pan**.

## Passport Control and Customs

I'm just passing through.

**Jestem tu tylko przejazdem.** <u>yeh</u>·stehm tuh <u>tyhl</u>·koh psheh·<u>yahz</u>·dehm

I would like to declare...

**Chciałbym♂/Chciałabym♀ zadeklarować...** hch'<u>yahw</u>·byhm♂/hch'yah·<u>wah</u>·byhm♀ zah·dehk·lah·<u>roh</u>·vahch'...

I have nothing to declare.

**Nie mam nic do oclenia.** n'yeh mahm n'eets doh ohts·<u>leh</u>·n'yah

### You May Hear...

**Czy ma pan coś do oclenia?** chyh mah pahn tsohsh' doh ohts·<u>leh</u>·n'yah

Anything to declare?

**Musi pan zapłacić za to cło.** <u>muh</u>·sh'ee pahn zah·<u>pwa</u>·ch'eech' zah toh tswoh

You must pay duty on this.

**Proszę otworzyć *torbę/walizkę.*** <u>proh</u>·sheh oht·<u>foh</u>·zhyhch' *<u>tohr</u>·beh/vah·<u>lees</u>·keh*

Please open your *bag/suitcase.*

### You May See...

| | |
|---|---|
| **ODPRAWA CELNA** | customs |
| **TOWARY BEZCŁOWE** | duty-free goods |
| **TOWARY DO OCLENIA** | goods to declare |
| **NIC DO OCLENIA** | nothing to declare |
| **KONTROLA PASZPORTOWA** | passport control |
| **POLICJA** | police |
| **DLA PERSONELU** | staff only |

# Money and Banking

## Essential

| Where's...? | **Gdzie jest...?** gdj'yeh yehst... |
|---|---|
| – the ATM | **– bankomat** bahn·<u>koh</u>·maht |
| – the bank | **– bank** bahnk |
| – the currency exchange office | **– kantor** <u>kahn</u>·tohr |
| When does the bank *open/close*? | **O której** *otwierają/zamykają* **bank?** oh <u>ktuh</u>·rehy *oht·fyeh·<u>rah</u>·yohm/ zah·myh·<u>kah</u>·yohm* bahnk |
| I'd like to change *dollars/pounds* into zlotys. | **Chciałbym♂/Chciałabym♀ wymienić** *dolary/funty* **na złotówki.** hch'yahw·byhm♂/ hch'yah·wah·byhm♀ vyh·<u>myeh</u>·n'eech' *do·<u>lah</u>·ryh/<u>fuhn</u>·tyh* nah zwoh·<u>tuhf</u>·kee |
| I want to cash some travelers checks [cheques]. | **Chcę zrealizować czeki podróżne.** htseh zreh·ah·lee·<u>zoh</u>·vahch' <u>cheh</u>·kee pohd·<u>ruhzh</u>·neh |

Prices in Poland generally include **VAT** (sales tax). The price you will pay is the price provided on the sales tag.

## ATM, Bank and Currency Exchange

| I'd like to change money. | **Chciałbym♂/Chciałabym♀ wymienić pieniądze.** <u>hch'yahw</u>·byhm♂/hch'yah·<u>wah</u>·byhm♀ vyh·<u>myeh</u>·n'eech' pyeh·<u>n'yohn</u>·dzeh |
|---|---|
| What's the exchange rate? | **Jaki jest kurs wymiany?** <u>yah</u>·kee yehst kurs vyh·<u>myah</u>·nyh |

| | |
|---|---|
| How much is the fee? | **Jaka jest prowizja?** <u>yah</u>·kah yest proh·<u>veez</u>·yah |
| I've lost my *travelers checks [cheques]/credit cards.* | **Zgubiłem♂/Zgubiłam♀ *czeki podróżne/ karty kredytowe.*** zguh·<u>bee</u>·wehm♂/ zguh·<u>bee</u>·wahm♀ *<u>cheh</u>·kee pohd·<u>ruhzh</u>·neh/ <u>kahr</u>·tyh kreh·dyh·<u>toh</u>·veh* |
| My card was stolen. | **Ukradli mi kartę.** uh·<u>krahd</u>·lee mee <u>kahr</u>·teh |
| My card doesn't work. | **Moja karta nie działa.** <u>moh</u>·yah <u>kahr</u>·tah n'yeh <u>dj'yah</u>·wah |

▶ For numbers, see page 168.

## You May See...

| | |
|---|---|
| **WŁÓŻ KARTĘ** | insert credit card |
| **WYBIERZ JĘZYK** | select language |
| **WPROWADŹ PIN** | enter your PIN |
| **WCIŚNIJ KLAWISZ** | press key |
| **WYPŁATA GOTÓWKI** | cash withdrawal |
| **INNA KWOTA** | different amount |
| **STAN RACHUNKU** | balance inquiry |
| **WOLNE ŚRODKI** | available balance |
| **AKCEPTUJ** | enter |
| **ANULUJ** | cancel |
| **POPRAW** | clear |
| **KONTYNUUJ** | next |
| **KONIEC** | end |
| **POTWIERDZENIE** | receipt |

*i* Banks are usually open between 8 a.m. and 6 p.m. When changing cash and travelers checks, you will need to show your passport. Numerous **kantory** (currency exchange offices) provide exchange services and usually have a better exchange rate than banks. Some large hotels will exchange cash and travelers checks for their guests. In cities and larger towns you'll find **bankomaty**, ATMs that accept various international bank and credit cards. Travelers checks are not currently accepted in stores and hotels.

## You May See...

Polish currency is currently the **złoty**; one **złoty** is made up of 100 **groszy**. Soon Poland may adopt the euro as its national currency; until then **złoty** is the accepted form of payment.
Coins: 1, 2, 5, 10, 20, 50 groszy; 1, 2, 5 zloty.
Bills: 10, 20, 50, 100, 200 zloty.

# Transportation

## Essential

| | |
|---|---|
| How do I get to town? | **Jak stąd dojechać do miasta?** yahk stohnt doh·yeh·hahch' doh myahs·tah |
| Where's...? | **Gdzie jest...?** gdj'yeh yehst... |
| – the airport | – **lotnisko** loht·n'ees·koh |
| – the train [railway] station | – **dworzec kolejowy** dvoh·zhehts koh·leh·yoh·vyh |
| – the bus station | – **dworzec autobusowy** dvoh·zhehts ahw·toh·buh·soh·vyh |
| – the subway [underground] station | – **stacja metra** stahts·yah meht·rah |
| Is it far from here? | **Czy to daleko stąd?** chyh toh dah·leh·koh stohnt |
| Where can I buy tickets? | **Gdzie mogę kupić bilety?** gdj'yeh moh·geh kuh·peech' bee·leh·tyh |
| A *one-way [single]/ round-trip [return]* ticket to... | **Bilet w jedną stonę/powrotny do...** bee·leht vyehd·nohm stroh·neh/pohv·roht·nyh doh... |
| Are there any discounts? | **Czy są zniżki?** chyh sohm zn'eesh·kee |
| Where can I get a taxi? | **Gdzie mogę złapać taksówkę?** gdj'yeh moh·geh zwah·pahch' tahk·suhf·keh |
| Please take me to this address. | **Proszę mnie zawieźć pod ten adres.** proh·sheh mn'yeh zah·vyehsh'ch' poht tehn ahd·rehs |
| Where can I rent a car? | **Gdzie mogę wynająć samochód?** gdj'yeh moh·geh vyh·nah·yohn'ch' sah·moh·hoot |
| A map, please. | **Poproszę mapę.** poh·proh·sheh mah·peh |

## Ticketing

| | |
|---|---|
| When's...to Cracow? | **O której jest...do Krakowa?** oh ktuh·rehy yehst...doh krah·koh·vah |
| – the (first) bus | – **(pierwszy) autobus** (pyehr·shyh) ahw·toh·buhs |
| – the (next) flight | – **(następny) samolot** (nahs·tehm·pnyh) sah·moh·loht |
| – the (last) train | – **(ostatni) pociąg** (ohs·taht·n'ee) poh·ch'yonk |
| Where can I buy a ticket? | **Gdzie mogę kupić bilet?** gdj'yeh moh·geh kuh·peech' bee·leht |
| One/two ticket(s), please. | *Jeden bilet/Dwa bilety proszę.* yeh·dehn bee·leht/dvah bee·leh·tyh proh·sheh |
| A...ticket. | **Bilet...** bee·leht... |
| – one-way [single] | – **w jedną stronę** vyehd·nohm stroh·neh |
| – round-trip [return] | – **powrotny** pohv·roht·nyh |
| – first class | – **w pierwszej klasie** fpyehr·shehy klah·sh'yeh |
| – economy class | – **w klasie turystycznej** fklah·sh'yeh tuh·ryhs·tyhch·nehy |
| How much? | **Ile to kosztuje?** ee·leh toh kohsh·tuh·yeh |
| Is there a discount for...? | **Czy jest zniżka dla...?** chyh yehst zn'eesh·kah dlah... |
| – children | – **dzieci** dj'ye·ch'ee |
| – students | – **studentów** stuh·dehn·tuhf |
| – senior citizens | – **emerytów** eh·meh·ryh·tuhf |
| I have an e-ticket. | **Mam bilet elektroniczny.** mahm bee·leht eh·lehk·troh·n'eech·nyh |
| Can I buy a ticket on the *bus/train*? | **Czy można kupić bilet w *autobusie/pociągu*?** chyh mohzh·nah kuh·peech' bee·leht v *ahw·toh·buh·sh'yeh/poh·ch'yohn·guh* |

| I'd like to...my reservation. | **Chciałbym** ♂/**Chciałabym** ♀ **...moją rezerwację.** hch'yahw·byhm♂/hch'yah·wah·byhm♀... moh·yohm reh·zehr·<u>vahts</u>·yeh |
| - cancel | **– odwołać** ohd·<u>voh</u>·wahch' |
| - change | **– zmienić** <u>zmyeh</u>·n'eech' |
| - confirm | **– potwierdzić** poh·<u>tfyehr</u>·dj'eech' |

## Plane

### Getting to the Airport

| How much is a taxi to the airport? | **Ile kosztuje taksówka na lotnisko?** <u>ee</u>·leh kohsh·<u>tuh</u>·yeh tahk·<u>suhf</u>·kah nah loht·<u>n'ees</u>·koh |
| To...Airport, please. | **Na lotnisko...proszę.** nah loht·<u>n'ees</u>·koh... <u>proh</u>·sheh |
| My airline is... | **Lecę liniami...** <u>leh</u>·tseh lee·<u>n'yah</u>·mee... |
| My flight leaves at... | **Mam samolot o...** mahm sah·<u>moh</u>·loht oh... |

▶ For time, see page 170.

| I'm in a hurry. | **Spieszę się.** <u>spyeh</u>·sheh sh'yeh |
| Can you drive *faster/slower*? | **Mógłby pan jechać *szybciej/wolniej*?** <u>muhgw</u>·byh pahn <u>yeh</u>·hahch' *<u>shyhp</u>·ch'yehy/ <u>vohl</u>·n'yehy* |

## You May Hear...

**Jakimi liniami pan leci?** yah·<u>kee</u>·mee
lee·<u>n'yah</u>·mee pahn <u>leh</u>·ch'ee

What airline are you
flying?

**Lot krajowy czy zagraniczny?** loht
krah·<u>yoh</u>·wyh chyh zah·grah·<u>n'eech</u>·nyh

Domestic or
international flight?

**Który terminal?** <u>ktuh</u>·ryh tehr·<u>mee</u>·nahl

What terminal?

## You May See...

| | |
|---|---|
| **PRZYLOTY** | arrivals |
| **ODLOTY** | departures |
| **ODBIÓR BAGAŻU** | baggage claim |
| **ODLOTY KRAJOWE** | domestic flights |
| **ODLOTY MIĘDZYNARODOWE** | international flights |
| **STANOWISKO ODPRAWY** | check-in |
| **WYJŚCIA** | departure gates |
| **NIC DO OCLENIA** | nothing to declare |
| **TOWARY DO OCLENIA** | goods to declare |
| **INFORMACJA CELNA** | customs information |
| **WOLNY OBSZAR CELNY** | duty-free zone |

### Check-in and Boarding

| | |
|---|---|
| Where's check-in? | **Gdzie jest stanowisko odprawy?** gdj'yeh yest stah·noh·<u>vees</u>·koh oht·<u>prah</u>·vyh |
| My name is... | **Nazywam się...** nah·<u>zyh</u>·vahm sh'yeh... |
| I'm going to... | **Lecę do...** <u>leh</u>·tseh doh... |
| How much luggage is allowed? | **Ile bagażu mogę wziąć?** <u>ee</u>·leh bah·<u>gah</u>·zhuh <u>moh</u>·geh wzh'yohn'ch' |

| | |
|---|---|
| Which terminal does flight...leave from? | **Z którego terminalu odlatuje lot numer...?** sktuh·<u>reh</u>·goh tehr·mee·<u>nah</u>·lah ohd·lah·<u>tuh</u>·yeh loht <u>nuh</u>·mehr... |
| Which gate does flight...leave from? | **Które wyjście jest dla lotu numer...?** <u>ktuh</u>·reh vyhy·sh'ch'yeh yehst dlah <u>loh</u>·tuh <u>nuh</u>·mehr... |
| I'd like *a window/ an aisle* seat. | **Chciałbym**♂/**Chciałabym**♀ **miejsce przy *oknie/przejściu.*** hch'yahw·byhm♂/ hch'yah·wah·byhm♀ myehys·tseh pshyh <u>ohk</u>·n'yeh/psheh·<u>sh'ch'yuh</u> |
| Can I take this on board? | **Czy mogę to wziąć jako bagaż podręczny?** chyh <u>moh</u>·geh toh vzh'yohn'ch' <u>yah</u>·koh <u>bah</u>·gahsh pohd·<u>rehn</u>·chnyh |
| When do we *leave/ arrive*? | **O której *startujemy/lądujemy?*** oh <u>ktuh</u>·rehy <u>stahr</u>·tuh·yeh·myh/lohn·duh·<u>yeh</u>·myh |
| Is flight...delayed? | **Czy lot...jest opóźniony?** chyh loht...yehst oh·puhzh'·<u>n'yoh</u>·nyh |
| How late will it be? | **O ile jest opóźniony?** oh <u>ee</u>·leh yehst oh·puhzh'·<u>n'yoh</u>·nyh |

## You May Hear...

| | |
|---|---|
| **Proszę następną osobę!** <u>proh</u>·sheh nah·<u>stehmp</u>·nohm oh·<u>soh</u>·beh | Next person, please! |
| **Poproszę *paszport/bilet.*** poh·<u>proh</u>·sheh <u>pahsh</u>·pohrt/<u>bee</u>·leht | Your *passport/ ticket*, please. |
| **Ma pan jakiś bagaż do nadania?** mah pahn <u>yah</u>·keesh' <u>bah</u>·gahsh doh nah·<u>dah</u>·n'yah | Are you checking any luggage? |
| **Ma pan nadbagaż.** mah pahn nahd·<u>bah</u>·gash | You have excess luggage. |
| **Czy pan się sam pakował?** chyh pahn sh'yeh sahm pah·<u>koh</u>·vahw | Did you pack these bags yourself? |

**Proszę opróżnić kieszenie.** <u>proh</u>·sheh ohp·<u>ruzh</u>·n'eech' kyeh·<u>sheh</u>·n'yeh

Please empty your pockets.

**Proszę zdjąć buty.** <u>proh</u>·sheh zdyohn'ch' <u>buh</u>·tyh

Please take off your shoes.

**Zapraszamy pasażerów na pokład samolotu do..., rejs numer...** zah·prah·<u>shah</u>·myh pah·sah·<u>zheh</u>·ruhv nah <u>pohk</u>·wahd sah·moh·<u>loh</u>·tuh doh...rehys <u>nuh</u>·mehr...

Now boarding flight number...to...

## Luggage

| | |
|---|---|
| Where *is/are*...? | **Gdzie *jest/są*...?** gdj'yeh *yehst/sohm*... |
| – the luggage carts [trolleys] | – **wózki bagażowe** <u>vuhs</u>·kee bah·gah·<u>zhoh</u>·veh |
| – luggage lockers/ baggage room | – **skrytki bagażowe/przechowalnia bagażu** <u>skryht</u>·kee bah·gah·<u>zhoh</u>·veh/ psheh·hoh·<u>vahl</u>·n'yah bah·<u>gah</u>·zhuh |
| – the baggage claim | – **odbiór bagażu** <u>ohd</u>·byuhr bah·<u>gah</u>·zhuh |
| My luggage has been lost. | **Zgubili mój bagaż.** zguh·<u>bee</u>·lee muy <u>bah</u>·gahsh |
| My baggage has been stolen. | **Ukradli mi bagaż.** uh·<u>krahd</u>·lee mee <u>bah</u>·gahsh |
| My suitcase was damaged. | **Moja walizka została uszkodzona.** <u>moh</u>·yah vah·<u>lees</u>·kah zohs·<u>tah</u>·wah uhsh·koh·<u>dzoh</u>·nah |

## Finding Your Way

| | |
|---|---|
| Where *is/are*...? | **Gdzie *jest/są*...?** gdj'yeh *yehst/sohm*... |
| – the currency exchange office | – **kantor** <u>kahn</u>·tohr |
| – the exit | – **wyjście** <u>vyhsh</u>'ch'yeh |
| – the taxis | – **taksówki** tahk·<u>suhf</u>·kee |

| Where is the car rental [hire]? | **Gdzie można wynająć samochód?** gdj'yeh <u>mohzh</u>·nah wyh·<u>nah</u>·yohn'ch' sah·<u>moh</u>·huht |
|---|---|
| Is there...into town? | **Czy można stąd dojechać...do centrum?** chyh <u>mohzh</u>·nah stohnt doh·<u>yeh</u>·hahch'...doh <u>tsehn</u>·truhm |
| – a bus | – **autobusem** ahw·toh·<u>buh</u>·sehm |
| – a train | – **pociągiem** poh·<u>ch'yohn</u>·gyehm |
| – a subway [underground] | – **metrem** <u>meht</u>·rehm |

▶ For directions, see page 33.

## Train

| Where's the train [railway] station? | **Gdzie jest dworzec kolejowy?** gdj'yeh yehst <u>dvoh</u>·zhehts koh·leh·<u>yoh</u>·vyh |
|---|---|
| Is it far from here? | **Czy to daleko stąd?** chyh toh dah·<u>leh</u>·koh stohnt |
| Where *is/are*...? | **Gdzie *jest/są*...?** gdj'yeh *yehst/sohm*... |
| – the ticket office | – **kasa biletowa** <u>kah</u>·sah bee·leh·<u>toh</u>·vah |
| – the information desk | – **informacja** een·fohr·<u>mah</u>·tsyah |
| – luggage lockers/ baggage room | – **skrytki bagażowe/przechowalnia bagażu** <u>skryht</u>·kee bah·gah·<u>zhoh</u>·veh/ psheh·hoh·<u>vahl</u>·n'yah bah·<u>gah</u>·zhuh |
| – the platforms | – **perony** peh·<u>roh</u>·nyh |

▶ For directions, see page 33.

▶ For ticketing, see page 19.

## You May See...

| | |
|---|---|
| **PERONY** | platforms |
| **INFORMACJA** | information |
| **REZERWACJE** | reservations |
| **PRZYJAZDY** | arrivals |
| **ODJAZDY** | departures |
| **KASA BILETOWA** (*CZYNNA/NIECZYNNA*) | ticket office (*open/closed*) |
| **ROZKŁAD JAZDY** | schedule [timetable] |
| **WYJŚCIE (EWAKUACYJNE)** | (emergency) exit |
| **TOALETY** | restroom [toilet] |
| **POSTÓJ TAKSÓWEK** | taxi stand |
| **BIURO RZECZY ZNALEZIONYCH** | lost-and-found [lost property office] |

## Questions

| | |
|---|---|
| Could I have a schedule [timetable]? | **Czy mogę prosić rozkład jazdy?** chyh <u>moh</u>·geh <u>proh</u>·sh'eech' <u>rohs</u>·kwaht <u>yahz</u>·dyh |
| How long is the trip [journey]? | **Jak długo trwa podróż?** yahk <u>dwuh</u>·goh trfah <u>poh</u>·druhsh |
| Do I have to change trains? | **Czy muszę się przesiadać?** chyh <u>muh</u>·sheh sh'yeh psheh·<u>sh'yah</u>·dahch' |
| Do I need a reservation for this train? | **Muszę kupować miejscówkę?** <u>muh</u>·sheh kuh·<u>poh</u>·vahch' myehys·<u>tsuhf</u>·keh |

25

## Departures

| | |
|---|---|
| Which track [platform] does the train to...leave from? | **Z którego toru odjeżdża pociąg do...?** sktuh·<u>reh</u>·goh toh·ruh ohd·<u>yehzh</u>·djah <u>poh</u>·ch'yohnk doh... |
| Is this the right track [platform] for...? | **Czy to z tego toru odjeżdża pociąg do...?** chyh toh <u>steh</u>·goh toh·ruh ohd·<u>yehzh</u>·djah <u>poh</u>·ch'yohnk doh... |
| Where is track [platform]...? | **Gdzie jest tor...?** gdj'yeh yehst tohr... |
| Where do I change for...? | **Gdzie mam się przesiąść na pociąg do...?** gdj'yeh mahm sh'yeh <u>psheh</u>·sh'yohn'sh'ch' nah <u>poh</u>·ch'yonk doh... |

## Boarding

| | |
|---|---|
| Is this seat free? | **Czy to miejsce jest wolne?** chyh toh <u>myehys</u>·tseh yehst <u>vohl</u>·neh |
| That's my seat. | **To moje miejsce.** toh <u>moh</u>·yeh <u>myehys</u>·tseh |

## You May Hear...

| | |
|---|---|
| **Proszę wsiadać!** <u>proh</u>·sheh fsh'yah·dahch' | **All aboard!** |
| **Proszę bilety do kontroli.** <u>proh</u>·sheh bee·<u>leh</u>·tyh doh kohn·<u>troh</u>·lee | **Tickets, please.** |
| **Musi pan się przesiąść w...** <u>muh</u>·sh'ee pahn sh'yeh <u>psheh</u>·sh'yohn'sh'ch' v... | **You have to change at...** |
| **Następna stacja...** nahs·<u>tehmp</u>·nah <u>stahts</u>·yah... | **Next stop...** |

## Bus

| | |
|---|---|
| Where's the bus station? | **Gdzie jest dworzec autobusowy?** gdj'yeh yehst <u>dvoh</u>·zhehts ahw·toh·buh·<u>soh</u>·vyh |
| Is it far from here? | **Czy to daleko stąd?** chyh toh dah·<u>leh</u>·koh stohnt |
| How do I get to...? | **Jak dojechać do...?** yahk doh·<u>yeh</u>·hahch' doh... |
| Does this bus stop at...? | **Czy ten autobus zatrzymuje się w...?** chyh tehn ahw·<u>toh</u>·buhs zah·tshyh·<u>muh</u>·yeh sh'yeh v... |
| Could you tell me when to get off? | **Czy może mi pan powiedzieć, kiedy wysiąść?** chyh <u>moh</u>·zhe mee pahn poh·<u>vyeh</u>·dj'yehch' <u>kyeh</u>·dyh vyh·sh'on'sh'ch' |
| Do I have to change buses? | **Czy muszę się przesiadać?** chyh <u>muh</u>·sheh sh'yeh psheh·<u>sh'yah</u>·dahch' |
| Stop here, please! | **Proszę się zatrzymać!** <u>proh</u>·sheh sh'yeh zaht·<u>shyh</u>·mahch' |

▶ For ticketing, see page 19.

Bus service in Poland is extensive. **PKS (Przedsiębiorstwo Komunikacji Samochodowej)** offers the widest range of routes; **Polski Express** also has numerous national routes. You can buy tickets for **PKS** buses at the bus station ticket office or from the driver. Tickets for **Polski Express** buses can be bought at bus stations or at special ticket offices in towns.

## You May See...

| | |
|---|---|
| **PRZYSTANEK AUTOBUSOWY** | bus stop |
| **OTWIERANIE DRZWI PRZYCISKIEM** | press to open door |
| **SKASUJ BILET** | validate your ticket |
| **HAMULEC BEZPIECZEŃSTWA** | emergency brake |
| **KASOWNIK** | validation machine |
| **WYJŚCIE AWARYJNE** | emergency exit |

## Subway [Underground]

Where's the nearest subway [underground] station?
**Gdzie jest najbliższa stacja metra?** gdj'yeh yehst nahy·<u>bleesh</u>·shah <u>stahts</u>·yah <u>meht</u>·rah

Where can I find a subway [underground] map?
**Gdzie mogę znaleźć mapę metra?** gdj'yeh <u>moh</u>·geh <u>znah</u>·lesh'ch' <u>mah</u>·peh <u>meht</u>·rah

Which subway goes in the direction of...?
**Które metro jedzie w stronę...?** <u>ktuh</u>·reh <u>meht</u>·roh <u>yeh</u>·dj'yeh fstroh·neh...

Do I have to transfer [change]?
**Czy muszę się przesiadać?** chyh <u>muh</u>·sheh sh'yeh psheh·<u>sh'yah</u>·dahch'

Is this the subway [train] to...?
**Czy to metro jedzie do...?** chyh toh·<u>meht</u>·roh <u>yeh</u>·dj'yeh doh...

Where are we?
**Gdzie jesteśmy?** gdj'yeh yehs·<u>tehsh'</u>·myh

▶ For ticketing, see page 19.

 Warsaw is the only Polish city with subway service. The line passes through **Centrum** (the city center), where visitors can admire **Pałac Kultury i Nauki** (Palace of Culture and Science). Maps are located throughout subway stations and inside trains. Above-ground **tramwaje** (trams) can be found in Warsaw, Gdańsk, Poznań and many other cities.

Tickets for the subway and trams should be bought before boarding from kiosks or local shops. On boarding you must validate your ticket in a **kasownik** (validation machine). Unvalidated tickets result in an on-the-spot fine. Different types of tickets are used in different cities, but usually single-trip tickets and multiple-trip travelcards are available. In some cities electronic cards are available as well.

## Boat and Ferry

| | |
|---|---|
| When is the ferry to...? | **Kiedy odpływa prom do...?** <u>kyeh</u>·dyh oht·<u>pwyh</u>·vah prohm doh... |
| Can I take my car? | **Czy mogę zabrać na pokład mój samochód?** chyh <u>moh</u>·geh <u>zahb</u>·rahch' nah <u>pohk</u>·wahd muy sah·<u>moh</u>·huht |

▶ For ticketing, see page 19.

## You May See...

| | |
|---|---|
| **ŁODZIE RATUNKOWE** | life boats |
| **KAPOKI** | life jackets |
| **POKŁAD** | deck |

Regular ferry services to and from Denmark and Sweden operate from Świnoujście, Gdańsk and Gdynia. There are several ferry operators who offer various cruises on the Baltic Sea on different days of the week.

## Bicycle and Motorcycle

| I'd like to rent... | **Chciałbym♂/Chciałabym♀ wynając...** <u>hch'yahw</u>·byhm♂/<u>hch'yah</u>·wah·byhm♀ vyh·<u>nah</u>·yohn'ch'... |
| --- | --- |
| – a bicycle | – **rower** <u>roh</u>·vehr |
| – a moped | – **motorower** moh·toh·<u>roh</u>·vehr |
| – a motorcycle | – **motor** <u>moh</u>·tohr |
| How much per day/week? | **Ile kosztuje wynajęcie na** *dzień/tydzień*? <u>ee</u>·leh kohsh·<u>tuh</u>·yeh vyh·nah·<u>yehn'</u>·ch'yeh nah *dj'yehn'/<u>tyh</u>·dj'yehn'* |
| Can I have a helmet/lock? | **Mogę prosić** *kask/blokadę*? <u>moh</u>·geh <u>proh</u>·sh'eech' *kahsk/bloh·<u>kah</u>·deh* |

## Taxi

| Where can I get a taxi? | **Gdzie mogę złapać taksówkę?** gdj'yeh <u>moh</u>·geh <u>zwah</u>·pahch' tahk·<u>suhf</u>·keh |
| --- | --- |
| I'd like a taxi *now/ for tomorrow at...* | **Chciałbym♂/Chciałabym♀ zamówić taksówkę** *na jak najszybciej/na jutro na godzinę...* <u>hch'yahw</u>·byhm♂/ <u>hch'yah</u>·wah·byhm♀ zah·<u>muh</u>·veech' tahk·<u>suhf</u>·keh *nah yahk nahy·<u>shyhp</u>·ch'yehy/ nah <u>yuht</u>·roh nah goh·<u>dj'ee</u>·neh...* |
| The pick-up address is... | **Proszę mnie odebrać z...** <u>proh</u>·sheh mn'yeh oh·<u>dehb</u>·rahch' z... |
| Please take me to... | **Proszę...** <u>proh</u>·sheh... |
| – this address | – **pod ten adres** poht tehn <u>ahd</u>·rehs |
| – the airport | – **na lotnisko** nah loht·<u>n'ees</u>·koh |
| – the train [railway] station | – **na dworzec kolejowy** nah <u>dvoh</u>·zhehts koh·leh·<u>yoh</u>·vyh |
| I'm late. | **Jestem spóźniony♂/spóźniona♀.** <u>yehs</u>·tehm spuhzh'·<u>n'yoh</u>·nyh♂/spuhzh'·<u>n'yoh</u>·nah♀ |

| | |
|---|---|
| Can you drive *faster/slower*? | **Mógłby pan jechać *szybciej/wolniej*?** <u>muhgw</u>·byh pahn <u>yeh</u>·hahch' *<u>shyhp</u>·ch'yehy/<u>vohl</u>·n'yey* |
| *Stop/Wait* here, please. | **Proszę się tu zatrzymać/tu zaczekać.** <u>proh</u>·sheh sh'yeh tuh zaht·<u>shyh</u>·mahch'/tuh zah·<u>cheh</u>·kahch' |
| How much? | **Ile płacę?** <u>ee</u>·leh <u>pwah</u>·tseh |
| You said it would cost... | **Mówił pan, że to będzie kosztowało...** <u>muh</u>·veew pahn zheh toh <u>behn'</u>·dj'yeh kohsh·toh·<u>vah</u>·woh... |
| Keep the change. | **Proszę zatrzymać resztę.** <u>proh</u>·sheh zah·<u>tshyh</u>·mahch' <u>rehsh</u>·teh |

## You May Hear...

| | |
|---|---|
| **Dokąd jedziemy?** <u>doh</u>·kohnt yeh·<u>dj'yeh</u>·myh | Where to? |
| **Jaki adres?** <u>yah</u>·kee <u>ahd</u>·rehs | What's the address? |

*i* Schedule a taxi pick up by calling a local company; check the phone book for listings. You may be able to hail a taxi but make sure it displays a recognized taxi company name and that the meter is started. A table of fares should be displayed in the taxi. Fares are higher on Sundays, public holidays and at night. Be careful about taking a taxi to suburbs of the city, as it may mean entering another fare zone. Most taxis take cash only. It is not customary to tip the taxi drivers.

## Car

### Car Rental [Hire]

| | |
|---|---|
| Where can I rent a car? | **Gdzie mogę wynająć samochód?** gdj'yeh <u>moh</u>·geh vyh·<u>nah</u>·yohnch' sah·<u>moh</u>·huht |

| I'd like to rent... | Chcę wynająć... htseh vyh·<u>nah</u>·yohn'ch'... |
|---|---|
| - an automatic/ a manual | - samochód z *automatyczną/ręczną* skrzynią biegów sah·<u>moh</u>·huht z ahw·toh·mah·<u>tyhch</u>·nohm/<u>rehnch</u>·nohm skshyh·n'yohm <u>byeh</u>·guhf |
| - a car with air conditioning | - samochód z klimatyzacją sah·<u>moh</u>·huht sklee·mah·tyh·<u>zahts</u>·yohm |
| - a car seat | - fotelik dziecięcy foh·<u>teh</u>·leek dj'yeh·<u>ch'yehn</u>·tsyh |
| How much...? | Ile to kosztuje...? <u>ee</u>·leh toh kohsh·<u>tuh</u>·yeh... |
| - per *day/week* | - za *dzień/tydzień* zah dj'yehn'/<u>tyh</u>·dj'yehn' |
| - per kilometer | - za kilometr zah kee·<u>loh</u>·mehtr |
| - for unlimited mileage | - bez limitu kilometrów behs lee·<u>mee</u>·tuh kee·loh·<u>meht</u>·ruhf |
| - with insurance | - z ubezpieczeniem zuh·behs·pyeh·<u>cheh</u>·n'yehm |
| Are there any discounts? | Czy są zniżki? chyh sohm <u>zn'eezh</u>·kee |

## Gas [Petrol] Station

| Where's the next gas [petrol] station? | **Gdzie jest najbliższa stacja benzynowa?** gdj'yeh yehst nahy·<u>bleesh</u>·shah <u>stah</u>·tsyah behn·zyh·<u>noh</u>·vah |
|---|---|
| Fill it up, please. | **Do pełna, proszę.** doh <u>pehw</u>·nah <u>proh</u>·sheh |
| ...liters, please. | **...litrów, proszę.** ...<u>leet</u>·ruhf <u>proh</u>·sheh |
| I'll pay *in cash/by credit card*. | **Zapłacę** *gotówką/kartą kredytową.* zap·<u>wah</u>·tseh goh·<u>tuhf</u>·kohm/<u>kahr</u>·tohm kreh·dyh·<u>toh</u>·vohm |

## You May See...

| Pb 95 | regular |
|---|---|
| Pb 98 | premium [super] |
| ON | diesel |
| LPG | autogas |

## Asking Directions

| Is this the right road to...? | **Czy to właściwa droga do...?** chyh toh vwahsh'·<u>ch'ee</u>·vah <u>droh</u>·gah doh... |
|---|---|
| How far is it to...? | **Jak daleko jest stąd do...?** yahk dah·<u>leh</u>·koh yehst stohnt doh... |
| Where's...? | **Gdzie jest...?** gdj'yeh yehst... |
| – ...Street | – **ulica...** uh·<u>lee</u>·tsah... |
| – this address | – **ten adres** tehn <u>ahd</u>·rehs |
| – the highway [motorway] | – **autostrada** ahw·toh·<u>strah</u>·dah |
| Can you show me on the map? | **Czy może mi pan pokazać na mapie?** chyh <u>moh</u>·zheh mee pahn poh·<u>kah</u>·zahch' nah <u>mah</u>·pyeh |
| I'm lost. | **Zgubiłem**♂/**Zgubiłam**♀ **się.** zguh·<u>bee</u>·wehm♂/zguh·<u>bee</u>·wahm sh'yeh♀ |

## You May Hear...

| | |
|---|---|
| Proszę jechać... <u>proh</u>·sheh <u>yeh</u>·hahch'... | You should go... |
| – prosto <u>prohs</u>·toh | – straight |
| – w lewo v<u>leh</u>·voh | – left |
| – w prawo <u>fprah</u>·voh | – right |
| – na północ/południe nah <u>puhw</u>·nohts/ poh·<u>wuhd</u>·n'yeh | – north/south |
| – na wschód/zachód na fs·huht/<u>zah</u>·huht | – east/west |
| To jest... toh yehst... | It's... |
| – na rogu/za rogiem nah <u>roh</u>·guh/zah <u>roh</u>·gyehm | – on/around the corner |
| – naprzeciwko... nah psheh·<u>ch'eef</u>·koh... | – opposite... |
| – za... zah... | – behind... |
| – przy... pshyh... | – next to... |

## You May See...

| | | |
|---|---|---|
| ↑ | DROGA JEDNOKIERUNKOWA | one way |
| ◇ | DROGA Z PIERWSZEŃSTWEM | right of way |
| 🚶 | PRZEJŚCIE DLA PIESZYCH | pedestrian crossing |
| STOP | STOP | stop |

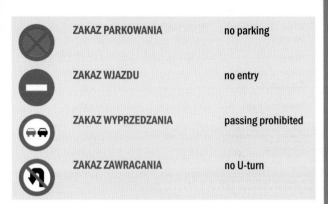

| | | |
|---|---|---|
| | **ZAKAZ PARKOWANIA** | no parking |
| | **ZAKAZ WJAZDU** | no entry |
| | **ZAKAZ WYPRZEDZANIA** | passing prohibited |
| | **ZAKAZ ZAWRACANIA** | no U-turn |

## Parking

| | |
|---|---|
| Can I park here? | **Czy mogę tu zaparkować?** chyh <u>moh</u>·geh tuh zah·pahr·<u>koh</u>·vahch' |
| Where is the nearest parking lot [car park]? | **Gdzie jest najbliższy parking?** gdj'yeh yehst nahy·<u>bleesh</u>·shyh <u>pahr</u>·keenk |
| How much...? | **Ile kosztuje...?** <u>ee</u>·leh kohsh·<u>tuh</u>·yeh... |
| – per hour | – **godzina** goh·<u>dj'ee</u>·nah |
| – per day | – **dzień** dj'yehn' |
| – for overnight | – **zostawienie samochodu na noc** zohs·tah·<u>vyeh</u>·n'yeh sah·moh·<u>hoh</u>·duh nah nohts |

## Breakdown and Repairs

| | |
|---|---|
| My car *broke down/won't start*. | **Mój samochód *się zepsuł/nie chce zapalić*.** muy sah·<u>moh</u>·huht *sh'yeh <u>zehp</u>·suhw/n'yeh htseh zah·<u>pah</u>·leech'* |
| Can you fix it (today)? | **Możecie to naprawić (dzisiaj)?** moh·<u>zheh</u>·ch'yeh toh nahp·<u>rah</u>·veech' (<u>dj'ee</u>·sh'ahy) |

| | |
|---|---|
| When can I pick up the car? | **Kiedy mogę odebrać samochód?** <u>kyeh</u>·dyh <u>moh</u>·geh oh·<u>dehb</u>·rahch' sah·<u>moh</u>·huht |
| How much? | **Ile to kosztuje?** <u>ee</u>·leh toh kohsh·<u>tuh</u>·yeh |

### Accidents

| | |
|---|---|
| There has been an accident. | **Był wypadek.** byhw vyh·<u>pah</u>·dehk |
| Call *an ambulance/ the police*. | **Proszę wezwać *karetkę/policję*.** <u>proh</u>·sheh <u>vehz</u>·vahch' kah·<u>reht</u>·keh/poh·<u>leets</u>·yeh |

# Accommodations

## Essential

| | |
|---|---|
| Can you recommend a hotel? | **Czy może mi pan polecić jakiś hotel?** chyh <u>moh</u>·zheh mee pahn poh·<u>leh</u>·ch'eech' <u>yah</u>·keesh' <u>hoh</u>·tehl |
| I have a reservation. | **Mam rezerwację.** mahm reh·zehr·<u>vahts</u>·yeh |
| My name is... | **Nazywam się...** nah·<u>zyh</u>·vahm sh'yeh... |
| I would like a room... | **Chciałbym♂/Chciałabym♀ wynająć pokój...** hch'yahw·byhm♂/hch'yah·wah·byhm♀ vyh·<u>nah</u>·yohn'ch' <u>poh</u>·kuy... |
| – for *one/two* | – **jednoosobowy/dwuosobowy** yehd·noh·oh·soh·<u>boh</u>·vyh/dvuh·oh·soh·<u>boh</u>·vyh |
| – with a bathroom | – **z łazienką** zwah·<u>zh'yehn</u>·kohm |
| – with air conditioning | – **z klimatyzacją** sklee·mah·tyh·<u>zahts</u>·yohm |
| For... | **Na...** nah... |
| – tonight | – **tę noc** teh nohts |
| – two nights | – **dwie noce** dvyeh <u>noh</u>·tseh |
| – one week | – **tydzień** <u>tyh</u>·dj'yehn' |

| | |
|---|---|
| How much? | **Ile to kosztuje?** ee·leh toh kohsh·<u>tuh</u>·yeh |
| Do you have anything cheaper? | **Czy są jakieś tańsze pokoje?** chyh sohm <u>yah</u>·kyehsh' <u>tahn'</u>·sheh poh·<u>koh</u>·yeh |
| When's check-out? | **O której mamy zwolnić pokój?** oh <u>ktuh</u>·rehy <u>mah</u>·myh <u>zvohl</u>·n'eech' <u>poh</u>·kuy |
| Can I leave this in the safe? | **Mogę zostawić to w sejfie?** <u>moh</u>·geh zohs·<u>tah</u>·veech' toh <u>fsehy</u>·fyeh |
| Can I leave my luggage? | **Mogę zostawić mój bagaż?** <u>moh</u>·geh zohs·<u>tah</u>·veech' muy <u>bah</u>·gahsh |
| Can I have *the bill/a receipt*? | **Czy mogę prosić o *rachunek/pokwitowanie*?** chyh <u>moh</u>·geh pro·sh'eech' oh rah·<u>huh</u>·nehk/ poh·kfee·toh·<u>vah</u>·n'yeh |
| I'll pay *in cash/by credit card*. | **Zapłacę *gotówką/kartą kredytową*.** <u>zahpwah</u>·tseh goh·<u>tuhf</u>·kohm/<u>kahr</u>·tohm kreh·dyh·<u>toh</u>·vohm |

*i*  If you didn't reserve accommodations before your trip, visit the local **Informacja Turystyczna** (Tourist Information Office) for recommendations on places to stay. These are usually located in the city center and/or near the train station.

## Finding Lodging

| | |
|---|---|
| Can you recommend a hotel? | **Czy może mi pan polecić jakiś hotel?** chyh <u>moh</u>·zheh me pahn poh·<u>leh</u>·ch'eech' <u>yah</u>·keesh' <u>hoh</u>·tehl |
| What is it near? | **Koło czego on się znajduje?** <u>koh</u>·woh <u>cheh</u>·goh ohn sh'yeh znahy·<u>duh</u>·yeh |
| How do I get there? | **Jak można się tam dostać?** yahk <u>mohzh</u>·nah sh'yeh tahm <u>dohs</u>·tahch' |

There is a wide choice of accommodation; prices vary according to facilities, location and season. Following are some places to stay.

Hotels: As any other country, Poland has numerous hotels catering to leisure and business travelers. In smaller towns you will mainly find lower class hotels.

Hostels: These are inexpensive, and usually offer both private and dormitory-style rooms.

Tourist Houses: **Domy Turysty** (guest houses), ideal for budget travelers, are run by the **PTTK** (Polish Tourist Country Lovers' Society), which also runs **schroniska górskie** (mountain hostels). These are found mainly in the countryside.

There are many **pensjonaty** (boarding houses) and **pokoje gościnne** (rooms in private houses) available in big towns and resorts, some of which can be found on the internet. In some towns you may book a room through certain tourist agencies, such as **Biuro Kwater Prywatnych** or **Agencja Promocji Miasta**. Most **pensjonaty** provide meals and/or cooking facilities. They can accommodate fewer guests than hotels but offer a friendly and cozy atmosphere.

## At the Hotel

| | |
|---|---|
| I have a reservation. | **Mam rezerwację.** mahm reh·zehr·<u>vahts</u>·yeh |
| My name is... | **Nazywam się...** nah·<u>zyh</u>·vahm sh'yeh... |
| I would like a room... | **Chciałbym**♂/**Chciałabym**♀ **wynająć pokój...** <u>hch'yahw</u>·byhm♂/<u>hch'yah</u>·wah·byhm♀ vyh·<u>nah</u>·yohn'ch' <u>poh</u>·kuy... |
| – with a bathroom | – **z łazienką** zwah·<u>zh'yehn</u>·kohm |
| – with air conditioning | – **z klimatyzacją** sklee·mah·tyh·<u>zahts</u>·yohm |
| – for *smokers/non-smokers* | – **dla** *palących/niepalących* dla pah·<u>lohn</u>·tsyhh/n'yeh·pah·<u>lohn</u>·tsyhh |

| For... | Na... nah... |
|---|---|
| - tonight | - **tę noc** teh nohts |
| - two nights | - **dwie noce** dvyeh <u>noh</u>·tseh |
| - one week | - **tydzień** <u>tyh</u>·dj'yehn' |

▶ For numbers, see page 168.

| Does the hotel have...? | **Czy jest u państwa...?** chyh yehst uh <u>pahn's</u>·tfah... |
|---|---|
| - a computer for guests | - **komputer dla gości** kohm·<u>puh</u>·tehr dlah <u>gohsh'</u>·ch'ee |
| - an elevator [lift] | - **winda** <u>veen</u>·dah |
| - (wireless) internet service | - **(bezprzewodowy) internet** (behs·psheh·voh·<u>doh</u>·vyh) een·<u>tehr</u>·neht |
| - room service | - **room service** ruhm <u>sehr</u>·vees |
| - a pool | - **basen** <u>bah</u>·sehn |
| - a gym | - **siłownia** sh'ee·<u>wohv</u>·n'yah |
| Could I have...? | **Czy mógłbym**♂**/mogłabym**♀ **dostać...?** chyh <u>muhgw</u>·byhm♂/<u>moh</u>·gwah·byhm♀ dohs·tahch'... |
| - an extra bed | - **dodatkowe łóżko** doh·daht·<u>koh</u>·veh wuhzh·koh |
| - a cot | - **rozkładane łóżko** rohs·kwah·<u>dah</u>·neh wuhzh·koh |
| - a crib [child's cot] | - **łóżeczko dziecięce** wuh·<u>zhehch</u>·koh dj'yeh·<u>ch'yehn</u>·tseh |

## You May Hear...

**Poproszę pana** *paszport/kartę kredytową.* poh·<u>proh</u>·sheh pah·nah *pahsh·pohrt/kahr·teh kreh·dyh·<u>toh</u>·vohm*

Your *passport/ credit card*, please.

**Proszę wypełnić ten formularz.** <u>proh</u>·sheh vyh·<u>pehw</u>·n'eech' tehn fohr·<u>muh</u>·lahsh

Please fill out this form.

**Proszę tutaj podpisać.** <u>proh</u>·sheh tuh·tahy poht·pee·sahch'

Please sign here.

## Price

| | |
|---|---|
| How much per *night/week*? | **Jaka jest cena za *noc/tydzień*?** yah·kah yehst <u>tseh</u>·nah zah nohts/<u>tyh</u>·dj'yehn' |
| Does the price include *breakfast/ sales tax [VAT]*? | **Czy w cenę *wliczone jest śniadanie/wliczony jest VAT*?** chyh f <u>tseh</u>·neh vlee·<u>choh</u>·neh yehst sh'n'yah·<u>dah</u>·n'yeh/vlee·<u>choh</u>·nyh yehst vaht |

## Questions

| | |
|---|---|
| Where *is/are*...? | **Gdzie *jest/są*...?** gdj'eh yehst/sohm... |
| – the bar | – **bar** bahr |
| – the bathrooms [toilets] | – **łazienki** wah·<u>zh'yehn</u>·kee |
| – the elevators [lifts] | – **windy** <u>veen</u>·dyh |
| Can I have...? | **Czy mogę dostać...?** chyh moh·<u>geh</u> <u>dohs</u>·tahch'... |
| – a blanket | – **koc** kohts |
| – an iron | – **żelazko** zheh·<u>lahs</u>·koh |

| – a pillow | – **poduszkę** poh·<u>duhsh</u>·keh |
| – soap | – **mydło** <u>myhd</u>·woh |
| – toilet paper | – **papier toaletowy** <u>pah</u>·pyehr toh·ah·leh·<u>toh</u>·vyh |
| – a towel | – **ręcznik** <u>rehnch</u>·n'eek |
| Do you have an adapter for this? | **Czy ma pan do tego przejściowkę?** chyh mah pahn doh <u>teh</u>·goh pshehysh'·<u>ch'yuhf</u>·keh |
| How do I turn on the lights? | **Jak się włącza światło?** yahk sh'yeh <u>vwohn</u>·chah <u>sh'fyaht</u>·woh |
| Please wake me at... | **Proszę mnie obudzić o...** <u>proh</u>·sheh mn'yeh oh·<u>buh</u>·dj'eech' oh... |
| Can I leave this in the safe? | **Czy mogę to zostawić w sejfie?** chyh <u>moh</u>·geh toh zohs·<u>tah</u>·veech' <u>fsehy</u>·fyeh |
| Could I have my things from the safe? | **Mógłbym♂/Mogłabym♀ wyjąć moje rzeczy z sejfu?** <u>muhgw</u>·byhm♂/<u>moh</u>·gwah·byhm♀ vyh·yohn'ch' <u>moh</u>·yeh zheh·chyh <u>ssehy</u>·fuh |
| Is there any mail [post] for me? | **Czy są jakieś listy do mnie?** chyh sohm <u>yah</u>·kyehsh' <u>lees</u>·tyh doh mn'yeh |
| Are there any messages for me? | **Czy są dla mnie jakieś wiadomości?** chyh sohm dlah mn'yeh <u>yah</u>·kyehsh' vyah·doh·<u>mosh'</u>·ch'ee |

## You May See...

| PCHAĆ/CIĄGNĄĆ | push/pull |
| TOALETA | restroom [toilet] |
| PRYSZNICE | showers |
| WINDY | elevators [lifts] |
| SCHODY | stairs |
| PRALNIA | laundry |
| NIE PRZESZKADZAĆ | do not disturb |

| DRZWI PRZECIWPOŻAROWE | fire door |
| WYJŚCIE (AWARYJNE) | (emergency) exit |
| BUDZENIE TELEFONICZNE | wake-up call |

## Problems

| There's a problem. | **Mam problem.** mahm <u>prohb</u>·lehm |
| I've lost my key. | **Zgubiłem♂/Zgubiłam♀ klucz.** zguh·<u>bee</u>·wehm♂/zguh·<u>bee</u>·wahm♀ kluhch |
| I've locked the key in my room. | **Zatrzasnąłem♂/Zatrzasnęłam♀ klucz w pokoju.** zah·tshahs·<u>noh</u>·wehm♂/ zah·tshahs·<u>neh</u>·wahm♀ kluhch fpoh·<u>koh</u>·yuh |
| There is no *hot water/toilet paper*. | **Nie ma *ciepłej wody/papieru toaletowego*.** n'yeh mah <u>ch'yehp</u>·wehy <u>voh</u>·dyh/pah·<u>pyeh</u>·ruh toh·ah·leh·toh·<u>veh</u>·goh |
| The room is dirty. | **Pokój jest brudny.** <u>poh</u>·kuy yehst <u>bruhd</u>·nyh |
| There are bugs in my room. | **W moim pokoju są robaki.** <u>vmoh</u>·eem poh·<u>koh</u>·yuh sohm roh·<u>bah</u>·kee |
| ...doesn't work. | **...nie działa.** ...n'yeh <u>dj'yah</u>·wah |
| Can you fix...? | **Mogą państwo naprawić...?** <u>moh</u>·gohm <u>pahn's</u>·tfoh nahp·<u>rah</u>·veech'... |
| – the air conditioning | – **klimatyzację** klee·mah·tyh·<u>zahts</u>·yeh |
| – the fan | – **wentylator** vehn·tyh·<u>lah</u>·rohr |
| – the heat [heating] | – **ogrzewanie** oh·gzheh·<u>vah</u>·n'yeh |
| – the light | – **światło** <u>sh'fyaht</u>·woh |
| – the TV | – **telewizor** teh·leh·<u>vee</u>·zohr |
| – the toilet | – **toaletę** toh·ah·<u>leh</u>·teh |
| I'd like another room. | **Chciałbym♂/Chciałabym♀ zmienić pokój.** hch'yahw·byhm♂/hch'yah·wah·byhm♀ <u>zmyeh</u>·n'eech' <u>poh</u>·kuy |

42

Poland's electricity is 230 volts. You may need a converter and/or an adapter for your appliances.

### Check-out

| | |
|---|---|
| When's check-out? | **O której mam zwolnić pokój?** oh <u>ktuh</u>·rehy *mahm* <u>zvohl</u>·n'eech' *poh*·kuy |
| Could I leave my baggage here until...? | **Czy mogę zostawić tutaj bagaż do...?** chyh <u>moh</u>·geh zohs·<u>tah</u>·veech' <u>tuh</u>·tahy <u>bah</u>·gahsh doh... |
| Can I have *an itemized bill/ a receipt*? | **Czy mogę dostać *szczegółowy rachunek/ pokwitowanie*?** chyh <u>moh</u>·geh <u>dohs</u>·tach' shcheh·guh·<u>woh</u>·vyh ra·<u>huh</u>·nehk/ poh·kfee·toh·<u>vah</u>·n'yeh |
| I think there's a mistake in this bill. | **Na tym rachunku chyba jest błąd.** nah tyhm rah·<u>huhn</u>·kuh <u>hyh</u>·bah yehst blohnt |
| I'll pay *in cash/by credit card*. | **Zapłacę *gotówką/kartą kredytową*.** zah·<u>pwah</u>·tseh goh·<u>tuhf</u>·kohm/<u>kahr</u>·tohm kreh·dyh·<u>toh</u>·vohm |

## Renting

| | |
|---|---|
| I've reserved *an apartment/a room*. | **Zarezerwowałem♂/Zarezerwowałam♀ *mieszkanie/pokój*.** zah·reh·zehr·voh·<u>vah</u>·wehm♂/ zah·reh·zehr·voh·vah·lahm♀ *myehsh·<u>kah</u>·n'yeh/ <u>poh</u>·kuy* |
| My name is... | **Nazywam się...** nah·<u>zyh</u>·vahm sh'yeh... |
| Can I have the *key/key card*? | **Czy mogę dostać *klucz/kartę*?** chyh <u>moh</u>·geh <u>dohs</u>·tach' *kluhch/<u>kahr</u>·teh* |
| Are there...? | **Czy są...?** chyh sohm... |
| – dishes [crockery] | – **naczynia** nah·<u>chyh</u>·n'yah |
| – pillows | – **poduszki** poh·<u>duhsh</u>·kee |

| Are there...? | Czy są...? chyh sohm... |
|---|---|
| – sheets | – **pościel** <u>pohsh'</u>·ch'yehl |
| – towels | – **ręczniki** rehnch·<u>n'ee</u>·kee |
| – utensils [cutlery] | – **sztućce** <u>shtuhch'</u>·tseh |
| When do I put out the trash [rubbish]? | **Kiedy wywożą śmieci?** <u>kyeh</u>·dyh vyh·<u>voh</u>·zhohm sh'myeh·ch'ee |
| ...is broken. | **...nie działa.** ...n'yeh <u>dj'yah</u>·wah |
| How does...work? | **Jak obsługiwać...?** yahk ohp·swuh·<u>gee</u>·vahch'... |
| – the air conditioner | – **klimatyzator** klee·mah·tyh·<u>zah</u>·tohr |
| – the dishwasher | – **zmywarkę** zmyh·<u>vahr</u>·keh |
| – the freezer | – **zamrażarkę** zahm·rah·<u>zhahr</u>·keh |
| – the heater | – **grzejnik** <u>gzhehy</u>·n'eek |
| – the microwave | – **mikrofalówkę** mee·kroh·fah·<u>luhf</u>·keh |
| – the refrigerator | – **lodówkę** loh·<u>duhf</u>·keh |
| – the stove | – **kuchenkę** kuh·<u>hehn</u>·keh |

▶ For oven temperatures, see page 173.

| – the washing machine | – **pralkę** <u>prahl</u>·keh |
|---|---|

## Household Items

| Could I have...? | Czy mogę dostać...? chyh <u>moh</u>·geh dohs·tahch'... |
|---|---|
| – an adapter | – **przejściówkę** pshehysh'·<u>ch'yuhf</u>·keh |
| – aluminum [kitchen] foil | – **folię aluminiową** <u>fohl</u>·yeh ah·luh·mee·<u>n'yoh</u>·vohm |
| – a bottle opener | – **otwieracz do butelek** oht·<u>fyeh</u>·rahch doh buh·<u>teh</u>·lehk |
| – a broom | – **zmiotkę** <u>zmyoht</u>·keh |
| – a can opener | – **otwieracz do puszek** oht·<u>fyeh</u>·rahch doh <u>puh</u>·shehk |
| – a corkscrew | – **korkociąg** kohr·<u>koh</u>·ch'yohnk |

| | |
|---|---|
| – garbage [rubbish] bags | – **worki na śmieci** <u>vohr</u>·kee nah <u>sh'myeh</u>·ch'ee |
| – matches | – **zapałki** zah·<u>pahw</u>·kee |
| – a mop | – **mopa** <u>moh</u>·pah |
| – napkins | – **serwetki** sehr·<u>veht</u>·kee |
| – paper towels | – **papierowe ręczniki** pah·pyeh·<u>roh</u>·veh rehnch·<u>n'ee</u>·kee |
| – plastic wrap [cling film] | – **folię do żywności** <u>fohl</u>·yeh doh zhyhv·<u>nohsh'</u>·ch'ee |
| – a plunger | – **przepychacz** psheh·<u>pyh</u>·hahch |
| – scissors | – **nożyczki** noh·<u>zhyhch</u>·kee |
| – a vacuum cleaner | – **odkurzacz** oht·<u>kuh</u>·zhahch |

▶ For dishes and utensils, see page 64.

## Hostel

| | |
|---|---|
| Do you have any places left for tonight? | **Czy są na dzisiaj wolne miejsca?** chyh sohm nah <u>dj'ee</u>·sh'yahy <u>vohl</u>·neh <u>myehys</u>·tsah |
| I would like a *single/double* room. | **Chciałbym♂/Chciałabym♀ pokój** *jednoosobowy/dwuosobowy.* <u>hch'yahw</u>·byhm♂/<u>hch'yah</u>·wah·byhm♀ <u>poh</u>·kuy yehd·noh·oh·soh·<u>boh</u>·vyh/dvuh·oh·soh·<u>boh</u>·vyh |
| Could I have...? | **Czy mógłbym♂/mogłabym♀ dostać...?** chyh <u>muhgw</u>·byhm♂/<u>moh</u>·gwah·byhm♀ dohs·tahch'... |
| – a blanket | – **koc** kohts |
| – a pillow | – **poduszkę** poh·<u>duhsh</u>·keh |
| – sheets | – **pościel** <u>pohsh'</u>·ch'yehl |
| – a towel | – **ręcznik** <u>rehnch</u>·n'eek |
| What time are the doors locked? | **O której zamykają państwo drzwi?** oh <u>ktuh</u>·rehy zah·myh·<u>kah</u>·yohm <u>pahn's</u>·tfoh djvee |

## Camping

| Can I camp here? | **Mogę tutaj rozbić namiot?** moh·<u>geh</u> tuh·tahy <u>rohz</u>·beech' <u>nah</u>·myoht |
|---|---|
| Is there a campsite near here? | **Czy jest tu w pobliżu jakiś camping?** chyh yehst tuh fpoh·<u>blee</u>·zhuh yah·keesh' <u>kehm</u>·peenk |
| What is the charge per *day/week*? | **Ile kosztuje *jedna noc/tydzień*?** ee·leh kohsh·<u>tuh</u>·yeh *yehd·nah nohts/tyh·dj'yehn'* |
| Are there *electric outlets/showers*? | **Czy są *gniazdka elektryczne/prysznice*?** chyh sohm *<u>gn'yahs</u>·tkah eh·lehk·<u>tryh</u>·chneh/ pryhsh·<u>n'ee</u>·tseh* |
| Where can I empty the chemical toilet? | **Gdzie mogę opróżnić chemiczną toaletę?** gd'yeh <u>moh</u>·geh ohp·<u>ruhzh</u>·n'eech' heh·<u>meech</u>·nohm toh·ah·<u>leh</u>·teh |

### You May See...

| WODA PITNA | potable water |
|---|---|
| ZAKAZ BIWAKOWANIA | no camping |
| ZAKAZ ROZPALANIA GRILLA I OGNISK | no fires or barbecues |
| ZAKAZ WSTĘPU | no trespassing |

# Internet and Communications

## Essential

| Is there an internet cafe nearby? | **Czy jest tu gdzieś w pobliżu kafejka internetowa?** chyh yehst tuh gj'yehsh' fpoh·<u>blee</u>·zhuh kah·<u>fehy</u>·kah een·tehr·neh·<u>toh</u>·vah |
| Can I *access the internet/check e-mail* here? | **Można tu *skorzystać z internetu/sprawdzić pocztę*?** <u>mohzh</u>·nah tuh *skoh·<u>zhyhs</u>·tahch' zeen·tehr·<u>neh</u>·tuh/<u>sprahw</u>·dj'eech' <u>pohch</u>·teh* |

| | |
|---|---|
| How much per *hour/half hour*? | **Ile kosztuje** *godzina/pół godziny*? ee·leh koh·<u>shtuh</u>·yeh goh·<u>dj'ee</u>·nah/puhw goh·<u>dj'ee</u>·nyh |
| How do I *connect/ log on*? | **Jak mam się** *połączyć z siecią/zalogować*? yahk mahm sh'yeh poh·<u>wohn</u>·chyhch' <u>ssh'yeh</u>·ch'yohm/zah·loh·<u>goh</u>·vahch' |
| Is there a password? | **Jest jakieś hasło?** yehst yah·kyehsh' <u>hahs</u>·woh |
| A phone card, please. | **Poproszę kartę telefoniczną.** poh·<u>proh</u>·sheh <u>kahr</u>·teh teh·leh·foh·<u>n'eech</u>·nohm |
| Can I have your phone number? | **Czy mogę prosić pana numer telefonu?** chyh <u>moh</u>·geh <u>proh</u>·sh'eech' <u>pah</u>·nah <u>nuh</u>·mehr teh·leh·<u>foh</u>·nuh |
| Here's my *number/ e-mail address*. | **To jest mój** *numer telefonu/adres e-mail*. toh yehst muy <u>nuh</u>·mehr teh·leh·<u>foh</u>·nuh/<u>ahd</u>·rehs <u>ee</u>·mehyl |
| Could you please *call/e-mail* me? | **Czy mógłby pan** *do mnie zadzwonić/napisać do mnie maila*? chyh <u>muhgw</u>·byh pahn doh mn'yeh zahdz·<u>voh</u>·n'eech'/nah·<u>pee</u>·sahch' doh mn'yeh <u>mehy</u>·lah |
| Hello. This is... | **Dzień dobry. Mówi...** dj'yehn' <u>dohb</u>·ryh muh·vee... |
| I'd like to speak to... | **Chciałbym♂/Chciałabym♀ rozmawiać z...** hch'yahw·byhm♂/hch'yah·wah·byhm♀ rohz·<u>mah</u>·vyahch' z... |
| Could you repeat that? | **Może pan powtórzyć?** <u>moh</u>·zheh pahn pohf·<u>tuh</u>·zhyhch' |
| I'll call back later. | **Zadzwonię później.** zahdz·<u>voh</u>·n'yeh <u>puhzh'</u>·n'yehy |
| Bye. | **Do widzenia.** doh vee·<u>dzeh</u>·n'yah |
| Where's the post office? | **Gdzie jest poczta?** Gdj'yeh yehst <u>pohch</u>·tah |
| I'd like to send this to... | **Chciałbym♂/Chciałabym♀ to wysłać do...** hch'yahw·byhm♂/hch'yah·wah·byhm♀ toh vyhs·<u>wahch'</u> doh... |

## Computer, Internet and E-mail

| | |
|---|---|
| Is there an internet cafe nearby? | **Czy jest tu gdzieś w pobliżu kafejka internetowa?** chyh yehst tuh gdj'yehsh' fpoh·<u>blee</u>·zhuh kah·<u>fehy</u>·kah een·tehr·neh·<u>toh</u>·vah |
| Does it have wireless internet? | **Jest tam bezprzewodowy internet?** yehst tahm behs·psheh·voh·<u>doh</u>·vyh een·<u>tehr</u>·neht |
| How do I turn the computer on/off? | **Jak _włączyć/wyłączyć_ komputer?** yah <u>_vwohn_</u>·_chyhch'_/_wyh_·<u>_wohn_</u>·_chyhch'_ kohm·puh·tehr |
| Can I...? | **Mogę...?** <u>moh</u>·geh... |
| – access the internet | – **skorzystać z internetu** skoh·<u>zhyhs</u>·tahch' zeen·tehr·<u>neh</u>·tuh |
| – check e-mail | – **sprawdzić pocztę** <u>sprahv</u>·dj'eech' <u>pohch</u>·teh |
| – print something | – **coś wydrukować** tsohsh' druh·<u>koh</u>·vahch' |
| How much per _hour/half hour_? | **Ile kosztuje _godzina/pół godziny_?** <u>ee</u>·leh kohsh·<u>tuh</u>·yeh zah goh·<u>dj'ee</u>·_nah_/puhw goh·<u>dj'ee</u>·_nyh_ |
| How do I...? | **Jak mam się...?** yahk mahm sh'yeh... |
| – connect/ disconnect | – **połączyć z siecią/rozłączyć** poh·<u>wohn</u>·chyhch' ssh'yeh·ch'yohm/rohz·<u>wohn</u>·chyhch' |

| | |
|---|---|
| – log *on/off* | – **zalogować/wylogować** zah·loh·<u>goh</u>·vahch'/ wyh·loh·<u>goh</u>·vahch' |
| How do I type this symbol? | **Jak wpisać ten symbol?** yahk <u>fpee</u>·sahch' tehn <u>syhm</u>·bohl |
| What's your e-mail? | **Jaki jest pana adres e-mail?** <u>yah</u>·kee yehst <u>pah</u>·nah <u>ahd</u>·rehs <u>ee</u>·mehyl |
| My e-mail is... | **Mój e-mail to...** muy <u>ee</u>·meyhl toh... |

## You May See...

| | |
|---|---|
| **ZAMKNIJ** | close |
| **USUŃ** | delete |
| **E-MAIL** | e-mail |
| **ZAKOŃCZ** | exit |
| **POMOC** | help |
| **KOMUNIKATOR** | instant messenger |
| **LOGIN** | login |
| **ANULUJ** | cancel |
| **OTWARTE** | open |
| **DRUKUJ** | print |
| **ZAPISZ** | save |
| **NAZWA UŻYTKOWNIKA** | username |
| **HASŁO** | password |
| **(BEZPRZEWODOWY) INTERNET** | (wireless) internet |

## Phone

| | |
|---|---|
| A phone card, please. | **Poproszę kartę telefoniczną.** poh·<u>proh</u>·sheh <u>kahr</u>·teh teh·leh·foh·<u>n'eech</u>·nohm |
| How much? | **Ile to kosztuje?** <u>ee</u>·leh toh kohsh·<u>tuh</u>·yeh |

| My phone doesn't work here. | **Mój telefon tu nie działa.** muy teh·<u>leh</u>·fohn tuh n'yeh dj'yah·wah |
|---|---|
| What's the country code for...? | **Jaki jest numer kierunkowy do...?** yah·kee yehst <u>nuh</u>·mehr kyeh·ruhn·<u>koh</u>·vyh doh... |
| What's the number for Information? | **Jaki jest numer do informacji?** yah·kee yehst <u>nuh</u>·mehr doh een·fohr·<u>mahts</u>·yee |
| I'd like the number for... | **Proszę o numer telefonu do...** proh·<u>sh'eh</u> oh <u>nuh</u>·mehr teh·leh·<u>foh</u>·nuh doh... |
| Can I have your phone number? | **Czy mogę prosić pana numer telefonu?** chyh <u>moh</u>·geh <u>proh</u>·sh'eech' <u>pah</u>·nah <u>nuh</u>·mehr teh·leh·<u>foh</u>·nuh |
| Here's my number. | **To jest mój numer telefonu.** toh yehst muhy <u>nuh</u>·mehr teh·leh·<u>foh</u>·nuh |

▶ For numbers, see page 168.

| Could you call me please? | **Czy mógłby pan do mnie zadzwonić?** chyh <u>muhgw</u>·byh pahn doh mn'yeh zahdz·<u>voh</u>·n'eech' |
|---|---|
| Text me. | **Napisz do mnie SMS-a.** <u>nah</u>·peesh doh mn'yeh eh·seh·<u>meh</u>·sah |
| I'll call you. | **Zadzwonię do pana.** zahdz·<u>voh</u>·n'yeh doh <u>pah</u>·nah |
| I'll text you. | **Napiszę do pana SMS-a.** nah·<u>pee</u>·sheh doh <u>pah</u>·nah es·seh·<u>meh</u>·sah |

## On the Phone

| Hello. This is... | **Dzień dobry. Mówi...** dj'yen' <u>dohb</u>·ryh <u>muh</u>·vee... |
|---|---|
| I'd like to speak to... | **Chciałbym♂/Chciałabym♀ rozmawiać z...** <u>hch'yahw</u>·byhm♂/<u>hch'yah</u>·wah·byhm♀ rohz·<u>mah</u>·vyahch' z... |
| Extension... | **Wewnętrzny...** vehv·<u>nehnch</u>·nyh... |

| | |
|---|---|
| Speak *louder/more slowly*, please. | **Proszę mówić *głośniej/wolniej*.** proh·<u>sh'eh</u> muh·veech' *<u>gwohsh'</u>·n'yehy/<u>vohl</u>·n'yehy* |
| Could you repeat that? | **Mógłby pan powtórzyć?** <u>muhgw</u>·byh pahn pohf·<u>tuh</u>·zhyhch' |
| I'll call back later. | **Zadzwonię później.** zahdz·<u>voh</u>·n'yeh <u>puhzh'</u>·n'yehy |
| Bye. | **Do widzenia.** doh vee·<u>dzeh</u>·n'yah |

► For business travel, see page 142.

## You May Hear...

| | |
|---|---|
| **Halo.** <u>hah</u>·loh | Hello. |
| **Przepraszam, kto mówi?** psheh·<u>prah</u>·shahm ktoh muh·vee | Who's calling, please? |
| **Proszę poczekać.** <u>proh</u>·sheh poh·<u>cheh</u>·kahch' | Please hold. |
| **Przełączę pana.** psheh·<u>wohn</u>·cheh <u>pah</u>·nah | I'll put you through. |
| **Nie może teraz podejść.** n'yeh <u>moh</u>·zheh <u>teh</u>·rahs poh·<u>deysh'ch'</u> | He/She can't come to the phone. |
| **Coś przekazać?** tsohsh' psheh·<u>kah</u>·zahch' | Would you like to leave a message? |

| | |
|---|---|
| **Czy może do pana oddzwonić?** chyh <u>moh</u>·zheh doh <u>pah</u>·nah ohd·<u>dzvoh</u>·n'eech' | Can he/she call you back? |
| **Jaki jest pana numer telefonu?** <u>yah</u>·kee yehst <u>pah</u>·nah <u>nuh</u>·mehr teh·leh·<u>foh</u>·nuh | What's your number? |

*i* Public phones are card operated. A local or international **karta telefoniczna** (phone card) can be purchased from kiosks or post offices. Be sure to break off the perforated corner before inserting the card into the phone.

## Fax

| | |
|---|---|
| Can I *send/receive* a fax here? | **Czy mogę *stąd wysłać/tu odebrać* faks?** chyh <u>moh</u>·geh *stohnt <u>vyhs</u>·wahch'/tuh oh·<u>dehb</u>·rahch'* fahks |
| What's the fax number? | **Jaki jest numer faksu?** <u>yah</u>·kee yehst <u>nuh</u>·mehr <u>fahk</u>·suh |
| Please fax this to... | **Proszę to przefaksować do...** <u>proh</u>·sheh toh psheh·fahk·<u>soh</u>·vahch' doh... |

## Post Office

| | |
|---|---|
| Where's the *post office/mailbox [postbox]*? | **Gdzie jest *poczta/skrzynka pocztowa*?** gdj'yeh yehst *<u>pohch</u>·tah/<u>skshyhn</u>·kah pohch·<u>toh</u>·vah* |
| A stamp for this *postcard/letter*, please. | **Poproszę znaczek na *tę pocztówkę/ten list*.** poh·<u>proh</u>·sheh <u>znah</u>·chehk nah *teh pohch·<u>tuhf</u>·keh/tehn leest* |
| How much? | **Ile to kosztuje?** <u>ee</u>·leh toh kohsh·<u>tuh</u>·yeh |
| I want to send this package by *airmail/express mail*. | **Chcę wysłać tę paczkę *pocztą lotniczą/priorytetem*.** htseh <u>vyhs</u>·wahch' teh <u>pahch</u>·keh *<u>pohch</u>·tohm loht·<u>n'ee</u>·chohm/pryoh·ryh·<u>teh</u>·tehm* |
| A receipt, please. | **Poproszę paragon.** poh·<u>proh</u>·sheh pah·<u>rah</u>·gohn |

## You May Hear...

| | |
|---|---|
| **Proszę wypełnić deklarację celną.** proh·sheh vyh·<u>pehw</u>·n'eech' deh·klah·<u>rahts</u>·yeh <u>tsehl</u>·nohm | **Please fill out the customs declaration form.** |
| **Jaka jest wartość przesyłki?** <u>yah</u>·kah yehst <u>wahr</u>·tohsh'ch' psheh·<u>syhw</u>·kee | **What's the value of the package?** |
| **Co jest w środku?** tsoh yehst <u>fsh'roht</u>·kuh | **What's inside?** |

**Poczta** (the post office) has locations throughout Poland. It handles mail and provides courier, phone and fax services. Stamps and postcards can be bought at the post office and at some kiosks. Mailboxes are red and display the logo **Poczta Polska**.

## ▼ Food

## Eating Out

## Essential

| | |
|---|---|
| Can you recommend a good *restaurant/cafe*? | **Czy może mi pan polecić dobrą** *restauracje/kawiarnię*? chyh <u>moh</u>·zheh mee pahn poh·<u>leh</u>·ch'eech' <u>dohb</u>·rohm rehs·tahw·<u>rahts</u>·yeh/kah·<u>vyahr</u>·n'yeh |
| Is there *a traditional Polish/ an inexpensive* restaurant nearby? | **Czy jest tu gdzieś w pobliżu** *tradycyjna polska/niedroga* **restauracja?** chyh yehst tuh gdj'yehsh' fpoh·<u>blee</u>·zhuh trah·dyh·<u>tsyhy</u>·nah <u>pohls</u>·kah/n'yeh·<u>droh</u>·gah rehs·tahw·<u>rahts</u>·yah |
| A table for *one/ two*, please. | **Stolik dla** *jednej osoby/dwóch osób*, **proszę.** <u>stoh</u>·leek dlah <u>yehd</u>·nehy oh·<u>soh</u>·byh/dvuhh <u>oh</u>·suhp <u>proh</u>·sheh |
| Could we sit...? | **Możemy usiąść...?** moh·<u>zheh</u>·myh uh·sh'yohn'sh'ch'... |
| – here/there | – **tu/tam** tuh/tahm |
| – outside | – **na zewnątrz** nah <u>zehv</u>·nohnch |
| – in a non-smoking area | – **w części dla niepalących** <u>fchehn'sh'</u>·ch'ee dlah n'yeh·pah·<u>lohn</u>·tsyhh |
| Where are the restrooms [toilets]? | **Gdzie są toalety?** gdj'yeh sohm toh·ah·<u>leh</u>·tyh |
| Can I have a menu? | **Mogę prosić menu?** <u>moh</u>·geh proh·sh'eech' meh·<u>n'ee</u> |
| What do you recommend? | **Co może pan polecić?** tsoh <u>moh</u>·zheh pahn poh·<u>leh</u>·ch'eech' |
| I'd like... | **Poproszę...** poh·<u>proh</u>·sheh... |
| Some more..., please. | **Poproszę trochę więcej...** poh·<u>proh</u>·sheh <u>troh</u>·heh <u>vyehn</u>·tsehy... |
| Enjoy your meal. | **Smacznego.** smahch·<u>neh</u>·goh |

| | |
|---|---|
| The check [bill], please. | **Poproszę rachunek.** poh·<u>proh</u>·sheh rah·<u>huh</u>·nehk |
| Is service included? | **Czy obsługa jest wliczona w cenę?** chyh ohp·<u>swuh</u>·gah yehst vlee·<u>choh</u>·nah ftseh·neh |
| Can I pay by credit card? | **Czy mogę zapłacić kartą kredytową?** chyh <u>moh</u>·geh zah·<u>pwah</u>·ch'eech' <u>kahr</u>·tohm kreh·dyh·<u>toh</u>·vohm |
| Can I have a receipt? | **Czy mogę prosić paragon?** chyh <u>moh</u>·geh <u>pro</u>·sh'eech' pah·<u>rah</u>·gohn |
| Thank you. | **Dziękuję.** dj'yehn·<u>kuh</u>·yeh |

## Restaurant Types

| | |
|---|---|
| Can you recommend...? | **Czy może pan polecić...?** chyh <u>moh</u>·zheh pahn poh·<u>leh</u>·ch'eech'... |
| – a restaurant | – **restaurację** rehs·tahw·<u>rahts</u>·yeh |
| – a cafe | – **kawiarnię** kah·<u>vyahr</u>·n'yeh |
| – a fast-food place | – **fast-food** <u>fahst</u>·fuht |
| – an ice-cream parlor | – **lodziarnię** loh·<u>dj'yahr</u>·n'yeh |
| – a pub | – **pub** pahp |

## Reservations and Questions

| | |
|---|---|
| I'd like to reserve a table... | **Chciałbym♂/Chciałabym♀ zarezerwować stolik...** hch'yahw·byhm♂/hch'yah·wah·byhm♀ zah·reh·zehr·<u>voh</u>·vahch' <u>stoh</u>·leek... |
| – for two | – **dla dwóch osób** dlah dvuhh <u>oh</u>·suhp |
| – for this evening | – **na dziś wieczór** nah dj'eesh <u>vyeh</u>·chuhr |
| – for tomorrow at... | – **na jutro na...** nah <u>yuht</u>·roh nah... |
| A table for two, please. | **Proszę stolik dla dwóch osób.** <u>proh</u>·sheh <u>stoh</u>·leek dlah dvuhh <u>oh</u>·suhp |

| We have a reservation. | **Mamy rezerwację.** <u>mah</u>·myh reh·zehr·<u>vahts</u>·yeh |
|---|---|
| My name is... | **Nazywam się...** nah·<u>zyh</u>·vahm sh'yeh... |
| Could we sit...? | **Możemy usiąść...?** moh·<u>zheh</u>·myh <u>uh</u>·sh'yohn'sh'ch'... |
| – here/there | **– tu/tam** tuh/tahm |
| – outside | **– na zewnątrz** nah <u>zehv</u>·nohnch |
| – in a non-smoking area | **– w części dla niepalących** <u>fchehnsh'</u>·ch'ee dlah n'yeh·pah·<u>lohn</u>·tsyhh |
| – by the window | **– przy oknie** pshyh <u>ohk</u>·n'yeh |
| Where are the restrooms [toilets]? | **Gdzie są toalety?** gdj'yeh sohm toh·ah·<u>leh</u>·tyh |

## You May Hear...

**Czy ma pan rezerwację?** chyh mah pahn reh·zehr·<u>vahts</u>·yeh — Do you have a reservation?

**Dla ilu osób?** dlah <u>ee</u>·luh <u>oh</u>·suhp — For how many?

**Co podać?** tsoh <u>poh</u>·dahch' — What would you like?

**Polecam...** poh·<u>leh</u>·tsahm... — I recommend...

**Smacznego.** smahch·<u>neh</u>·goh — Enjoy your meal.

## Ordering

| | | |
|---|---|---|
| Excuse me! | **Przepraszam!** psheh·<u>prah</u>·shahm | |
| I'm ready to order. | **Chciałbym♂/Chciałabym♀ już zamówić.** <u>hch'yahw</u>·byhm♂/<u>hch'yah</u>·wah·byhm♀ yuhsh zah·<u>muh</u>·veech' | |
| May I see the wine list? | **Mogę prosić kartę win?** <u>moh</u>·geh <u>proh</u>·sheech' <u>kahr</u>·teh veen | |
| I'd like... | **Poproszę...** poh·<u>proh</u>·sheh... | |
| – a bottle of... | **– butelkę...** buh·<u>tehl</u>·keh... | |
| – a carafe of... | **– karafkę...** kah·<u>rahf</u>·keh... | |
| – a glass of wine | **– kieliszek wina** kyeh·<u>lee</u>·shehk <u>vee</u>·nah | |
| – a glass of water | **– szklankę wody** <u>shklahn</u>·keh <u>voh</u>·dyh | |

▶ For alcoholic and non-alcoholic drinks, see page 76.

| | | |
|---|---|---|
| Can I have a menu? | **Mogę prosić menu?** <u>moh</u>·geh <u>proh</u>·sh'eech' meh·<u>n'ee</u> | |
| Do you have...? | **Czy mają państwo...?** chyh <u>mah</u>·yohm <u>pahn's</u>·tfoh... | |
| – a menu in English | **– menu po angielsku** meh·<u>n'ee</u> poh ahn·<u>gyehls</u>·kuh | |
| – a fixed-price menu | **– zestawy** zehs·<u>tah</u>·vyh | |
| – a children's menu | **– dania dla dzieci** <u>dah</u>·n'yah dlah <u>dj'yeh</u>·ch'ee | |

| | |
|---|---|
| What do you recommend? | **Co może pan polecić?** tsoh <u>moh</u>·zheh pahn poh·<u>leh</u>·ch'eech' |
| What's this? | **Co to jest?** tso toh yehst |
| What's in it? | **Z czego to jest zrobione?** <u>scheh</u>·goh toh yehst zroh·<u>byoh</u>·neh |
| It's to go [take away]. | **Na wynos, poproszę.** nah <u>vyh</u>·nohs poh·<u>proh</u>·sheh |

## You May See...

| | |
|---|---|
| **DANIA DNIA** | menu of the day |
| **OBSŁUGA (NIE)WLICZONA W CENĘ** | service (not) included |
| **SZEF KUCHNI POLECA** | specials |

## Cooking Methods

| | |
|---|---|
| baked | **pieczony** pyeh·<u>choh</u>·nyh |
| boiled | **gotowany** goh·toh·<u>vah</u>·nyh |
| braised | **duszony** duh·<u>shoh</u>·nyh |
| breaded | **panierowany** pah·n'yeh·roh·<u>vah</u>·nyh |
| creamed | **starty** <u>stahr</u>·tyh |
| diced | **pokrojony w kostkę** poh·kroh·<u>yoh</u>·nyh <u>fkohs</u>·tkeh |
| fried | **smażony** smah·<u>zhoh</u>·nyh |
| grilled | **grillowany** gree·loh·<u>vah</u>·nyh |
| poached | **z wody** <u>zvoh</u>·dyh |
| roasted | **pieczony** pyeh·<u>choh</u>·nyh |
| smoked | **wędzony** vehn·<u>dzoh</u>·nyh |
| steamed | **gotowany na parze** goh·toh·<u>vah</u>·nyh nah <u>pah</u>·zheh |
| stewed | **duszony** duh·<u>shoh</u>·nyh |
| stuffed | **faszerowany** fah·sheh·roh·vah·nyh |

## Special Requirements

| | |
|---|---|
| I'm... | **Jestem...** <u>yehs</u>·tehm... |
| - allergic to... | - **uczulony na...** uh·chuh·<u>loh</u>·nyh nah... |
| - diabetic | - **cukrzykiem** <u>yehs</u>·tehm tsuhk·<u>shyh</u>·kyehm |
| - a vegetarian | - **wegetarianinem**♂/**wegetarianką**♀ veh·geh·tahr·yah·<u>n'ee</u>·nehm♂/ veg·geh·tah·<u>ryahn</u>·kohm♀ |
| I'm lactose intolerant. | **Mam nietolerancję laktozy.** mahm n'yeh·toh·leh·<u>rahn</u>·tsyeh lahk·<u>toh</u>·zyh |
| I can't eat... | **Nie mogę jeść...** n'yeh <u>moh</u>·geh yehsh'ch'... |
| - dairy | - **produktów mlecznych** proh·<u>duhk</u>·tuhf <u>mlehch</u>·nyhh |
| - gluten | - **glutenu** gluh·<u>teh</u>·nuh |
| - nuts | - **orzechów** oh·<u>zheh</u>·huhf |
| - pork | - **wieprzowiny** vyehp·shoh·<u>vee</u>·nyh |
| - shellfish | - **owoców morza** oh·<u>voh</u>·tsuhf <u>moh</u>·zhah |
| - spicy food | - **pikantnych potraw** pee·<u>kahnt</u>·nyhh <u>poht</u>·rahf |
| - wheat | - **pszenicy** psheh·<u>n'ee</u>·tsyh |
| Is it kosher? | **Czy to jest koszerne?** chyh toh yehst koh·<u>shehr</u>·neh |

## Dining with Kids

| | |
|---|---|
| Do you have children's portions? | **Mają państwo porcje dla dzieci?** <u>mah</u>·yohm <u>pahn's</u>·tfoh <u>pohr</u>·tsyeh dlah <u>dj'yeh</u>·ch'ee |
| Can I have a *highchair/child's seat*? | **Mógłbym**♂/**Mogłabym**♀ **dostać** *wysokie krzesełko/krzesełko dla dziecka*? <u>muhgw</u>·byhm♂/<u>moh</u>·gwah·byhm♀ dohs·tahch' vyh·<u>soh</u>·kyeh ksheh·<u>sehw</u>·koh/ksheh·<u>sehw</u>·koh dlah <u>dj'yehts</u>·kah |

| Where can I *feed/ change* the baby? | **Gdzie mogę *nakarmić/przewinąć* dziecko?** gdj'yeh <u>moh</u>·geh nah·<u>kahr</u>·meech'/ psheh·<u>vee</u>·nohn'ch' <u>dj'yehts</u>·koh |
| Can you warm this? | **Może pan to podgrzać?** <u>moh</u>·zheh pahn toh <u>pohd</u>·gzhahch' |

▶ For travel with children, see page 145.

## Complaints

| How much longer will our food be? | **Jak długo jeszcze będziemy czekać na nasze zamówienie?** yahk <u>dwuh</u>·goh <u>yehsh</u>·cheh behn'·<u>dj'yeh</u>·myh <u>cheh</u>·kahch' nah <u>nah</u>·sheh zah·muh·<u>vyeh</u>·n'yeh |
| We can't wait any longer. | **Nie możemy dłużej czekać.** n'yeh moh·<u>zheh</u>·myh <u>dwuh</u>·zhehy <u>cheh</u>·kach' |
| We're leaving. | **Wychodzimy.** vyh·hoh·<u>dj'ee</u>·myh |
| That's not what I ordered. | **Nie zamawiałem♂/zamawiałam♀ tego.** n'yeh zah·mah·<u>vyah</u>·wehm♂/ zah·mah·<u>vyah</u>·wahm♀ <u>teh</u>·goh |
| I ordered... | **Zamawiałem♂/Zamawiałam♀...** zah·mah·<u>vyah</u>·wehm♂/zah·mah·<u>vyah</u>·wahm♀... |
| I can't eat this. | **Nie mogę tego jeść.** n'yeh <u>moh</u>·geh teh·goh yehsh'ch' |
| This is too... | **To jest za...** toh yehst zah... |
| – cold/hot | – **zimne/gorące** <u>zh'eem</u>·neh/goh·<u>rohn</u>·tseh |
| – salty/spicy | – **słone/ostre** <u>swoh</u>·neh/<u>ohs</u>·treh |
| – tough/bland | – **twarde/mdłe** <u>tfahr</u>·deh/mdweh |
| This isn't fresh. | **To jest nieświeże.** toh yehst n'yeh·<u>sh'fyeh</u>·zheh |
| This is dirty. | **To jest brudne.** toh yehst <u>bruhd</u>·neh |

## Paying

| | |
|---|---|
| The check [bill], please. | **Poproszę rachunek.** poh·<u>proh</u>·sheh rah·<u>huh</u>·nehk |
| We'd like to pay separately. | **Chcielibyśmy zapłacić osobno.** hch'yeh·lee·<u>byhsh'</u>·myh zah·<u>pwah</u>·ch'eech' oh·<u>sohb</u>·noh |
| It's all together. | **Proszę policzyć wszystko razem.** <u>proh</u>·sheh poh·<u>lee</u>·chyhch' <u>fshyhst</u>·koh rah·zehm |
| Is service included? | **Czy obługa jest wliczona w cenę?** chyh ohp·<u>swuh</u>·gah yehst vlee·<u>choh</u>·nah <u>ftseh</u>·neh |
| What's this amount for? | **Za co jest ta kwota?** zah tsoh yehst tah <u>kfoh</u>·tah |
| Can I pay by credit card? | **Można płacić kartą kredytową?** <u>mohzh</u>·nah <u>pwah</u>·ch'eech' <u>kahr</u>·tohm kreh·deeh·<u>toh</u>·vohm |
| Can I have an itemized bill/ a receipt? | **Czy mogę dostać szczegółowy rachunek/ pokwitowanie?** chyh <u>moh</u>·geh <u>dohs</u>·tahch' shcheh·guh·<u>woh</u>·vyh rah·<u>huh</u>·nehk/ pohk·fee·toh·<u>vah</u>·n'yeh |
| That was delicious. | **Bardzo mi smakowało.** <u>bahr</u>·dzoh mee smah·koh·<u>vah</u>·woh |

It is customary to tip your server 10% of the total bill. In more expensive restaurants the head waiter should also be tipped.

## Market

| | |
|---|---|
| Where are the *carts [trolleys]/baskets*? | **Gdzie są *wózki/koszyki*?** gdj'yeh sohm <u>*vuhs*</u>·kee/koh·<u>*shyh*</u>·kee |
| Where *is/are*...? | **Gdzie *jest/są*...?** gdj'yeh *yehst/sohm*... |

▶ For food items, see page 81.

| I'd like some... | **Poproszę trochę...** poh·proh·sheh troh·heh... |
|---|---|
| Can I taste it? | **Mogę spróbować?** moh·geh spruh·boh·vahch' |
| I'd like... | **Poproszę...** poh·proh·sheh... |
| – a *kilo/half-kilo* of... | **– kilo/pół kilo...** kee·loh/puhw kee·loh... |
| – a *liter/half-liter* of... | **– litr/pół litra...** leetr/puhw leet·rah... |

▶ For conversion tables, see page 173.

| – a piece of... | **– kawałek...** kah·vah·wehk... |
|---|---|
| – a slice of... | **– plasterek...** plahs·teh·rehk... |
| More/Less. | **Trochę *więcej/mniej*.** troh·heh *vyehn·tsehy/ mn'yehy* |
| How much? | **Ile to kosztuje?** ee·leh toh kohsh·tuh·yeh |
| Where do I pay? | **Gdzie się płaci?** gdj'yeh sh'yeh pwah·ch'ee |
| A bag, please. | **Poproszę siatkę.** poh·proh·sheh sh'yaht·keh |
| I'm being helped. | **Już jestem obsługiwany♂/obsługiwana♀.** juhsh yehs·tehm ohp·swuh·gee·vah·nyh♂/ ohp·swuh·gee·vah·nah♀ |

## You May Hear...

| **Czym mogę służyć?** chyhm moh·geh swuh·zhyhch' | Can I help you? |
|---|---|
| **Co dla pana?** tsoh dlah pah·nah | What would you like? |
| **Coś jeszcze?** tsohsh' yehsh·cheh | Anything else? |
| **To wszystko?** toh fshyhs·tkoh | Is that all? |
| **(To będzie)...złotych.** (toh behn·dj'yeh)... zwoh·tyhh | (That's)...zlotys. |

## You May See...

| | |
|---|---|
| NAJLEPIEJ SPOŻYĆ PRZED... | best if used by... |
| KALORIE | calories |
| BEZ TŁUSZCZU | fat free |
| PRZECHOWYWAĆ W LODÓWCE | keep refrigerated |
| MOŻE ZAWIERAĆ ŚLADOWE ILOŚCI... | may contain traces of... |
| SPRZEDAĆ PRZED | sell by |

## Dishes, Utensils and Kitchen Tools

| | | |
|---|---|---|
| bottle opener | otwieracz do butelek | oht·<u>fyeh</u>·rahch doh buh·<u>teh</u>·lehk |
| bowl | miska | <u>mees</u>·kah |
| can opener | otwieracz do puszek | oht·<u>fyeh</u>·rahch doh <u>puh</u>·shehk |
| corkscrew | korkociąg | kohr·<u>koh</u>·ch'yohnk |
| cup | filiżanka | fee·lee·<u>zhahn</u>·kah |
| fork | widelec | vee·<u>deh</u>·lehts |
| frying pan | patelnia | pah·<u>tehl</u>·n'yah |
| glass (non-alcoholic/ alcoholic) | szklanka/kieliszek | <u>shklahn</u>·kah/ kyeh·<u>lee</u>·shehk |
| knife | nóż | nuhsh |
| measuring cup | miarka kuchenna | <u>myahr</u>·kah kuh·<u>hehn</u>·nah |
| napkin | serwetka | sehr·<u>veht</u>·kah |
| plate | talerz | <u>tah</u>·lehsh |
| pot | garnek | <u>gahr</u>·nehk |
| saucepan | rondel | <u>rohn</u>·dehl |
| spatula | łopatka | woh·<u>paht</u>·kah |
| spoon | łyżka | <u>wyhsh</u>·kah |
| teaspoon | łyżeczka | wyh·<u>zhehch'</u>·kah |

# Meals

**Śniadanie** (breakfast) is usually served between 7 and 10 a.m. **Obiad** (lunch) is the main meal, traditionally enjoyed between 1 and 5 p.m., but with changing working habits more and more people have their main meal in the evening. **Kolacja** (supper) is typically served from 6 p.m. onwards. It can be either a cold or hot meal.

## Breakfast

| | |
|---|---|
| **boczek** boh·chehk | bacon |
| **bułki** buhw·kee | rolls |
| **chleb** hlehp | bread |
| **dżem** djehm | jam |
| **herbata** hehr·bah·tah | tea |
| **jajecznica** yah·yehch·n'ee·tsah | scrambled eggs |
| **jajka sadzone** yahy·kah sah·dzoh·neh | fried eggs |
| **jajko na *twardo/miękko*** yahy·koh nah *tfahr·doh/myehnk·koh* | *hard-boiled/soft-boiled* egg |
| **jogurt** yoh·guhrt | yogurt |
| **kawa** kah·vah | coffee |
| **marmolada** mahr·moh·lah·dah | marmalade |
| **masło** mahs·woh | butter |
| **miód** myuht | honey |
| **mleko** mleh·koh | milk |

| | |
|---|---|
| I'd like... | **Poproszę...** poh·proh·sheh... |
| More...please. | **Poproszę więcej...** poh·proh·sheh vyehn·tsehy... |
| With/Without...please. | **Poproszę z/*bez*...** poh·proh·sheh z/*behs*... |
| I can't eat... | **Nie mogę jeść...** n'yeh moh·geh yehsh'ch'... |

| | |
|---|---|
| **omlet** <u>ohm</u>·leht | omelet |
| **parówki** pah·<u>ruhf</u>·kee | sausage |
| **płatki śniadaniowe** <u>pwaht</u>·kee shn'yah·dah·<u>n'yoh</u>·veh | cereal |
| **ser** sehr | cheese |
| **tost** tohst | toast |
| **woda** <u>voh</u>·dah | water |

## Appetizers [Starters] and Salads

| | |
|---|---|
| **grillowany oscypek** gree·<u>loh</u>·vah·nyh ohs·<u>tsyh</u>·pehk | grilled and smoked ewe's milk cheese |
| **grzybki marynowane** <u>gzhyhp</u>·kee mah·ryh·noh·<u>vah</u>·neh | marinated wild mushrooms |
| **naleśniki z kapustą i grzybami** nah·lehsh'·<u>n'ee</u>·kee skah·<u>puhs</u>·tohm ee gzhyh·<u>bah</u>·mee | thin pancakes with sauerkraut and mushrooms |
| **pieczarki w śmietanie** pyeh·<u>chahr</u>·kee fsh'myeh·<u>tah</u>·n'yeh | mushrooms in a cream sauce |
| **sałatka** sah·<u>waht</u>·kah | mixed salad |
| **sałatka jarzynowa** sah·<u>waht</u>·kah yah·zhyh·<u>noh</u>·vah | mixed vegetable salad in mayonnaise |
| **sałatka pomidorowa z cebulą** sah·<u>waht</u>·kah poh·mee·doh·<u>roh</u>·vah stseh·<u>buh</u>·lohm | tomato and onion salad |
| **sałatka ziemniaczana** sah·<u>waht</u>·kah zh'yehm·n'yah·<u>chah</u>·nah | potato salad |
| **śledź w oleju** sh'lehch' voh·<u>leh</u>·yuh | herring in oil |
| **śledź w śmietanie** sh'lehch' fsh'myeh·<u>tah</u>·n'yeh | herring in sour cream |
| **węgorz wędzony** <u>vehn</u>·gohsh vehn·<u>dzoh</u>·nyh | smoked eel |

| | |
|---|---|
| I'd like... | **Poproszę...** poh·<u>proh</u>·sheh... |
| More...please. | **Poproszę więcej...** poh·<u>proh</u>·sheh <u>vyehn</u>·tsehy... |

## Soup

**barszcz czerwony** bahrshch chehr·<u>voh</u>·nyh

beet soup

**bulion z pasztecikiem** <u>buhl</u>·yohn
spahsh·teh·<u>ch'ee</u>·kyehm

consommé with
meat-filled pastries

**chłodnik z botwinki** <u>hwohd</u>·n'eek
sboht·<u>feen</u>·kih

a cold soup with
sour cream, beets
and dill, served
with boiled eggs

**grochówka** groh·<u>huhf</u>·kah

pea soup

**jarzynowa** yah·zhyh·<u>noh</u>·vah

vegetable soup

**kapuśniak** kah·<u>puh</u>·<u>sh'</u>·n'yahk

sauerkraut soup

**ogórkowa** oh·guhr·<u>koh</u>·vah

pickled cucumber
soup

**pomidorowa z *ryżem/makaronem***
poh·mee·doh·<u>roh</u>·vah <u>z ryh</u>·zhehm/
mah·kah·<u>roh</u>·nehm

tomato soup with
*rice/noodles*

**rosół (z kury)** <u>roh</u>·suhw (<u>skuh</u>·ryh)

(chicken) broth

**szczawiowa** shchah·<u>vyoh</u>·vah

sorrel soup with
boiled eggs

**żurek (z białą kiełbasą)** <u>zhuh</u>·rehk
(<u>zbyah</u>·whom kyehw·<u>bah</u>·sohm)

sour rye soup (with
white sausage)

## Fish and Seafood

**dorsz** dohrsh

cod

**flądra** <u>flohn</u>·drah

flounder [plaice]

**homar** <u>hoh</u>·mahr

lobster

**karp** kahrp

carp

| | |
|---|---|
| *With/Without*...please. | **Poproszę *z/bez*...** poh·<u>proh</u>·sheh *z/behs*... |
| I can't eat... | **Nie mogę jeść...** n'yeh <u>moh</u>·geh yehsh'ch'... |

| | |
|---|---|
| **karp po żydowsku** kahrp poh zhyh·<u>doh</u>·skuh | carp Jewish style: seasoned and cooked in beer |
| **karp smażony** kahrp smah·<u>zhoh</u>·nyh | fried carp |
| **krewetki** kreh·<u>veht</u>·kee | shrimp [prawns] |
| **leszcz** lehshch | bream |
| **łosoś** <u>woh</u>·sohsh' | salmon |
| **łupacz** wuh·pahch' | haddock |
| **makrela** mahk·<u>reh</u>·lah | mackerel |
| **owoce morza** oh·<u>voh</u>·tseh <u>moh</u>·zhah | seafood |
| **pstrąg** pstrohnk | trout |
| **rak** rahk | crayfish |
| **ryba** <u>ryh</u>·bah | fish |
| **sandacz** <u>sahn</u>·dahch | perch |
| **sandacz po polsku** <u>sahn</u>·dahch poh <u>pohls</u>·kuh | perch in vegetable stock served with boiled eggs |
| **śledź** sh'lehdj' | herring |
| **szczupak (faszerowany)** <u>shchuh</u>·pahk (fah·sheh·roh·vah·nyh) | (stuffed) pike |
| **tuńczyk** <u>tuhn'</u>·chyhk | tuna |
| **węgorz** <u>vehn</u>·gohsh | eel |

## Meat and Poultry

| | |
|---|---|
| **baranina** bah·rah·<u>n'eeh</u>·nah | mutton |
| **boczek** <u>boh</u>·chehk | bacon |

| | |
|---|---|
| I'd like... | **Poproszę...** poh·<u>proh</u>·sheh... |
| More...please. | **Poproszę więcej...** poh·<u>proh</u>·sheh <u>vyehn</u>·tsehy... |

| | |
|---|---|
| **cielęcina** ch'yeh·lehn'·<u>ch'ee</u>·nah | veal |
| **drób** druhp | poultry |
| **gęś** gehn'sh' | goose |
| **gołąbki** goh·<u>wohmp</u>·kee | cabbage leaves stuffed with ground meat and rice |
| **golonka** goh·<u>lohn</u>·kah | pork shank |

| | |
|---|---|
| rare | **krwisty** <u>krfees</u>·tyh |
| medium | **średnio wysmażony** <u>sh'rehd</u>·n'yoh vyhs·mah·<u>zhoh</u>·nyh |
| well-done | **dobrze wysmażony** <u>dohb</u>·zheh vyhs·mah·<u>zhoh</u>-nyh |

| | |
|---|---|
| With/Without...please. | **Poproszę z/bez...** poh·<u>proh</u>·sheh z/behs... |
| I can't eat... | **Nie mogę jeść...** n'yeh <u>moh</u>·geh yehsh'ch'... |

| | |
|---|---|
| **gulasz wieprzowy** <u>guh</u>·lahsh vyehp·<u>shoh</u>·vyh | chopped pork with onions, pepper, garlic and tomato purée |
| **indyk** <u>een</u>·dyhk | turkey |
| **jagnię** <u>yahg</u>·n'yeh | lamb |
| **kaczka** <u>kahch</u>·kah | duck |
| **kaczka pieczona z jabłkami** <u>kahch</u>·kah pyeh·<u>choh</u>·nah zyahp·<u>kah</u>·mee | roast duck with apples |
| **kiełbasa** kyehw·<u>bah</u>·sah | sausage |
| **klopsy** <u>klohp</u>·syh | meatballs |
| **kotlety schabowe** koht·<u>leh</u>·tyh s·hah·<u>boh</u>·veh | breaded pork chops |
| **kurczak** <u>kuhr</u>·chahk | chicken |
| **mięso** myehn·soh | meat |
| **ozór** <u>oh</u>·zuhr | tongue |
| **schab pieczony ze śliwkami** s·hahp pyeh·<u>choh</u>·nyh zeh sh'leef·<u>kah</u>·mee | roast pork loin with prunes |
| **stek** stehk | steak |
| **szynka** <u>shyhn</u>·kah | ham |
| **wieprzowina** vyehp·shoh·<u>vee</u>·nah | pork |
| **wołowina** voh·woh·<u>vee</u>·nah | beef |
| **zrazy** zrah·zyh | rolled beef fillets |

## Traditional Dishes

| | |
|---|---|
| **bigos** <u>bee</u>·gohs | sauerkraut with meat, prunes and mushrooms |

| | |
|---|---|
| I'd like... | **Poproszę...** poh·<u>proh</u>·sheh... |
| More...please. | **Poproszę więcej...** poh·<u>proh</u>·sheh <u>vyehn</u>·tsehy... |

| | |
|---|---|
| **knedle ze śliwkami** <u>knehd</u>·leh zeh sh'leef·<u>kah</u>·mee | dumplings stuffed with plums |
| **kluski śląskie** <u>kluhs</u>·kee <u>sh'lohns</u>·kyeh | dumplings with bacon and onions |
| **leniwe pierogi** leh·<u>n'ee</u>·veh pyeh·<u>roh</u>·gee | large dumplings made with flour, potatoes and curd cheese |
| **pierogi z...** pyeh·<u>roh</u>·gee z... | dumplings stuffed with... |
| – **mięsem** <u>myehn</u>·sehm | – meat |
| – **grzybami** gzhyh·<u>bah</u>·mee | – mushrooms |
| – **kapustą** kah·<u>puhs</u>·tohm | – sauerkraut |
| – **serem** <u>seh</u>·rehm | – curd cheese |
| – **owocami** oh·voh·<u>tsah</u>·mee | – fruit |
| **pierogi ruskie** pyeh·<u>roh</u>·gee <u>ruhs</u>·kyeh | potato and curd cheese dumplings |
| **placki ziemniaczane** <u>plahts</u>·kee zyehm·n'yah·<u>chah</u>·neh | potato pancakes |

---

*i* Traditional Polish cuisine was influenced by the climate and location of Poland. Many dishes owe much to neighboring Russia, Germany and Hungary. Heavy soup, meat with root and/or pickled vegetables, cabbage, preserved fruit and dry and pickled mushrooms are still popular. So too are dumpling and noodle dishes. Modern Polish cuisine offers imaginative, healthy derivatives of traditional dishes. Salads and healthy snacks are popular, and vegetarian dishes are now common in restaurants.

---

| | |
|---|---|
| *With/Without*...please. | **Poproszę** *z/bez*... poh·<u>proh</u>·sheh *z/behs*... |
| I can't eat... | **Nie mogę jeść...** n'yeh <u>moh</u>·geh yehsh'ch'... |

## Vegetables

| | |
|---|---|
| **bakłażan** bahk·<u>wah</u>·zhahn | eggplant [aubergine] |
| **brokuł** broh·<u>kuhw</u> | broccoli |
| **brukselka** bruhk·<u>sehl</u>·kah | Brussel sprout |
| **burak** <u>buh</u>·rahk | beet |
| **cebula** tseh·<u>buh</u>·lah | onion |
| **cukinia** tsuh·<u>kee</u>·n'yah | zucchini [courgette] |
| **czosnek** <u>chohs</u>·nehk | garlic |
| **fasolka szparagowa** fah·<u>sohl</u>·kah shpah·rah·<u>goh</u>·vah | green bean |
| **groszek** <u>groh</u>·shehk | pea |
| **jarzyna** yah·<u>zhyh</u>·nah | vegetable |
| **kalafior** kah·<u>lah</u>·fyohr | cauliflower |
| **kapusta** kah·<u>puhs</u>·tah | cabbage |
| **marchew** <u>mahr</u>·hehf | carrot |
| **mieszane jarzyny** myeh·<u>shah</u>·neh yah·<u>zhyh</u>·nyh | mixed vegetables |
| **ogórek** oh·<u>guh</u>·rehk | cucumber |
| **papryka** pahp·<u>ryh</u>·kah | pepper |
| **pieczarka/grzyb** pyeh·<u>chahr</u>·kah/gzhyhb | mushroom/wild mushroom |
| **pomidor** poh·<u>mee</u>·dohr | tomato |
| **rzepa** <u>zheh</u>·pah | turnip |
| **sałata** sah·<u>wah</u>·tah | lettuce |
| **seler naciowy** <u>seh</u>·lehr nah·<u>ch'yoh</u>·vyh | celery |
| **ziemniak** <u>z'yehm</u>·n'yahk | potato |

| | |
|---|---|
| I'd like... | **Poproszę...** poh·<u>proh</u>·sheh... |
| More...please. | **Poproszę więcej...** poh·<u>proh</u>·sheh <u>vyehn</u>·tsehy... |

## Spices and Staples

| | |
|---|---|
| **chleb** hlehp | bread |
| **cukier** <u>tsuh</u>·kyehr | sugar |
| **keczup** <u>keh</u>·chuhp | ketchup |
| **majonez** mah·<u>yoh</u>·nehs | mayonnaise |
| **mąka (pszenna)** <u>mohn</u>·kah (<u>pshehn</u>·nah) | (wheat) flour |
| **makaron** mah·<u>kah</u>·rohn | pasta |
| **musztarda** muhsh·<u>tahr</u>·dah | mustard |
| **ocet** <u>oh</u>·tseht | vinegar |
| **oliwa** oh·<u>lee</u>·vah | oil |
| **pieprz** pyehpsh | pepper |
| **przyprawy** pshyh·<u>prah</u>·vyh | seasoning |
| **ryż** ryhsh | rice |
| **sól** suhl | salt |

## Fruit

| | |
|---|---|
| **agrest** <u>ahg</u>·rehst | gooseberry |
| **ananas** ah·<u>nah</u>·nahs | pineapple |
| **arbuz** <u>ahr</u>·buhs | watermelon |
| **banan** <u>bah</u>·nahn | banana |
| **brzoskwinia** bzhohs·<u>kfee</u>·n'yah | peach |
| **cytryna** tsyh·<u>tryh</u>·nah | lemon |
| **czereśnia** cheh·<u>resh'</u>·n'yah | cherry |
| **grejpfrut** <u>grehy</u>·fruht | grapefruit |
| **jabłko** <u>yahp</u>·koh | apple |

| | |
|---|---|
| With/Without...please. | **Poproszę z/bez...** poh·<u>proh</u>·sheh z/behs... |
| I can't eat... | **Nie mogę jeść...** n'yeh <u>moh</u>·geh yehsh'ch'... |

| | |
|---|---|
| **limonka** lee·<u>mohn</u>·kah | lime |
| **malina** mah·<u>lee</u>·nah | raspberry |
| **morela** mo·<u>reh</u>·lah | apricot |
| **owoce** oh·<u>voh</u>·tseh | fruit |
| **pomarańcza** poh·mah·<u>rahn'</u>·chah | orange |
| **porzeczka** *czarna/czerwona* poh·<u>zhech</u>·kah <u>chahr</u>·nah/chehr·<u>voh</u>·nah | *black/red* currant |
| **śliwka** sh'leef·kah | plum |
| **truskawka** truhs·<u>kahf</u>·kah | strawberry |
| **winogrono** vee·noh·<u>groh</u>·noh | grape |

## Cheese

| | |
|---|---|
| **biały ser** <u>byah</u>·wyh sehr | cottage cheese |
| **bryndza** <u>bryhn</u>·dzah | ewe's milk cheese |
| **camembert** kah·<u>mehm</u>·behr | camembert |
| **ser** sehr | cheese |
| **ser pleśniowy** sehr plehsh'·<u>n'yoh</u>·vyh | blue cheese |
| **ser topiony** <u>seh</u>·ryh tohp·<u>yoh</u>·nyh | processed cheese |
| **ser żółty** <u>seh</u>·ryh zhuhw·tyh | hard cheese |
| **twarożek** tfah·<u>roh</u>·zhehk | curd cheese |

## Dessert

| | |
|---|---|
| **deser** <u>deh</u>·sehr | dessert |
| **galaretka z bitą śmietaną** gah·lah·<u>reht</u>·kah <u>zbee</u>·tohm sh'myeh·<u>tah</u>·nohm | fruit jelly with whipped cream |
| **gruszki w syropie** <u>gruhsh</u>·kee fsyh·<u>roh</u>·pyeh | pears in syrup |

| | |
|---|---|
| I'd like... | **Poproszę...** poh·<u>proh</u>·sheh... |
| More...please. | **Poproszę więcej...** poh·<u>proh</u>·sheh <u>vyehn</u>·tsehy... |

| | |
|---|---|
| **kompot owocowy** <u>kohm</u>·poht oh·voh·<u>tsoh</u>·vyh | fruit compote |
| **lody...** <u>loh</u>·dyh... | ...ice cream |
| – **czekoladowe** cheh·koh·lah·<u>doh</u>·veh | – chocolate |
| – **malinowe** mah·lee·<u>noh</u>·veh | – raspberry |
| – **pistacjowe** pees·tats·<u>yoh</u>·veh | – pistachio |
| – **śmietankowe** sh'myeh·tahn·<u>koh</u>·veh· | – cream flavored |
| – **truskawkowe** truhs·kahf·<u>koh</u>·veh | – strawberry |
| – **waniliowe** vah·n'eel·<u>yoh</u>·veh | – vanilla |
| **murzynek** muh·<u>zhyh</u>·nek | chocolate cake with chocolate icing |
| **naleśniki** nah·lesh'·<u>n'ee</u>·kee | thin pancakes |
| **owoce z bitą śmietaną** oh·<u>voh</u>·tseh zbee·tohm sh'myeh·<u>tah</u>·nohm | fruit with whipped cream |
| **racuchy z jabłkami** rah·<u>tsuh</u>·hyh z yahp·<u>kah</u>·mee | small fried pancakes made with sliced apples |
| **sernik** <u>sehr</u>·n'eek | cheesecake |
| **szarlotka** shahr·<u>loht</u>·kah | apple tart |

---

| | |
|---|---|
| *With/Without*...please. | **Poproszę z/bez...** poh·<u>proh</u>·sheh *z/behs*... |
| I can't eat... | **Nie mogę jeść...** n'yeh <u>moh</u>·geh yehsh'ch'... |

# Drinks

## Essential

| | |
|---|---|
| May I see the *wine list/drink menu*? | **Czy mogę prosić *kartę win/listę drinków*?** chyh <u>moh</u>·geh proh·sheech' <u>*kahr*</u>·*teh veen/ <u>lees</u>·teh <u>dreen</u>·kuhf* |
| What do you recommend? | **Co może pan polecić?** tsoh <u>moh</u>·zheh pahn poh·<u>leh</u>·ch'eech' |
| I'd like a *bottle/ glass* of *red/white* wine. | **Poproszę *butelkę/kieliszek czerwonego/ białego wina*.** poh·<u>proh</u>·sheh buh·<u>tehl</u>·keh/ kyeh·<u>lee</u>·shehk chehr·voh·<u>neh</u>·goh/ byah·<u>weh</u>·goh <u>vee</u>·nah |
| The house wine, please. | **Poproszę wino stołowe.** poh·<u>proh</u>·sheh <u>vee</u>·noh stoh·<u>woh</u>·veh |
| Another *bottle/ glass*, please. | **Poproszę jeszcze *jedną butelkę/jeden kieliszek*.** poh·<u>proh</u>·sheh yehsh·cheh <u>*jehd*</u>·*nohm buh·<u>tehl</u>·keh/<u>yeh</u>·dehn kyeh·<u>lee</u>·shehk* |
| I'd like a local beer. | **Poproszę lokalne piwo.** poh·<u>proh</u>·sheh loh·<u>kahl</u>·neh <u>pee</u>·voh |
| Can I buy you a drink? | **Mogę postawić panu drinka?** <u>moh</u>·geh pohs·<u>tah</u>·veech' <u>pah</u>·nuh <u>dreen</u>·kah |
| Cheers! | **Na zdrowie!** nah <u>zdroh</u>·vyeh |
| A *coffee/tea*, please. | **Poproszę *kawę/herbatę*.** poh·<u>proh</u>·sheh <u>*kah*</u>·*veh/hehr·<u>bah</u>·teh* |
| A coffee with..., please. | **Poproszę kawę z...** poh·<u>proh</u>·sheh <u>kah</u>·veh z... |
| – milk | **– mlekiem** <u>mleh</u>·kyehm |
| – sugar | **– cukrem** <u>tsuhk</u>·rehm |
| – artificial sweetener | **– słodzikiem** swoh·<u>dj'ee</u>·kyehm |

| I'd like... | **Poproszę...** poh·<u>proh</u>·sheh... |
|---|---|
| – a juice | – **sok** sohk |
| – a cola | – **colę** <u>koh</u>·leh |
| – a (sparkling/still) water | – **wodę (gazowaną/niegazowaną)** <u>voh</u>·deh (gah·zoh·<u>vah</u>·nohm/n'yeh·gah·zoh·<u>vah</u>·nohm) |
| Is the tap water safe to drink? | **Można pić wodę z kranu?** <u>mohzh</u>·nah peech' <u>voh</u>·deh <u>skrah</u>·nuh |

## Non-alcoholic Drinks ───────────────

| | |
|---|---|
| **cola** <u>koh</u>·lah | cola |
| **gorąca czekolada** goh·<u>rohn</u>·tsah cheh·koh·<u>lah</u>·dah | hot chocolate |
| **herbata...** hehr·<u>bah</u>·tah... | tea... |
| – **czarna** <u>chahr</u>·nah | – black |
| – **owocowa** oh·voh·<u>tsoh</u>·vah | – fruit |
| – **zielona** zh'yeh·<u>loh</u>·nah | – green |
| – **ziołowa** zh'yoh·<u>woh</u>·vah | – herbal |
| – **z cukrem** <u>stsuhk</u>·rehm | – with sugar |
| – **z cytryną** stsyht·<u>ryh</u>·nohm | – with lemon |
| **kawa...** <u>kah</u>·vah... | coffee... |
| – **z mlekiem** <u>zmleh</u>·kyehm | – with milk |
| – **z cukrem** <u>stsuhk</u>·rehm | – with sugar |
| – **czarna** <u>chahr</u>·nah | – black |
| – **bezkofeinowa** behs·koh·feh·ee·<u>noh</u>·vah | – decaffeinated |
| – **z ekspresu** zehks·<u>preh</u>·suh | – espresso |
| – **po turecku** poh tuh·<u>rehts</u>·kuh | – Turkish |
| **lemoniada** leh·moh·<u>n'yah</u>·dah | lemonade |
| **mleko** <u>mleh</u>·koh | milk |

| | |
|---|---|
| **shake** shehyk | milk shake |
| **sok...** sohk... | ...juice |
| – **grejpfrutowy** grehy·fruh·<u>toh</u>·vyh | – grapefruit |
| – **pomarańczowy** poh·mah·rahn'·<u>choh</u>·vyh | – orange |
| – **jabłkowy** yahp·<u>koh</u>·vyh | – apple |
| – **owocowy** sohk oh·voh·<u>tsoh</u>·vyh | – juice |
| – **świeżo wyciskany** <u>sh'feh</u>·zho vyh·ch'ees·<u>kah</u>·nyh | – fresh squeezed |
| **woda** *gazowana/niegazowana* <u>voh</u>·dah gah·zoh·<u>vah</u>·nah/n'yeh·gah·zoh·<u>vah</u>·nah | *sparkling/still* water |

*i* Tea is a popular beverage in Poland, usually enjoyed black or with lemon. Traditionally, **esencja** (the essence) was brewed in a small ceramic teapot over a boiling kettle. The essence was poured into a glass or cup and boiling water was added. Nowadays, tea bags are frequently used. Other types of tea, such as green, fruit or herbal tea, have become increasingly popular. Coffee is also popular; many drink instant coffee at home. Specialty coffee, including espresso and mocha, is available at many of the numerous **kawiarnie** (coffee shops) in town.

## You May Hear...

**Czy mogę postawić panu coś do picia?** chyh <u>moh</u>·geh pohs·<u>tah</u>·vich' <u>pah</u>·nuh tsosh' doh <u>pee</u>·ch'yah

Can I get you a drink?

**Z mlekiem i z cukrem?** z <u>mleh</u>·kyehm ee <u>stsuhk</u>·rehm

With milk and sugar?

**Gazowana czy niegazowana?** gah·zoh·<u>vah</u>·nah chyh n'yeh gah·zoh·<u>vah</u>·nah

Sparkling or still water?

## Aperitifs, Cocktails and Liqueurs

| | |
|---|---|
| **ajerkoniak** ah·yehr·<u>koh</u>·n'yahk | egg-yolk liqueur |
| **gin** djeen | gin |
| **koniak** <u>koh</u>·n'yahk | imported brandy |
| **miód pitny** myuht <u>peet</u>·nyh | mead |
| **szarlotka** shahr·<u>loht</u>·kah | grass-flavored vodka and apple juice |
| **śliwowica** sh'lee·voh·<u>vee</u>·tsah | plum brandy |
| **whisky** <u>wees</u>·kee | whisky |
| **winiak** <u>vee</u>·n'yahk | Polish brandy |
| **wódka...** <u>vuht</u>·kah... | vodka... |
| – **czysta** <u>chyhs</u>·tah | – straight [neat] |
| – **z lodem** z <u>loh</u>·dehm | – on the rocks [with ice] |
| – **z wodą/tonikiem** z <u>voh</u>·dohm/ toh·<u>n'ee</u>·kyehm | – with *water/tonic water* |
| **żubrówka** zhuhb·<u>ruhf</u>·kah | vodka flavored with bison grass |

## Beer

**piwo...** <u>pee</u>·voh...                          beer...

– **bezalkoholowe** behz·ahl·koh·hoh·<u>loh</u>·veh      – non-alcoholic

– **butelkowe/beczkowe** buh·tehl·<u>koh</u>·veh/     – bottled/draft
   behch·<u>koh</u>·veh                                  [draught]

– **ciemne/jasne** <u>ch'yehm</u>·neh/<u>yahs</u>·neh   – dark/light

– **jasne pełne** <u>yahs</u>·neh <u>pehw</u>·neh       – lager

– **lokalne** loh·<u>kahl</u>·neh                     – local

– **pilsner** <u>peel</u>·znehr                       – pilsner

---

*i* Vodka is one of the best known Polish exports. Several brands,
such as Chopin® and Sobieski®, are very popular in the U.S.
and U.K. However, the greatest Polish specialty is Żubrówka®,
vodka flavored with a unique grass growing only in **Puszcza
Białowieska** (Białowieża Forest) in eastern Poland. The grass
lends Bison Vodka its unmistakeable taste and characteristic
yellowish color. Vodka is served cold and enjoyed from small
glasses or mixed with juice or soda. Flavored vodka is also
popular.
Vodka, made from either potatoes or rye, is still the national
drink, but beer has recently become equally popular.
Polish beer includes Żywiec™, Tyskie™, Lech™ and Warka™;
most well-known international brands can also be found.

---

## Wine

**wino...** <u>vee</u>·noh...                         ...wine

– **białe** <u>byah</u>·weh                           – white

– **czerwone** chehr·<u>voh</u>·neh                   – red

– **deserowe** deh·seh·<u>roh</u>·veh                 – dessert

– **musujące** muh·suh·<u>yohn</u>·tseh               – sparkling

# *Menu Reader*

| | |
|---|---|
| **ajerkoniak** ah·yehr·<u>koh</u>·n'yahk | liqueur made from egg yolks, aromatic spirits, sugar, vanilla and brandy |
| **agrest** <u>ahg</u>·rehst | gooseberry |
| **alkohol** ahl·<u>koh</u>·hohl | alcohol |
| **ananas** ah·<u>nah</u>·nahs | pineapple |
| **anchois** ahn·shuh·<u>wah</u> | anchovy |
| **arbuz** <u>ahr</u>·buhs | watermelon |
| **awokado** ah·voh·<u>kah</u>·doh | avocado |
| **babeczka** bah·<u>behch</u>·kah | scone |
| **bakłażan** bahk·<u>wah</u>·zhahn | eggplant [aubergine] |
| **banan** <u>bah</u>·nahn | banana |
| **baranina** bah·rah·<u>n'ee</u>·nah | mutton |
| **baranina pieczona ze śmietaną** bah·rah·<u>n'ee</u>·nah pyeh·<u>choh</u>·nah zeh sh'myeh·<u>tah</u>·nohm | roast mutton with sour cream |
| **barszcz (czerwony)** bahrshch (chehr·<u>voh</u>·nyh) | (red) beet [beetroot] soup |
| **bażant** <u>bah</u>·zhahnt | pheasant |
| **bazylia** bah·<u>zyhl</u>·yah | basil |
| **befsztyk tatarski** <u>behf</u>·shtyhk tah·<u>tahrs</u>·kee | steak tartare |
| **beza** <u>beh</u>·zah | meringue |
| **bezkofeinowa** behs·koh·feh·ee·<u>noh</u>·vah | decaffeinated |
| **biała kapusta** <u>byah</u>·wah kah·<u>puhs</u>·tah | white cabbage |
| **białko** <u>byahw</u>·koh | egg white |
| **biały ser** <u>byah</u>·wyh sehr | cottage cheese |

| | |
|---|---|
| **bigos** <u>bee</u>·gohs | sauerkraut with slices of meat, pork sausage, prunes and mushrooms |
| **biszkopt** <u>beesh</u>·kohpt | sponge cake |
| **bita śmietana** <u>bee</u>·tah sh'myeh·<u>tah</u>·nah | whipped cream |
| **boczek** <u>boh</u>·chehk | bacon |
| **brokuł** <u>broh</u>·kuhw | broccoli |
| **brukiew** <u>bruh</u>·kyehf | rutabaga [swede] |
| **brukselka** bruhk·<u>sehl</u>·kah | Brussel sprout |

| | |
|---|---|
| **bryndza** <u>bryhn</u>·dzah | ewe's milk cheese |
| **brzoskwinia** bzhohs·<u>kfee</u>·n'yah | peach |
| **budyń** <u>buh</u>·dyhn' | pudding |
| **budyń z karmelem** <u>buh</u>·dyhn' skahr·<u>meh</u>·lehm | caramel pudding |
| **bulion** <u>buh</u>·lyohn | clear soup |
| **bułka** <u>buhw</u>·kah | roll |
| **bułka tarta** <u>buhw</u>·kah <u>tahr</u>·tah | bread crumbs |
| **burak** <u>buh</u>·rahk | beet [beetroot] |
| **cebula** tseh·<u>buh</u>·lah | onion |
| **chipsy** <u>cheep</u>·syh | chips [crisps] |
| **chleb** hlehp | bread |
| **chleb pszenny** hlehp <u>pshehn</u>·nyh | wheat bread |
| **chleb razowy** hlehp rah·<u>zoh</u>·vyh | whole-wheat [wholemeal] bread |
| **chleb żytni** hlehp <u>zhyht</u>·nee | rye bread |
| **chłodnik** <u>hwohd</u>·n'eek | cold yogurt, dill and beet [beetroot] soup |
| **chrupki** <u>hruhp</u>·kee | corn snacks |
| **chrzan** hshahn | horseradish |
| **ciasteczko** ch'yahs·<u>tehch</u>·koh | cookie [biscuit] |
| **ciasto** <u>ch'yahs</u>·toh | pastry, cake |
| **ciasto francuskie** <u>ch'yahs</u>·toh frahn·<u>tsuhs</u>·kyeh | puff pastry |
| **ciasto z bakaliami** <u>ch'yahs</u>·toh zbah·kahl·<u>yah</u>·mee | dried fruit cake |
| **ciecierzyca** ch'yeh·ch'yeh·<u>zhyh</u>·tsah | chick pea |
| **cielęcina** ch'yeh·lehn'·<u>ch'ee</u>·nah | veal |
| **comber** <u>cohm</u>·behr | loin (usually game) |
| **cukier** <u>tsuh</u>·kyehr | sugar |

| | |
|---|---|
| **cukinia** tsuh·<u>kee</u>·n'yah | zucchini [courgette] |
| **ćwikła** <u>ch'feek</u>·wah | horseradish with beets [beetroot] |
| **cykoria** tsyh·<u>koh</u>·ryah | endive |
| **cynamon** tsyh·<u>nah</u>·mohn | cinnamon |
| **cytryna** tsyh·<u>tryh</u>·nah | lemon |
| **czarna** <u>chahr</u>·nah | black (coffee) |
| **czarna porzeczka** <u>chahr</u>·nah poh·<u>zhehch</u>·kah | black currant |
| **czarny chleb** <u>czahr</u>·nyh hlehp | dark bread |
| **czekolada** cheh·koh·<u>lah</u>·dah | chocolate |
| **czereśnia** cheh·<u>rehsh'</u>·n'yah | cherry |
| **czerwona fasola** chehr·<u>voh</u>·nah fah·<u>soh</u>·lah | kidney bean |
| **czerwona kapusta** chehr·<u>voh</u>·nah kah·<u>puhs</u>·tah | red cabbage |
| **czerwone** chehr·<u>voh</u>·neh | red (wine) |
| **czerwony pieprz** cher·<u>voh</u>·nyh pyehpsh | chilli pepper |
| **czosnek** <u>chohs</u>·nehk | garlic |
| **daktyl** <u>dahk</u>·tyhl | date |
| **deser** <u>deh</u>·sehr | dessert |
| **domowy** doh·<u>moh</u>·vyh | homemade |
| **dorsz** dohrsh | cod |
| **drink** dreenk | alcoholic drink |
| **drób** druhp | poultry |
| **dymka** <u>dyhm</u>·kah | spring onion |
| **dynia** <u>dyh</u>·n'yah | pumpkin |
| **dżem** djehm | jam |
| **dziczyzna** dj'ee·<u>chyhz</u>·nah | game |
| **dzik** dj'eek | wild boar |

**estragon** ehs·trah·gohn — tarragon

**fasola** fah·soh·lah — bean

**fasolka szparagowa** fah·sohl·kah shpah·rah·goh·vah — green bean

**figa** *suszona/świeża* fee·gah *suh·shoh·nah/ sh'vyeh·zhah* — *dried/fresh* fig

**flądra** flohn·drah — flounder [plaice]

**flaki** flah·kee — tripe

**frytki** fryht·kee — French fries [chips]

**galaretka** gah·lah·reht·kah — jelly

**gałka muszkatołowa** gaw·kah muhsh·kah·toh·woh·vah — nutmeg

**gęś** gehn'sh' — goose

**gęsty** gehns·tyh — rich (sauce)

**gin z tonikiem** djeen stoh·nee·kyehm — gin and tonic

**głowizna** gwoh·veez·nah — pig's head [brawn]

**gołąbki** goh·whomp·kee — ground [minced] meat with rice rolled in cabbage leaves

**golonka** goh·lohn·kah — pork shank

**gorąca czekolada** goh·rohn·tsah cheh·koh·lah·dah — hot chocolate

**gorzki** gohsh·kee — bitter

**goździki** gozh'·dj'ee·kee — cloves

**grejpfrut** grey·fruht — grapefruit

**grochówka** groh·huhf·kah — pea soup

**groszek** groh·shehk — pea

**groszek cukrowy** groh·shehk tsuhk·roh·vyh — sugarsnap pea [mangetout]

|  |  |  |
|---|---|---|
| **gruszka** gruhsh·kah | | pear |
| **gruszki w syropie** gruhsh·kee fsyh·roh·pyeh | | pears in syrup |
| **grzane wino** gzhah·neh vee·noh | | mulled wine |
| **grzyb** gzhyhb | | wild mushroom |
| **gulasz** guh·lahsh | | meat stewed in gravy |
| **gulasz wieprzowy** guh·lahsh vyep·shoh·vyh | | pork stew |
| **gulasz z jagnięcia** guh·lahsh zyahg·nyehn'·ch'yah | | lamb stew |
| **herbata** hehr·bah·tah | | tea |
| **herbatnik** hehr·baht·n'eek | | tea cookie [tea biscuit] |
| **homar** hoh·mahr | | lobster |
| **imbir** eem·beer | | ginger |
| **indyk** een·dyhk | | turkey |
| **jabłko** yahp·koh | | apple |
| **jagnię** yahg·n'yeh | | lamb |
| **jagoda** yah·goh·dah | | blueberry |
| **jajecznica** yah·yehch·n'ee·tsah | | scrambled eggs |
| **jajko** yahy·koh | | egg |
| **jajko na miękko** yahy·koh nah myenk·koh | | soft-boiled egg |
| **jajko na twardo** yahy·koh nah tfahr·doh | | hard-boiled egg |
| **jajko sadzone** yahy·koh sah·dzoh·neh | | fried egg |
| **jarzyna** yah·zhyh·nah | | vegetable |
| **jeżyna** yeh·zhyh·nah | | blackberry |
| **jogurt** yoh·guhrt | | yogurt |
| **kabaczek** kah·bah·chehk | | marrow |
| **kaczka** kahch·kah | | duck |
| **kaczka pieczona z jabłkami** kahch·kah pyeh·choh·nah z yahp·kah·mee | | roast duck with apples |

| | |
|---|---|
| **kalafior** kah·<u>lah</u>·fyohr | cauliflower |
| **kałamarnica** kah·wah·mahr·<u>n'ee</u>·tsah | squid |
| **kanapka** kah·<u>nahp</u>·kah | sandwich |
| **kapary** kah·<u>pah</u>·ryh | capers |
| **kapuśniak** kah·<u>puhsh'</u>·n'yahk | sauerkraut soup |
| **kapusta** kah·<u>puhs</u>·tah | cabbage |
| **kapusta kiszona** kah·<u>puhs</u>·tah kee·<u>shoh</u>·nah | sauerkraut |
| **karczoch** <u>kahr</u>·chohh | artichoke |
| **karp** kahrp | carp |
| **karp po żydowsku** kahrp poh zhyh·<u>dohs</u>·kuh | carp with spices cooked in beer |
| **karp smażony** kahrp smah·<u>zhoh</u>·nyh | fried carp |
| **kaszanka** kah·<u>shahn</u>·kah | black pudding |
| **kasztan** kahsh·<u>tah</u>·nyh | chestnut (sweet) |
| **kawa** <u>kah</u>·vah | coffee |
| **kawa rozpuszczalna** <u>kah</u>·vah rohs·puhsh·<u>chahl</u>·nah | instant coffee |
| **kawior** <u>kah</u>·vyohr | caviar |
| **kefir** <u>keh</u>·feer | thin yogurt |
| **kiełbasa** kyehw·<u>bah</u>·sah | sausage |
| **kiełbaska wieprzowa** kyehw·<u>bahs</u>·kah vyehp·<u>shoh</u>·vah | pork sausage |
| **kiełek fasoli** <u>kyeh</u>·wehk fah·<u>soh</u>·lee | bean sprout |
| **kisiel** <u>kee</u>·sh'ehl | jelly |
| **kiwi** <u>kee</u>·vee | kiwi |
| **klops** klohps | meatball |
| **kluski** <u>kluhs</u>·kee | noodles, dumplings |
| **kluski śląskie** <u>kluhs</u>·kee <u>sh'lohns</u>·kyeh | dumplings with bacon and onions |

| | |
|---|---|
| **kminek** <u>kmee</u>·nehk | caraway |
| **knedle ze śliwkami** <u>knehd</u>·leh zeh shleef·<u>kah</u>·mee | dumplings stuffed with plums |
| **kokos** <u>koh</u>·kohs | coconut |
| **kompot** <u>kohm</u>·poht | stewed fruit |
| **koper** <u>koh</u>·pehr | fennel |
| **koperek** koh·<u>peh</u>·rehk | dill |
| **kopytka** koh·<u>pyht</u>·kah | small potato dumplings |
| **korniszon** kohr·<u>n'ee</u>·shohn | gherkin |
| **kość** kohsh'ch' | bone |
| **kotlet** <u>koht</u>·leht | chop |
| **kotlet schabowy** <u>koht</u>·leht s·hah·<u>boh</u>·vyh | pork chop fried and breaded |
| **kozie mleko** <u>koh</u>·zh'yeh <u>mleh</u>·koh | goat's milk |
| **krab** krahp | crab |
| **krakers** <u>krah</u>·kehrs | cracker |
| **krewetka** kreh·<u>veht</u>·kah | shrimp [prawn] |
| **krokiet** <u>kroh</u>·kyeht | croquette |
| **królik** <u>kruh</u>·leek | rabbit |
| **krupnik** <u>kruhp</u>·neek | barley soup |
| **kukurydza** kuh·kuh·<u>ryh</u>·dzah | corn |
| **kurczak** <u>kuhr</u>·chahk | chicken |
| **kurczak grillowany** <u>kuhr</u>·chahk gree·loh·<u>vah</u>·nyh | grilled chicken |
| **kurczak pieczony** <u>kuhr</u>·chahk pyeh·<u>choh</u>·nyh | roast chicken |
| **kurczak smażony** <u>kuhr</u>·chahk smah·<u>zhoh</u>·nyh | fried chicken |
| **kurka** <u>kuhr</u>·kah | chanterelle mushroom |

| | |
|---|---|
| **kuropatwa** kuh·roh·<u>paht</u>·fah | partridge |
| **kwaśny** <u>kfahsh'</u>·nyh | sour (taste) |
| **łagodny** wah·<u>gohd</u>·neh | mild (flavor) |
| **langusta** lahn·<u>guhs</u>·tah | lobster |
| **lekki** <u>lehk</u>·kee | light (sauce) |
| **lemoniada** leh·moh·<u>n'yah</u>·dah | lemonade |
| **leniwe pierogi** leh·<u>n'ee</u>·veh pyeh·<u>roh</u>·gee | flour, potato and curd cheese dumplings |
| **leszcz** lehshch | bream |
| **likier** <u>lee</u>·kyehr | liqueur |
| **limonka** lee·<u>mohn</u>·kah | lime |
| **liść laurowy** leesh'ch' lahw·<u>roh</u>·vyh | bay leaf |
| **lód** luht | ice |
| **lody** <u>loh</u>·dyh | ice cream |
| **łopatka** woh·<u>paht</u>·kah | shoulder (cut of meat) |
| **łosoś** woh·sohsh' | salmon |
| **łosoś wędzony** <u>woh</u>·sohsh' vehn·<u>dzoh</u>·nyh | smoked salmon |
| **lukier** <u>luh</u>·kyehr | icing |
| **łupacz** <u>wuh</u>·pahch | haddock |
| **majonez** mah·<u>yoh</u>·nehs | mayonnaise |
| **majonez czosnkowy** mah·<u>yoh</u>·nehs chohsn·<u>koh</u>·vyh | garlic mayonnaise |
| **mąka** <u>mohn</u>·kah | flour |
| **mąka pszenna** <u>mohn</u>·kah <u>pshehn</u>·nah | wheat flour |
| **mąka razowa** <u>mohn</u>·kah rah·<u>zoh</u>·vah | whole-wheat [wholemeal] flour |
| **makaron** mah·<u>kah</u>·rohn | pasta |

| | |
|---|---|
| **makrela** mahk·<u>reh</u>·lah | mackerel |
| **malina** mah·<u>lee</u>·nah | raspberry |
| **małża** <u>mahw</u>·zhah | mussel |
| **mandarynka** mahn·dah·<u>ryhn</u>·kah | tangerine |
| **marcepan** mahr·<u>tseh</u>·pahn | marzipan |
| **marchew** <u>mahr</u>·hehf | carrot |
| **margaryna** mahr·gah·<u>ryh</u>·nah | margarine |
| **marmolada** mahr·moh·<u>lah</u>·dah | marmalade |
| **marynowany w occie** mah·ryh·noh·<u>vah</u>·nyh <u>voh</u>hts·ch'yeh | marinated in vinegar |
| **maślanka** mahsh'·<u>lahn</u>·kah | buttermilk |
| **masło** <u>mahs</u>·woh | butter |
| **mazurek** mah·<u>zuh</u>·rehk | Easter shortcake (various flavors) |
| **melasa** meh·<u>lah</u>·sah | molasses [treacle] |
| **melon** <u>meh</u>·lohn | melon |
| **miecznik** <u>myehch</u>·n'eek | swordfish |
| **mielona wołowina** myeh·<u>loh</u>·nah voh·woh·<u>vee</u>·nah | ground beef [minced meat] |
| **mięso** <u>myehn</u>·soh | meat |
| **mięso grillowane** <u>myehn</u>·soh gree·loh·<u>vah</u>·neh | grilled meat |
| **mieszane jarzyny** myeh·<u>shah</u>·neh yah·<u>zhyh</u>·nyh | mixed vegetables |
| **mięta** <u>myehn</u>·tah | mint |
| **migdał** <u>meeg</u>·dahw | almond |
| **migdały w cukrze** meeg·<u>dah</u>·wyh <u>ftsuhk</u>·sheh | sugared almonds |
| **miód** myuht | honey |
| **miód pitny** myuht <u>peet</u>·nyh | mead |

**mizeria** mee·<u>zeh</u>·ryah — cucumber salad with sour cream

**mleko** <u>mle</u>·koh — milk

**młoda kapusta** <u>mwoh</u>·dah kah·<u>puhs</u>·tah — spring cabbage

**młody kurczak** <u>mwoh</u>·dyh <u>kuhr</u>·chahk — spring chicken

**mocny** <u>mohyts</u>·nyh — full-bodied (wine), strong (beer)

**morela** moh·<u>reh</u>·lah — apricot

**morwa** <u>mohr</u>·vah — mulberry

**mrożony** mroh·<u>zhoh</u>·nyh — iced (drinks)

**mus** muhs — mousse

**musujący** muh·suh·<u>yohn</u>·tsyh — sparkling

**musztarda** muhsh·<u>tahr</u>·dah — mustard

**naleśnik** nah·<u>lehsh'</u>·n'eek — thin pancake

**naleśniki z kapustą i grzybami** nah·lehsh'·<u>n'ee</u>·kee skah·<u>puhs</u>·tohm ee gzhyh·<u>bah</u>·mee — thin pancakes with sauerkraut and mushrooms

**napój** <u>nah</u>·puy — soft drink

**nektarynka** nehk·tah·<u>ryhn</u>·kah — nectarine

**nerka** <u>nehr</u>·kah — kidney

**nerkówka** nehr·<u>kuhf</u>·kah — loin (cut of meat)

**noga** <u>noh</u>·gah — leg (cut of meat)

**nóżki** <u>nuhsh</u>·kee — pigs' feet

**nugat** <u>nuh</u>·gaht — nougat

**ogon** <u>oh</u>·gohn — oxtail

**ogórek** oh·<u>guh</u>·rehk — cucumber

**ogórek kiszony** oh·<u>guh</u>·rehk kee·<u>shoh</u>·nyh — dill pickle

| | |
|---|---|
| **ogórek konserwowy** oh·<u>guh</u>·rehk kohn·sehr·<u>voh</u>·vyh | pickle |
| **ogórkowa** oh·guhr·<u>koh</u>·vah | pickled cucumber soup |
| **okoń** <u>oh</u>·kohn' | bass |
| **oliwka** oh·<u>leef</u>·kah | olive |
| **oliwki nadziewane** oh·<u>leef</u>·kee nah·dj'yeh·<u>vah</u>·neh | stuffed olives |
| **omlet** <u>ohm</u>·leht | omelet |
| **opieniek** oh·<u>pyeh</u>·n'yehk | oyster mushroom |
| **oranżada** oh·rahn·<u>zhah</u>·dah | orangeade |
| **orzech** <u>oh</u>·zhehh | nut |
| **orzech laskowy** <u>oh</u>·zhehh lahs·<u>koh</u>·vyh | hazelnut |
| **orzech nerkowca** <u>oh</u>·zhehh nehr·<u>kohf</u>·tsah | cashew |
| **orzech włoski** <u>oh</u>·zhehh <u>vwohs</u>·kee | walnut |
| **orzechy mieszane** oh·<u>zheh</u>·hyh myeh·<u>shah</u>·neh | assorted nuts |
| **orzeszek ziemny** oh·<u>zheh</u>·shehk <u>z'yehm</u>·nyh | peanut |
| **orzeszki ziemne solone** oh·<u>zhehsh</u>·kee <u>z'yehm</u>·neh soh·<u>loh</u>·neh | salted peanuts |
| **ośmiornica** ohsh'·myohr·<u>nee</u>·tsah | octopus |
| **ostra kiełbaska** <u>ohs</u>·trah kyehw·<u>bahs</u>·kah | spicy sausage |
| **ostry (smak)** <u>ohs</u>·tryh | hot, spicy (flavor) |
| **ostryga** ohs·<u>tryh</u>·gah | oyster |
| **owoce** oh·<u>voh</u>·tseh | fruit |
| **owoce kandyzowane** oh·<u>voh</u>·tseh kahn·dyh·zoh·<u>vah</u>·neh | candied fruit |
| **owoce morza** oh·<u>voh</u>·tseh <u>moh</u>·zhah | seafood |
| **owoce z puszki** oh·<u>voh</u>·tseh <u>spuhsh</u>·kee | canned fruit |

| | |
|---|---|
| **owsianka** ohf·<u>sh'yahn</u>·kah | porridge |
| **ozór** <u>oh</u>·zuhr | tongue |
| **pączek** <u>pohn</u>·chehk | donut [doughnut] |
| **papryka *zielona/czerwona*** pahp·<u>ryh</u>·kah zh'yeh·<u>loh</u>·nah/chehr·<u>voh</u>·nah | *green/red* pepper |
| **parówka** pah·<u>ruhf</u>·kah | sausage |
| **pasternak** pah·<u>stehr</u>·nahk | parsnip |
| **paszteciki** pahsh·teh·<u>ch'ee</u>·kee | pastries filled with meat, fish or cabbage |
| **pasztet** <u>pahsh</u>·teht | pâté |
| **pasztet w galarecie** <u>pahsh</u>·teht vgah·lah·<u>reh</u>·ch'yeh | pâté in aspic |
| **perliczka** pehr·<u>leech</u>·kah | guinea fowl |
| **pieczarka** pyeh·<u>chahr</u>·kah | mushroom |
| **pieczarki w śmietanie** pyeh·<u>chahr</u>·kee vsh'myeh·<u>tah</u>·n'yeh | mushrooms in cream |
| **pieczeń** pyeh·chehn' | pot roast |
| **pieczona wołowina** pyeh·<u>choh</u>·nah voh·woh·<u>vee</u>·nah | roast beef |
| **pieprz** pyehpsh | pepper (condiment) |
| **pieprzny sos** <u>pyehp</u>·shnyh sohs | hot pepper sauce |
| **piernik** <u>pyehr</u>·n'eek | ginger cake |
| **pierogi** pyeh·<u>roh</u>·gee | stuffed dumplings |
| **pierogi ruskie** pyeh·<u>roh</u>·gee <u>ruhs</u>·kyeh | dumplings with cheese and onion |
| **pierogi z kapustą i z grzybami** pyeh·<u>roh</u>·gee skah·<u>puhs</u>·tohm ee zgzhyh·<u>bah</u>·mee | dumplings with sauerkraut and mushrooms |
| **pierogi z mięsem** pyeh·<u>roh</u>·gee <u>zmyehn</u>·sehm | dumplings with meat |

| | |
|---|---|
| **pierogi z owocami** pyeh·<u>roh</u>·gee zoh·voh·<u>tsah</u>·mee | dumplings with fruit |
| **pierogi z serem** pyeh·<u>roh</u>·gee sseh·rehm | dumplings with curd cheese |
| **pierś** pyehrsh' | breast |
| **pierś z kurczaka** pyehrsh' skuhr·<u>chah</u>·kah | breast of chicken |
| **pietruszka zielona** pyeht·<u>ruhsh</u>·kah zh'yeh·<u>loh</u>·nah | parsley |
| **pikantny** pee·<u>kahnt</u>·nyh | spicy |
| **piwo** <u>pee</u>·voh | beer |
| **piwo jasne pełne** <u>pee</u>·voh <u>yahs</u>·neh pehw·neh | lager |
| **placek** <u>plah</u>·tsehk | tart, pie |
| **placki ziemniaczane** <u>plahts</u>·kee zh'yehm·n'yah·<u>chah</u>·neh | potato pancakes |
| **płatki śniadaniowe** <u>pwaht</u>·kee sh'nyah·dah·<u>n'yoh</u>·veh | cereal |
| **podroby** pohd·<u>roh</u>·byh | giblets |
| **polędwica** poh·lehnd·<u>vee</u>·tsah | tenderloin (cut of meat) |
| **pomarańcza** poh·mah·<u>rahn'</u>·chah | orange |
| **pomidor** poh·<u>mee</u>·dohr | tomato |
| **pomidorowa z *makaronem/ryżem*** poh·mee·doh·<u>roh</u>·vah z *mah·kah·<u>roh</u>·nehm/ <u>ryh</u>·zhehm* | tomato soup with *noodles/rice* |
| **poncz** pohnch | punch |
| **por** pohr | leek |
| **porcja** <u>pohr</u>·tsyah | portion |
| **porto** <u>pohr</u>·toh | port |
| **potrawa** poh·<u>trah</u>·vah | dish |
| **potrawka** poh·<u>trahf</u>·kah | casserole |

**prosiak** proh·sh'yahk — suckling pig

**przekąski** psheh·<u>kohns</u>·kee — snacks

**przepiórka** psheh·<u>pyuhr</u>·kah — quail

**przyprawy** pshyh·<u>prah</u>·vyh — seasoning, spices

**przysmak regionalny** <u>pshyhs</u>·mahk reh·gyoh·<u>nahl</u>·nyh — local specialty

**pstrąg** pstrohnk — trout

**purée** pee·<u>reh</u> — purée

**purée z ziemniaków** pee·<u>reh</u> zzh'yehm·<u>n'yah</u>·kuhf — potato purée

**pyzy** <u>pyh</u>·zyh — large potato dumplings, sometimes with meat stuffing

**rabarbar** rah·<u>bahr</u>·bahr — rhubarb

**racuch** <u>rah</u>·tsuhh — small pancake

**racuchy z jabłkami** rah·<u>tsuh</u>·hyh zyahp·<u>kah</u>·mee — apple pancakes, fritters

**rak** rahk — crayfish

**rodzynki** roh·<u>dzyhn</u>·kee — raisins

**rolmops** <u>rohl</u>·mohps — pickled herring filet [rollmop herring]

**rosół** <u>roh</u>·suhw — consommé, broth

**rosół z kury** <u>roh</u>·suhw <u>skuh</u>·ryh — chicken broth

**rosół z mięsem i jarzynami** <u>roh</u>·suhw <u>zmyehn</u>·shem ee yah·zhyh·<u>nah</u>·mee — meat and vegetable broth

**rostbef** <u>rohst</u>·behf — roast beef

**rozmaryn** rohz·<u>mah</u>·ryhn — rosemary

**rumsztyk** <u>ruhm</u>·shtyhk — rumpsteak

**ryba** <u>ryh</u>·bah — fish

| | |
|---|---|
| **ryż** rysh | rice |
| **rzepa** <u>zheh</u>·pah | turnip |
| **rzeżucha** zheh·<u>zhuh</u>·hah | cress |
| **rzeżucha wodna** zheh·<u>zhuh</u>·hah <u>vohd</u>·nah | watercress |
| **rzodkiewka** zhoht·<u>kyehf</u>·kah | radish |
| **sałata** sah·<u>wahh</u>·tah | lettuce |
| **sałatka jarzynowa** sah·<u>waht</u>·kah yah·zhyh·<u>noh</u>·vah | mixed vegetable salad |
| **sałatka z kapusty** sah·<u>waht</u>·kah skah·<u>puhs</u>·tyh | coleslaw |
| **salceson** sahl·<u>tseh</u>·sohn | headcheese [brawn] |
| **sandacz** <u>sahn</u>·dahch | perch |
| **sandacz po polsku** <u>sahn</u>·dahch poh <u>pohl</u>·skuh | perch in vegetable stock with eggs |
| **sardynka** sahr·<u>dyhn</u>·kah | sardine |
| **sarnina** sahr·<u>nee</u>·nah | venison |
| **schab** s·hahp | loin of pork |
| **schab pieczony ze śliwkami** s·hahp pyeh·<u>choh</u>·nyh zeh sh'leef·<u>kah</u>·mee | roast pork sirloin with prunes |
| **schłodzony** s·hwoh·<u>dzoh</u>·nyh | chilled |
| **seler naciowy** <u>seh</u>·lehr nah·<u>ch'yoh</u>·vyh | celery |
| **ser** sehr | cheese |
| **ser kozi** sehr <u>koh</u>·zh'ee | goat's cheese |
| **ser owczy** sehr <u>ohf</u>·chyh | ewe's milk cheese |
| **ser pleśniowy** sehr pleh·sh'<u>n'yoh</u>·vyh | blue cheese |
| **ser topiony** <u>seh</u>·ryh toh·<u>pyoh</u>·nyh | processed cheese |
| **serce** <u>sehr</u>·tseh | heart |
| **sernik** <u>sehr</u>·n'eek | cheesecake |
| **shake** shehyk | milkshake |

| | |
|---|---|
| **śledź** sh'lehch' | herring |
| **śledź marynowany** sh'lehch' mah·ryh·noh·<u>vah</u>·nyh | marinated herring |
| **śledź w oleju** sh'lehch' voh·<u>leh</u>·yuh | herring in oil |
| **śledź w śmietanie** sh'lehch' fsh'myeh·<u>tah</u>·n'yeh | herring in sour cream |
| **ślimak** <u>sh'lee</u>·mahk | snail |
| **śliwka** <u>sh'leef</u>·kah | plum |
| **śliwowica** sh'lee·voh·<u>vee</u>·tsah | plum brandy |
| **słodka papryka** <u>swoht</u>·kah pah·<u>pryh</u>·kah | sweet red pepper |
| **słodki** <u>swoht</u>·kee | sweet |
| **słodycze** swoh·<u>dyh</u>·cheh | candies [sweets] |
| **słodzik** <u>swoh</u>·dj'eek | sweetener |
| **śmietana** sh'myeh·<u>tah</u>·nah | cream |
| **soczewica** soh·cheh·<u>vee</u>·tsah | lentil |
| **sok** sohk | juice |
| **sok cytrynowy** sohk tsyh·tryh·<u>noh</u>·vyh | lemon juice |
| **sok owocowy** sohk oh·voh·<u>tsoh</u>·vyh | fruit juice |
| **sok pomarańczowy** sohk poh·mah·ran'·<u>choh</u>·vyh | orange juice |
| **sok z limonki** sohk zlee·<u>mohn</u>·kee | lime juice |
| **sól** suhl | salt |
| **sola** <u>soh</u>·lah | sole |
| **solony** soh·<u>loh</u>·nyh | salted |
| **sos** sohs | sauce |
| **sos czosnkowy** sohs chohsn·<u>koh</u>·vyh | garlic sauce |
| **sos pomidorowy** sohs poh·mee·doh·<u>roh</u>·vyh | tomato sauce |
| **sos słodko-kwaśny** sohs <u>swoht</u>·koh·<u>kfahsh'</u>·nyh | sweet and sour sauce |
| **sos winegret** sohs vee·<u>neh</u>·greh | vinaigrette [French dressing] |

| | |
|---|---|
| **sos z pieczeni** sohs spyeh·<u>cheh</u>·n'ee | gravy |
| **specjalność szefa kuchni** spehts·<u>yahl</u>·nohsh'ch' <u>sheh</u>·fah <u>kuhh</u>·n'ee | special |
| **stek** stehk | steak |
| **stek z polędwicy** stehk spoh·lehnd·<u>vee</u>·tsyh | fillet steak |
| **strucla** <u>struhts</u>·lah | strudel |
| **suflet** <u>suhf</u>·leht | soufflé |
| **surówka** suh·<u>ruhf</u>·kah | fresh vegetable salad |
| **surowy** suh·<u>roh</u>·vyh | raw |
| **suszone daktyle** suh·<u>shoh</u>·neh dahk·<u>tyh</u>·leh | dried dates |
| **suszone śliwki** suh·<u>shoh</u>·neh sh'leef·kee | prunes |
| **świeże owoce** <u>sh'fyeh</u>·zheh oh·<u>voh</u>·tseh | fresh fruit |
| **świeży** <u>sh'fyeh</u>·zhyh | fresh |
| **świeży daktyl** <u>sh'fyeh</u>·zhyh <u>dahk</u>·tyhl | fresh date |
| **syrop** <u>syh</u>·rohp | syrup |
| **szafran** <u>shahf</u>·rahn | saffron |
| **szalotka** shah·<u>loht</u>·kah | shallot |
| **szałwia** <u>shahw</u>·vyah | sage |
| **szarlotka** shahr·<u>loht</u>·kah | apple pie; grass-flavored vodka with apple juice |
| **szaszłyk** <u>shahsh</u>·wyhk | lamb or mutton kebab |
| **szczaw** shchahf | sorrel |
| **szczawiowa zupa** shchah·<u>vyoh</u>·vah <u>zuh</u>·pah | sorrel soup |
| **szczupak** <u>shchuh</u>·pahk | pike |
| **szczupak nadziewany** <u>shchuh</u>·pahk nah·dj'yeh·<u>vah</u>·nyh | stuffed pike |

| | |
|---|---|
| **szczupak w galarecie** <u>shchuh</u>·pahk vgah·lah·<u>reh</u>·ch'yeh | pike in aspic |
| **szczypiorek** shchyh·<u>pyoh</u>·rehk | chives |
| **szklanka** <u>shklahn</u>·kah | glass |
| **sznycel** <u>shnyh</u>·tsehl | breaded pork or veal cutlet |
| **szparag** <u>shpah</u>·rahg | asparagus |
| **szpinak** <u>shpee</u>·nahk | spinach |
| **szprotka** <u>shproht</u>·kah | sprat (small herring) |
| **sztuka mięsa** <u>shtuh</u>·kah <u>myehn</u>·sah | portion of meat |
| **szynka** <u>shyhn</u>·kah | ham |
| **tłusty** <u>twuhs</u>·tyh | fatty |
| **tonik** <u>toh</u>·neek | tonic water |
| **tort** tohrt | rich cake |
| **tost** tohst | toast |
| **trufla** <u>truhf</u>·lah | truffle |
| **truskawka** trus·<u>kahf</u>·kah | strawberry |
| **tuńczyk** <u>tuhn'</u>·chyhk | tuna |
| **twarożek** tfah·<u>roh</u>·zhehk | fresh curd cheese |
| **tymianek** tyh·<u>myah</u>·nehk | thyme |
| **udko** <u>uht</u>·koh | leg (cut of meat) |
| **w cieście** <u>fch'yehsh'</u>·ch'yeh | in batter |
| **w czosnku** <u>fchohsn</u>·kuh | in garlic |
| **w oliwie** voh·<u>lee</u>·vyeh | in olive oil |
| **wafel** <u>vah</u>·felh | waffle |
| **wanilia** vah·<u>n'eel</u>·yah | vanilla |
| **wątróbka** vohn·<u>truhp</u>·kah | liver |

| | |
|---|---|
| **wątróbka z kurczaka** vohn·truhp·kah skuhr·chah·kah | chicken liver |
| **wędlina** vehn·dlee·nah | cold cuts |
| **węgorz** vehn·gohsh | eel |
| **węgorz wędzony** vehn·gohsh vehn·dzoh·nyh | smoked eel |
| **wieprzowina** vyehp·shoh·vee·nah | pork |
| **winiak** vee·n'yahk | Polish brandy |
| **wino** vee·noh | wine |
| **wino deserowe** vee·noh deh·seh·roh·veh | dessert wine |
| **wino musujące** vee·noh muh·suh·yohn·tseh | sparkling wine |
| **wino stołowe** vee·noh stoh·woh·veh | table wine |
| **winogrono** vee·noh·groh·noh | grape |
| **winogrono czerwone** vee·noh·groh·noh chehr·voh·neh | red grape |
| **winogrono zielone** vee·noh·groh·noh zh'yeh·loh·neh | white grape |
| **wiśnia** veesh'·n'yah | cherry |
| **woda** voh·dah | water |
| **woda gazowana** voh·dah gas·how·ana | sparkling water |
| **woda gorąca** voh·dah goh·rohn·tsah | hot water |
| **woda mineralna** voh·dah mee·neh·rahl·nah | mineral water |
| **woda niegazowana** voh·dah nie·gas·how·ana | still water |
| **woda sodowa** voh·dah soh·doh·vah | soda water |
| **woda z lodem** voh·dah zloh·dehm | iced water |
| **wódka** vuht·kah | vodka |
| **wódki** vuht·kee | spirits |
| **wół** vuhw | ox |
| **wołowina** voh·woh·vee·nah | beef |

| | |
|---|---|
| **z cukrem** <u>stsuh</u>·krehm | with sugar |
| **z cytryną** stsyh·<u>tryh</u>·nohm | with lemon |
| **z kością** <u>skohsh'</u>·ch'yohm | on the bone |
| **zając** <u>zah</u>·yohnts | hare |
| **zakąski** zah·<u>kohns</u>·kee | appetizers |
| **zapiekany** zah·pyeh·<u>kah</u>·nyh | gratin |
| **zboże** <u>zboh</u>·zheh | grain |
| **żeberka** zheh·<u>behr</u>·kah | spare ribs |
| **zielona fasolka** zh'yeh·<u>loh</u>·nah fah·<u>sohl</u>·kah | green bean |
| **zielona sałata** zh'yeh·<u>loh</u>·nah sah·<u>wah</u>·tah | lettuce |
| **zielony pieprz** zh'yeh·<u>loh</u>·nyh pyehpsh | green pepper |
| **ziemniak** <u>zh'yehm</u>·n'yahk | potato |
| **ziemniak pieczony** zh'yehm·<u>n'yahk</u> pyeh·<u>choh</u>·nyh | baked potato |
| **ziemniaki gotowane** zh'yehm·<u>n'yah</u>·kee goh·toh·<u>vah</u>·neh | boiled potatoes |
| **zioła mieszane** <u>zh'yoh</u>·wah myeh·<u>shah</u>·neh | mixed herbs |
| **zioło** <u>zh'yoh</u>·woh | herb |
| **żółtko** <u>zhuhw</u>·tkoh | egg yolk |
| **żółty ser** <u>zhuhw</u>·tyh sehr | hard cheese |
| **Żubrówka** zhuh·<u>bruhf</u>·kah | grass-flavoured vodka |
| **zupa** <u>zuh</u>·pah | soup |
| **zupa jarzynowa** <u>zuh</u>·pah yah·zhyh·<u>noh</u>·vah | vegetable soup |
| **zupa krem** <u>zuh</u>·pah krehm | cream soup |
| **zupa na zimno** <u>zuh</u>·pah nah zh'eem·noh | cold soup |
| **żurek (z białą kiełbasą)** <u>zhuh</u>·rehk (<u>zbyah</u>·wohm kyeh·<u>bah</u>·sohm) | sour rye soup (with white sausage) |

# ▼ People

## Essential

| | |
|---|---|
| Hello. | **Dzień dobry.** dj'yehn' <u>dohb</u>·ryh |
| How are you? | **Jak się pan ma?** yahk sh'yeh pahn mah |
| Fine, thanks. | **W porządku, dziękuję.** fpoh·<u>zhohnt</u>·kuh dz'yehn·kuh·yeh |
| Excuse me! | **Przepraszam!** psheh·<u>prah</u>·shahm |
| Do you speak English? | **Mówi pan po angielsku?** <u>muh</u>·vee pahn poh ahn·<u>gyehl</u>·skuh |
| What's your name? | **Jak się pan nazywa?** yahk sh'yeh pahn nah·<u>zyh</u>·vah |
| My name is... | **Nazywam się...** nah·<u>zyh</u>·vahm sh'yeh... |
| Pleased to meet you. | **Miło mi pana poznać.** <u>mee</u>·woh mee <u>pah</u>·nah <u>pohz</u>·nahch' |
| Where are you from? | **Skąd pan jest?** skohnt pahn yehst |
| I'm from the U.S./U.K. | **Jestem z *USA/Wielkiej Brytanii.*** <u>yehs</u>·tehm z uh·ehs·<u>ah</u>/<u>vyehl</u>·kyehy bryh·<u>tah</u>·n'ee |
| What do you do? | **Czym się pan zajmuje?** chyhm sh'yeh pahn zahy·<u>muh</u>·yeh |
| I work for... | **Pracuję w...** prah·<u>tsuh</u>·yeh v... |
| I'm a student. | **Studiuję.** stuh·<u>dyuh</u>·yeh |
| I'm retired. | **Jestem na emeryturze.** <u>yehs</u>·tehm nah eh·meh·ryh·<u>tuh</u>·zheh |
| Do you like...? | **Lubi pan...?** <u>luh</u>·bee pahn... |
| Goodbye. | **Do widzenia.** doh vee·<u>dzeh</u>·n'yah |
| See you later. | **Do zobaczenia.** doh zoh·bah·<u>cheh</u>·n'yah |

## Communication Difficulties

| | |
|---|---|
| Do you speak English? | **Mówi pan po angielsku?** <u>muh</u>·vee pahn po ahn·<u>gyehls</u>·kuh |
| Does anyone here speak English? | **Czy ktoś tu zna angielski?** chyh ktohsh' tuh znah ahn·<u>gyehls</u>·kee |
| I don't speak much Polish. | **Słabo mówię po polsku.** <u>swah</u>·boh <u>muh</u>·vyeh poh <u>pohls</u>·kuh |
| Please speak more slowly. | **Proszę mówić wolniej.** <u>proh</u>·sheh <u>muh</u>·veech' <u>vohl</u>·n'yehy |
| Please repeat that. | **Proszę powtórzyć.** <u>proh</u>·sheh pohf·<u>tuh</u>·zhyhch' |
| Excuse me? [Pardon?] | **Słucham?** <u>swuh</u>·hahm |
| What was that? | **Co pan powiedział?** tsoh pahn poh·<u>vyeh</u>·dj'yahw |
| Can you spell it? | **Może pan to przeliterować?** <u>moh</u>·zheh pahn toh psheh·leeh·teh·<u>roh</u>·vahch' |
| Can you write it down? | **Może pan mi to napisać?** <u>moh</u>·zheh pahn mee toh nah·<u>pee</u>·sahch' |
| Can you translate this for me? | **Może pan mi to przetłumaczyć?** <u>moh</u>·zheh pahn mee toh psheh·twuh·<u>mah</u>·chyhch' |
| What does this mean? | **Co to znaczy?** tsoh toh znah·chyh |
| I understand. | **Rozumiem.** roh·<u>zuh</u>·myehm |
| I don't understand. | **Nie rozumiem.** n'yeh roh·<u>zuh</u>·myehm |
| Do you understand? | **Rozumie pan?** roh·<u>zuh</u>·myeh pahn |

## You May Hear...

| | |
|---|---|
| **Słabo mówię po angielsku.** <u>swah</u>·boh <u>muh</u>·vyeh poh ahn·<u>gyehls</u>·kuh | I speak only a little English. |
| **Nie mówię po angielsku.** n'yeh <u>muh</u>·vyeh poh ahn·<u>gyehls</u>·kuh | I don't speak English. |

## Making Friends

| | |
|---|---|
| Hello./Hi! | **Dzień dobry./Cześć!** dj'yehn' <u>dohb</u>·ryh/ chehsh'ch' |
| Good morning. | **Dzień dobry.** dj'yehn' <u>dohb</u>·ryh |
| Good evening. | **Dobry wieczór.** <u>dohb</u>·ryh <u>vyeh</u>·chuhr |
| My name is... | **Nazywam się...** nah·<u>zyh</u>·vahm sh'yeh... |
| What's your name? | **Jak się pan nazywa?** yahk sh'yeh pahn nah·<u>zyh</u>·vah |
| I'd like to introduce you to... | **Chciałbym♂/Chciałabym♀ pana przedstawić...** hch'yahw·byhm♂/ hch'yah·wah·byhm♀ <u>pah</u>·nah psheht·<u>stah</u>·veech'... |
| Pleased to meet you. | **Miło mi pana poznać.** <u>mee</u>·woh mee <u>pah</u>·nah <u>pohz</u>·nahch' |
| How are you? | **Jak się pan ma?** yahk sh'yeh pahn mah |
| Fine, thanks. | **W porządku, dziękuję.** fpoh·<u>zhohnt</u>·kuh dz'yehn·kuh·yeh |
| And you? | **A pan?** ah pahn |

Greetings between Polish men and women have changed during recent years. In the past men kissed women's hands as a sign of respect. Today men and women say hello or kiss each other on the cheek if they are good friends. In most situations you usually say **dzień dobry**, good morning or hello. With relatives, friends and children you can simply say **cześć**, hi.

## Travel Talk

| | |
|---|---|
| Where are you from? | **Skąd pan jest?** skohnt pahn yehst |
| I'm from... | **Jestem z...** <u>yehs</u>·tehm z... |

| I'm here on business/vacation [holiday]. | **Jestem tutaj _służbowo/na wakacjach._** yehs·tehm tuh·tay swuhzh·boh·voh/nah vah·_kahts_·yahh |
|---|---|
| I'm a student. | **Studiuję.** stuhd·_yuh_·yeh |
| I'm staying for... | **Będę tu...** _beh_·deh tuh... |
| I've been here... | **Jestem tu...** _yehs_·tehm tuh... |
| – a day | **– jeden dzień** _yeh_·dehn dj'yehn' |
| – a week | **– tydzień** _tyh_·dj'yehn' |
| – a month | **– miesiąc** _myeh_·sh'yohnts |

▶ For numbers, see page 168.

▶ For dates, see page 171.

## Relationships

| Who are you with? | **Z kim pan tu jest?** skeem pahn tuh yehst |
|---|---|
| I'm on my own. | **Jestem sam♂/sama♀.** _yehs_·tehm sahm♂/_sah_·mah♀ |
| I'm with... | **Jestem z...** _yehs_·tehm z... |
| – my husband/ my wife | **– moim mężem/moją żoną** _moh_·eem _mehn_·zhehm/_moh_·yohm _zhoh_·nohm |
| – my boyfriend/ my girlfriend | **– moim chłopakiem/moją dziewczyną** _moh_·eem _hwoh_·pah·kyehm/_moh_·yohm dj'yehf·_chyh_·nohm |
| – a friend | **– przyjacielem♂/przyjaciółką♀** pshyh·yah·_ch'yeh_·lehm♂/ pshyh·yah·_ch'yuhw_·kohm♀ |
| – a colleague | **– kolegą♂/koleżanką♀ z pracy** koh·_leh_·gohm♂/koh·leh·_zhahn_·kohm♀ _sprah_·tsyh |
| When's your birthday? | **Kiedy ma pan urodziny?** _k'yeh_·dyh mah pahn uh·roh·_dj'ee_·nyh |

| How old are you? | **Ile ma pan lat?** <u>ee</u>·leh mah pahn laht |
| I'm... | **Mam...lat.** mahm...laht |

▶ For numbers, see page 168.

| I'm... | **Jestem...** <u>yehs</u>·tehm... |
| – single | – **wolny**♂/**wolna** ♀ <u>vohl</u>·nyh♂/vohl·<u>nah</u> ♀ |
| – married | – **żonaty**♂/**mężatką** ♀ zhoh·<u>nah</u>·tyh♂/ mehn·<u>zhaht</u>·kohm ♀ |
| – divorced | – **rozwiedziony**♂/**rozwiedziona** ♀ rohz·vyeh·<u>dj'yoh</u>·nyh♂/rohz·vyeh·<u>dj'yoh</u>·nah ♀ |
| – separated | – **w separacji** fseh·pah·<u>rah</u>·tsee |
| Do you have *children/ grandchildren*? | **Ma pan *dzieci/wnuki*?** mah pahn <u>dj'yeh</u>·ch'ee/<u>vnuh</u>·kee |

## Work and School

| What do you do? | **Czym się pan zajmuje?** chyhm sh'yeh pahn zahy·<u>muh</u>·yeh? |
| What are you studying? | **Co pan studiuje?** tsoh pahn stuhd·<u>yuh</u>·yeh |
| I'm studying... | **Studiuję...** stuhd·<u>yuh</u>·yeh... |
| I work *full time/ part time*. | **Pracuję na *pełny etat/część etatu*.** prah·<u>tsuh</u>·yeh nah <u>pehw</u>·nyh eh·taht/ chehn'sh'ch' eh·<u>tah</u>·tuh |
| Who do you work for? | **Gdzie pan pracuje?** gdj'yeh pahn prah·<u>tsuh</u>·yeh |
| I work for... | **Pracuję w...** prah·<u>tsuh</u>·yeh v... |

▶ For business travel, see page 142.

## Weather

| What's the weather forecast? | **Jaka jest prognoza pogody?** yah·kah yehst prohg·<u>noh</u>·zah poh·<u>goh</u>·dyh |
| What *beautiful/ terrible* weather! | **Jaka *piękna/okropna* pogoda!** <u>yah</u>·kah *<u>pyehnk</u>·nah/oh·<u>krohp</u>·nah* poh·<u>goh</u>·dah |
| It's *cool/warm*. | **Jest *chłodno/ciepło*.** yehst *<u>hwohd</u>·noh/ <u>ch'yehp</u>·woh* |
| It's sunny. | **Świeci słońce.** sh'vyeh·ch'ee swohn'·tseh |
| It's *rainy/snowy*. | **Pada *deszcz/śnieg*.** <u>pah</u>·dah *dehshch/sh'n'yehk* |
| Do I need *a jacket/ an umbrella*? | **Mam wziąć *kurtkę/parasol*?** mahm vzyohn'ch' *<u>kuhrt</u>·keh/pah·<u>rah</u>·sohl* |

▶ For temperature, see page 173.

# *Romance*

## Essential

| Would you like to go out for a *drink/ meal*? | **Może pójdziemy *na drinka/coś zjeść*?** moh·zheh <u>pohsh</u>·lee·<u>byhsh</u>'·myh *nah <u>dreen</u>·kah/tsohsh' zyehsh'ch'* |
| What are your plans for *tonight/tomorrow*? | **Masz jakieś plany na *wieczór/jutro*?** mahsh <u>yah</u>·kyehsh' <u>plah</u>·nyh nah *<u>vyeh</u>·chuhr/<u>yuht</u>·roh* |
| Can I have your number? | **Podasz mi swój numer telefonu?** <u>poh</u>·dahsh mee sfuy <u>nuh</u>·mehr teh·leh·<u>foh</u>·nuh |
| Can I join you? | **Mogę się dosiąść?** <u>moh</u>·geh sh'yeh <u>doh</u>·sh'yohn'sh'ch' |
| Can I buy you a drink? | **Mogę postawić ci drinka?** <u>moh</u>·geh pohs·<u>tah</u>·veech' ch'ee <u>dree</u>·nkah |
| I *like/love* you. | ***Lubię/Kocham* cię.** *<u>luh</u>·bieh/<u>koh</u>·hahm* ch'yeh |

▶ For informal and formal usage, see page 163.

## Making Plans

| | |
|---|---|
| Would you like to go out for...? | **Może pójdziemy na...?** moh·zheh puy·<u>dj'yeh</u>·myh nah... |
| – coffee | – **kawę** <u>kah</u>·veh |
| – a drink | – **drinka** <u>dreen</u>·kah |
| – dinner | – **kolację** koh·<u>lahts</u>·yeh |
| What are your plans for...? | **Masz jakieś plany na...?** mahsh <u>yah</u>·kyehsh' <u>plah</u>·nyh nah... |
| – tonight | – **wieczór** <u>vyeh</u>·chuhr |
| – tomorrow | – **jutro** <u>yuht</u>·roh |
| – this weekend | – **weekend** <u>wee</u>·kehnt |
| Can I have your number? | **Podasz mi swój numer telefonu?** <u>poh</u>·dahsh mee sfuy <u>nuh</u>·mehr teh·leh·<u>foh</u>·nuh |
| Can I have your e-mail? | **Podasz mi swój e-mail?** <u>poh</u>·dahsh mee sfuy <u>ee</u>·mehyl |

▶ For e-mail and phone, see page 48.

## Pick-up [Chat-up] Lines

| | |
|---|---|
| Can I join you? | **Mogę się dosiąść?** <u>moh</u>·geh sh'yeh <u>doh</u>·sh'yohn'sh'ch' |
| Is this seat free? | **To miejsce jest wolne?** toh <u>myehys</u>·tseh yehst <u>vohl</u>·neh |
| You look great! | **Świetnie wyglądasz!** sh'<u>vyeht</u>·n'yeh wyh·<u>glohn</u>·dahsh |
| Shall we go somewhere quieter? | **Może pójdziemy w jakieś spokojniejsze miejsce?** <u>moh</u>·zheh puy·<u>dj'yeh</u>·myh vyah·kyehsh' spoh·kohy·<u>n'yehy</u>·sheh <u>myehys</u>·tseh |

## Accepting and Rejecting

| | |
|---|---|
| I'd love to. | **Bardzo chętnie.** <u>bahr</u>·dzoh <u>chehnt</u>·n'yeh |
| Where shall we meet? | **Gdzie możemy się spotkać?** gdj'eh moh·<u>zheh</u>·myh sh'yeh <u>spoht</u>·kach' |
| I'll meet you at your hotel. | **Spotkamy się w twoim hotelu.** spoht·<u>kah</u>·myh sh'yeh <u>tfoh</u>·eem hoh·<u>teh</u>·luh |
| I'll come by at... | **Przyjdę o...** <u>pshyhy</u>·deh oh... |
| What's your address? | **Gdzie mieszkasz?** gdj'yeh <u>myehsh</u>·kahsh |
| I'm busy. | **Jestem zajęty♂/zajęta♀.** <u>yehs</u>·tehm zah·<u>yehn</u>·tyh♂/zah·<u>yehn</u>·tah♀ |
| I'm not interested. | **Nie jestem zainteresowany♂/ zainteresowana♀.** n'yeh yehs·tehm zah·een·teh·reh·soh·<u>vah</u>·nyh♂/ zah·een·teh·reh·soh·<u>vah</u>·nah♀ |
| Leave me alone, please! | **Zostaw mnie w spokoju!** <u>zohs</u>·tahf mn'yeh fspoh·<u>koh</u>·yuh |
| Stop bothering me! | **Odczep się!** <u>oht</u>·chehp sh'yeh |

## Getting Physical

| | |
|---|---|
| Can I *hug/kiss* you? | **Mogę cię *przytulić/pocałować*?** <u>moh</u>·geh ch'yeh pshyh·<u>tuh</u>·leech'/poh·tsah·<u>woh</u>·vahch' |
| Yes. | **Tak.** tahk |
| No. | **Nie.** n'yeh |
| Stop! | **Przestań!** <u>pshehs</u>·tahn' |

## Sexual Preferences

| | |
|---|---|
| Are you gay? | **Jesteś gejem♂/lesbijką♀?** yehs·tehsh' <u>geh</u>·yehm♂/lehs·<u>beey</u>·kohm♀ |
| I'm... | **Jestem...** <u>yehs</u>·tehm... |
| – gay | – **gejem♂/lesbijką♀** <u>geh</u>·yehm♂/ lehs·<u>beey</u>·kohm♀ |
| – bisexual | – **biseksualny♂/biseksualna♀** bee·sehk·suh·<u>ahl</u>·nyh♂/ bee·sehk·suh·<u>ahl</u>·nah♀ |
| Do you like *men/women*? | **Wolisz *mężczyzn/kobiety*?** <u>voh</u>·leesh <u>mehnzh</u>·chyhzn/koh·<u>byeh</u>·tyh |

▶ For informal and formal usage, see page 163.

# ▼ *Fun*

# Sightseeing

## Essential

| | |
|---|---|
| Where's the tourist information office? | **Gdzie jest biuro informacji turystycznej?** gdj'yeh yehst <u>byuh</u>·roh een·fohr·<u>mah</u>·tsyee tuh·ryhs·<u>tyhch</u>·ney |
| What are the main points of interest? | **Co tu warto zobaczyć?** tsoh tuh <u>vahr</u>·toh zoh·<u>bah</u>·chyhch' |
| Are there tours in English? | **Czy są wycieczki po angielsku?** chyh sohm vyh·<u>ch'yech</u>·kee poh ahn·<u>gyehl</u>·skuh |
| Could I have a *map/ guide* please? | **Czy mogę prosić mapę/przewodnik?** chyh <u>moh</u>·geh <u>proh</u>·sh'eech' <u>mah</u>·peh/psheh·<u>vohd</u>·n'eek |

## Tourist Information Office

| | |
|---|---|
| Do you have any information on...? | **Czy ma pan jakieś informacje o...?** chyh mah pahn <u>yah</u>·kyehsh' een·fohr·<u>mah</u>·tsyeh oh... |
| Can you recommend...? | **Czy może pan polecić...?** chyh <u>moh</u>·zheh pahn poh·<u>leh</u>·ch'eech'... |
| – a boat trip | – **rejs statkiem** reys <u>staht</u>·kyehm |
| – an excursion | – **wycieczkę** vyh·<u>ch'yehch</u>·keh |
| – sightseeing tour | – **wycieczkę po mieście** vyh·<u>ch'yehch</u>·keh poh <u>myehsh'</u>·ch'yeh |

*i* Most cities and large towns have a tourist information office. They are usually located in the center of town; some display the sign **it (informacja turystyczna)**. Tourist information can also be obtained from **Orbis** and **PTTK** (Polish Tourist Organization) offices. Most bookstores and tourist offices sell road, regional and local maps. Town maps are displayed on kiosks in major squares and streets and at tourist information offices.

## Tours

| | |
|---|---|
| I'd like to go on the tour to... | **Interesuje mnie wycieczka do...** een·teh·reh·<u>suh</u>·yeh mn'yeh vyh·<u>ch'yehch</u>·kah doh... |
| When's the next tour? | **Kiedy będzie następna wycieczka?** <u>kyeh</u>·dyh <u>behn</u>·dj'yeh nahs·<u>tehmp</u>·nah vyh·<u>ch'yech</u>·kah |
| Are there tours in English? | **Czy są wycieczki po angielsku?** chyh sohm vyh·<u>ch'yech</u>·kee poh ahn·<u>gyehl</u>·skuh |
| What time do we *leave/return*? | **O której *wyruszamy/wracamy*?** oh <u>ktuh</u>·rey vyh·ruh·<u>shah</u>·myh/vrah·<u>tsah</u>·myh |
| We'd like to see the... | **Chcielibyśmy zobaczyć...** hch'yeh·lee·<u>byhsh</u>'·myh zoh·<u>bah</u>·chyhch'... |
| Can we stop here...? | **Czy możemy się tu zatrzymać...?** chyh moh·<u>zheh</u>·myh sh'yeh tuh zaht·<u>shyh</u>·mahch'... |
| – to take photos | – **żeby zrobić zdjęcia** <u>zheh</u>·byh <u>zroh</u>·beech' <u>zdyehn</u>·ch'yah |
| – to buy souvenirs | – **żeby kupić pamiątki** <u>zheh</u>·byh <u>kuh</u>·peech' pah·<u>myohnt</u>·kee |
| – to use the restrooms [toilets] | – **żeby skorzystać z toalety** <u>zheh</u>·byh skoh·<u>zhyhs</u>·tahch' stoh·ah·<u>leh</u>·tyh |

▶ For ticketing, see page 19.

## Sights

| Where *is/are*...? | **Gdzie *jest/są*...?** gdj'yeh *yehst/sohm* |
|---|---|
| - the battleground | - **pole bitwy** <u>poh</u>·leh <u>beet</u>·fyh |
| - the botanical garden | - **ogród botaniczny** <u>oh</u>·gruht boh·tah·<u>n'eech</u>·nyh |
| - the castle | - **zamek** <u>zah</u>·mehk |
| - the cathedral | - **katedra** kah·<u>teh</u>·drah |
| - the church | - **kościół** <u>kosh</u>'·ch'yuhw |
| - the downtown area | - **centrum** <u>tsehn</u>·truhm |
| - the market | - **bazar** <u>bah</u>·zahr |
| - the monument | - **pomnik** <u>pohm</u>·n'eek |
| - the museum | - **muzeum** muh·<u>zeh</u>·uhm |
| - the old town | - **stare miasto** <u>stah</u>·reh <u>myahs</u>·toh |
| - the palace | - **pałac** <u>pah</u>·wahts |
| - the park | - **park** pahrk |
| - the ruins | - **ruiny** ruh·<u>ee</u>·nyh |
| - the shopping area | - **centrum handlowe** <u>tsehn</u>·truhm hahn·<u>dloh</u>·veh |
| - the town square | - **rynek** <u>ryh</u>·nehk |
| - the town hall | - **ratusz** <u>rah</u>·tuhsh |
| Can you show me on the map? | **Czy może mi pan pokazać na mapie?** chyh <u>moh</u>·zheh mee pahn poh·<u>kah</u>·zahch' nah <u>mah</u>·pyeh |

▶ For directions, see page 33.

## Impressions

| It's... | **To jest...** toh yehst... |
|---|---|
| - beautiful | - **piękne** <u>pyehnk</u>·neh |
| - interesting | - **interesujące** een·teh·reh·suh·<u>yohn</u>·tseh |
| - romantic | - **romantyczne** roh·mahn·<u>tyhch</u>·neh |

| It's... | **To jest...** toh yehst... |
|---|---|
| – strange | – **dziwne** dj'eev·neh |
| – stunning | – **olśniewające** ohl·sh'n'yeh·vah·<u>yohn</u>·tseh |
| – terrible | – **okropne** ohk·<u>rohp</u>·neh |
| I (don't) like it. | **(Nie) Podoba mi się to.** (n'yeh) poh·<u>doh</u>·bah mee sh'yeh toh |

## Religion

| Where's...? | **Gdzie jest...?** gdj'yeh yehst |
|---|---|
| – the church | – **kościół** <u>kosh</u>'·ch'yuhw |
| – the mosque | – **meczet** <u>meh</u>·cheht |
| – the shrine | – **kapliczka** kah·<u>pleech</u>·kah |
| – the synagogue | – **synagoga** syh·nah·<u>goh</u>·gah |
| What time is *mass/ the service*? | **O której jest *msza/nabożeństwo*?** oh <u>ktuh</u>·rey yehst *mshah/nah·boh·<u>zhehn</u>'·stfoh* |

# Shopping

## Essential

| Where is the *market/mall [shopping centre]*? | **Gdzie jest *targ/centrum handlowe*?** gdj'yeh yehst *tahrk/<u>tsehn</u>·truhm hahn·<u>dloh</u>·veh* |
|---|---|
| I'm just browsing. | **Tylko się rozglądam.** <u>tyhl</u>·koh sh'yeh rohz·<u>glohn</u>·dahm |
| Can you help me? | **Czy może mi pan pomóc?** chyh <u>moh</u>·zheh mee pahn <u>poh</u>·muhts |
| I'm being helped. | **Jestem już obsługiwany**♂**/obsługiwana**♀**.** <u>yehs</u>·tehm yuhsh ohp·swuh·gee·<u>vah</u>·nyh♂/ ohp·swuh·gee·<u>vah</u>·nah♀ |

| | |
|---|---|
| How much is *this/that*? | **Ile *to/tamto* kosztuje?** ee·leh *toh/tahm*·toh kosh·<u>tuh</u>·yeh |
| Can you show me...? | **Może mi pan pokazać...?** moh·zheh mee pahn poh·<u>kah</u>·zahch'... |
| *This/That* one, please. | **Proszę *to/tamto*.** proh·sheh *toh/tahm*·toh |
| That's all, thanks. | **To wszystko, dziękuję.** toh <u>fshyhs</u>·tkoh dj'yehn·<u>kuh</u>·yeh |
| Where can I pay? | **Gdzie mogę zapłacić?** gdj'yeh <u>moh</u>·geh zah·<u>pwah</u>·ch'eech' |
| I'll pay *in cash/by credit card*. | **Zapłacę *gotówką/kartą kredytową*.** zah·<u>pwah</u>·tseh goh·<u>tuhf</u>·kohm/<u>kahr</u>·tohm kreh·dh·<u>toh</u>·vohm |
| A receipt, please. | **Proszę paragon.** <u>proh</u>·sheh pah·<u>rah</u>·gohn |

## Stores ─────────────────────

| Where *is/are*...? | **Gdzie *jest/są*...?** gdj'yeh *yehst/sohm*... |
|---|---|
| When does...*open/ close*? | *Od/Do* **której czynny jest...?** ohd/doh <u>ktuh</u>·rey <u>chyhn</u>·nyh yehst... |

– the antiques store
: **– antykwariat** ahn·tyh·<u>kfah</u>·ryaht

– the bakery
: **– piekarnia** pyeh·<u>kahr</u>·n'yah

– the butcher shop
: **– sklep mięsny** sklehp <u>myehn</u>·snyh

– the bookstore
: **– księgarnia** ksh'yehn·<u>gahr</u>·n'yah

– the camera shop
: **– sklep fotograficzny** sklehp foh·toh·grah·<u>feech</u>·nyh

– the clothing store
: **– sklep odzieżowy** sklehp oh·dj'yeh·<u>zhoh</u>·vyh

– the florist
: **– kwiaciarnia** kfyah·<u>ch'yahr</u>·n'yah

– grocery store
: **– sklep spożywczy** sklehp spoh·<u>zhyhf</u>·chyh

– the health food store
: **– sklep ze zdrową żywnością** sklehp zeh <u>zdroh</u>·vohm zhyhv·<u>nohsh'</u>·ch'yohm

– the jeweler
: **– jubiler** yuh·<u>bee</u>·lehr

– the liquor store [off-licence]
: **– sklep monopolowy** sklehp moh·noh·poh·<u>loh</u>·vyh

– market
: **– bazar** <u>bah</u>·zahr

– the pastry shop
: **– cukiernia** tsuh·<u>kyehr</u>·n'yah

– the pharmacy [chemist]
: **– apteka** ahp·<u>teh</u>·kah

– the shoe store
: **– sklep obuwniczy** sklehp oh·buhv·<u>n'ee</u>·chyh

– the shopping mall [centre]
: **– centrum handlowe** <u>tsehn</u>·truhm hahn·<u>dloh</u>·veh

– the souvenir store
: **– sklep z pamiątkami** sklehp spahm·yohnt·<u>kah</u>·mee

– the sporting store
: **– sklep sportowy** sklehp spohr·<u>toh</u>·vyh

– the supermarket
: **– supermarket** suh·pehr·<u>mahr</u>·keht

– the tobacconist
: **– sklep tytoniowy** sklehp tyh·toh·<u>n'yoh</u>·vyh

| - the newsstand | - **kiosk z gazetami** kyohsk zgah·zeh·<u>tah</u>·mee |
| - the toy store | - **sklep z zabawkami** sklehp z zah·bahf·<u>kah</u>·mee |

## Services

| Can you recommend...? | **Czy może pan polecić...?** chyh moh·zheh pahn poh·<u>leh</u>·ch'eech'... |
| - a barber | - **fryzjera męskiego** fryh·<u>zyeh</u>·rah mehn·<u>skyeh</u>·goh |
| - a dry cleaner | - **pralnię chemiczną** <u>prahl</u>·n'yeh heh·<u>meech</u>·nohm |
| - a hairdresser | - **fryzjera** fryh·<u>zyeh</u>·rah |
| - a laundromat [launderette] | - **pralnię samoobsługową** <u>prahl</u>·n'yeh sah·moh·ohp·swuh·<u>goh</u>·vohm |
| - a nail salon | - **manikiurzystkę** mah·nee·kyuh·<u>zhyhs</u>·tkeh |
| - a spa | - **spa** spah |
| - a travel agency | - **biuro podróży** <u>byuh</u>·roh pohd·<u>ruh</u>·zhyh |
| Can you...this? | **Może pan to...?** <u>moh</u>·zheh pahn toh... |
| - alter | - **poprawić** poh·<u>prah</u>·veech' |
| - clean | - **wyczyścić** vyh·<u>chyhsh</u>'·ch'eech' |
| - mend | - **załatać** zah·<u>wah</u>·tahch' |
| - press | - **wyprasować** vyh·prah·<u>soh</u>·vahch' |
| When will it be ready? | **Na kiedy to będzie gotowe?** nah <u>kyeh</u>·dyh toh <u>behn</u>·dj'yeh goh·<u>toh</u>·veh |

## Spa

| I'd like... | **Poproszę o...** poh·<u>proh</u>·sheh oh... |
| - an *eyebrow/ bikini* wax | - **depilację** *brwi/bikini* **woskiem** deh·pee·<u>lahts</u>·yeh *brvee/bee·<u>kee</u>·n'ee* <u>vohs</u>·kyehm |
| - a facial | - **zabieg na twarz** <u>zah</u>·byehk nah tfahsh |

119

| I'd like... | **Poproszę o...** poh·<u>proh</u>·sheh oh... |
|---|---|
| – a manicure/ pedicure | – **manicure/pedicure** mah·<u>n'ee</u>·kyuhr/ peh·<u>dee</u>·kyuhr |
| – a (sports) massage | – **masaż (sportowy)** <u>mah</u>·sash (spohr·<u>toh</u>·vyh) |
| Do you do...? | **Czy prowadzą państwo...?** chyh proh·<u>vah</u>·dzohm <u>pahn's</u>·tfoh... |
| – acupuncture | – **akupunkturę** ah·kuh·puhn·<u>ktuh</u>·reh |
| – aromatherapy | – **aromaterapię** ah·roh·mah·teh·<u>rah</u>·pyeh |
| – oxygen treatment | – **terapię tlenową** teh·<u>rah</u>·pyeh tleh·<u>noh</u>·vohm |
| Is there a sauna? | **Czy jest sauna?** chyh yehst <u>sahw</u>·nah |

*i* Throughout Poland, there are many popular health resorts of long-standing tradition (Busko-Zdrój, Konstancin Jeziorna, Duszniki Zdrój, Krynica, Nałęczów, Szczawnica) where the waters are known to have healing qualities. Spas and wellness centers, day and overnight, can be found in large cities and seaside resorts (Jurata, Jastarnia, Łeba, Sopot, Ustka), the lake region (Augustów) and the mountains (Zakopane, Bielsko-Biała). These offer a wide range of high-quality services and are usually relatively expensive.

## Hair Salon

| I'd like an appointment for *today/tomorrow*. | **Chciałbym**♂/**Chciałabym**♀ **umówić się na** *dzisiaj/jutro.* hch'yahw·byhm♂/hch'yah·wah·byhm♀ uh·<u>muh</u>·veech' sh'yeh nah <u>dj'ee</u>·sh'yay/<u>yuht</u>·roh |
| I'd like... | **Poproszę o...** poh·<u>proh</u>·sheh oh... |
| – my hair styled | – **ułożenie włosów** uh·woh·<u>zheh</u>·n'yeh <u>vwoh</u>·suhf |
| – a haircut | – **strzyżenie** st·shyh·<u>zheh</u>·n'yeh |
| – a trim | – **podcięcie włosów** poht·<u>ch'yen'</u>·ch'yeh <u>vwoh</u>·suhf |

## Sales Help

| | |
|---|---|
| What are the opening hours? | **Jakie są godziny otwarcia?** <u>yah</u>·kyeh sohm goh·<u>dj'ee</u>·nyh oht·<u>fahr</u>·ch'yah |
| Where *is/are*...? | **Gdzie *jest/są*...?** gdj'yeh *yehst/sohm*... |
| - the cashier | - **kasa** <u>kah</u>·sah |
| - the escalators | - **schody ruchome** <u>shoh</u>·dyh ruh·<u>hoh</u>·meh |
| - the elevator [lift] | - **winda** <u>veen</u>·dah |
| - the fitting room | - **przymierzalnia** pshyh·myeh·<u>zhahl</u>·n'yah |
| - the store directory [guide] | - **tablica informacyjna** tah·<u>blee</u>·tsah een·fohr·mah·<u>tsyh</u>·nah |
| Can you help me? | **Czy może mi pan pomóc?** chyh <u>moh</u>·zheh mee pahn <u>poh</u>·muhts |
| I'm being helped. | **Jestem już obsługiwany♂/obsługiwana♀.** <u>yehs</u>·tehm yuhsh ohp·swuh·gee·<u>vah</u>·nyh♂/ ohp·swuh·gee·<u>vah</u>·nah♀ |
| Do you have...? | **Czy mają państwo...?** chyh <u>mah</u>·yohm <u>pahn'</u>·stfoh... |
| Can you show me...? | **Czy może mi pan pokazać...?** chyh <u>moh</u>·zheh mee pahnpoh·<u>kah</u>·zahch'... |
| Can you *ship/wrap* it? | **Można prosić o *wysłanie/opakowanie*?** <u>mohzh</u>·nah <u>proh</u>·sh'eech' oh *vyh·<u>swah</u>·n'yeh/ oh·pah·koh·<u>vah</u>·n'yeh* |
| How much? | **Ile to kosztuje?** <u>ee</u>·leh toh kohsh·<u>tuh</u>·yeh |
| That's all, thanks. | **To wszystko, dziękuję.** toh <u>fshyhst</u>·koh dj'yehn·<u>kuh</u>·yeh |

▶ For clothing items, see page 128.

▶ For food items, see page 81.

▶ For souvenirs, see page 124.

## Preferences

| | |
|---|---|
| I want something... | **Chciałbym♂/Chciałabym♀ coś...** <u>hch'yahw</u>·byhm♂/<u>hch'yah</u>·wah·byhm♀ tsohsh'... |
| – cheap/expensive | – **taniego/drogiego** tah·<u>n'yeh</u>·goh/ droh·<u>gyeh</u>·goh |
| – larger/smaller | – **większego/mniejszego** vyehn·<u>ksheh</u>·goh/ mn'yey·<u>sheh</u>·goh |
| – from this region | – **miejscowego** myey·stsoh·<u>veh</u>·goh |
| Is it *real/fake*? | **Czy to jest *prawdziwe/sztuczne*?** chyh toh yehst *prahv·<u>dj'ee</u>·veh/<u>shtuh</u>·chneh* |
| Could I see *this/ that*? | **Czy mogę zobaczyć *to/tamto*?** chyh <u>moh</u>·geh zoh·<u>bah</u>·chyhch' *toh/<u>tahm</u>·toh* |

## Decisions

| | |
|---|---|
| That's not quite what I want. | **To nie to, czego szukam.** toh n'yeh toh <u>cheh</u>·goh <u>shuh</u>·kahm |
| I don't like it. | **To mi się nie podoba.** toh mee sh'yeh n'yeh poh·<u>doh</u>·bah |
| I'd like to think about it. | **Chcę się nad tym zastanowić.** htseh sh'yeh naht tyhm zahs·tah·<u>noh</u>·veech' |
| I'll take it. | **Wezmę to.** <u>vehz</u>·meh toh |

## Bargaining

| | |
|---|---|
| That's too much. | **To za drogo.** toh zah <u>droh</u>·goh |
| I'll give you... | **Dam panu...** dahm <u>pah</u>·nuh... |
| I only have...zlotys. | **Mam tylko...złotych.** mahm <u>tyhl</u>·koh...<u>zwoh</u>·tyh |
| Is that your best price? | **To najniższa cena?** toh nay·<u>n'eezh</u>·shah <u>tseh</u>·nah |
| Can you give me a discount? | **Da mi pan zniżkę?** dah mee pahn <u>zn'eezh</u>·keh |

▶ For numbers, see page 168.

## Paying

| | |
|---|---|
| How much? | **Ile to kosztuje?** <u>ee</u>·leh toh kosh·<u>tuh</u>·yeh |
| I'll pay *in cash/by credit card*. | **Zapłacę *gotówką/kartą kredytową*.** zah·<u>pwah</u>·tseh goh·<u>tuhf</u>·kohm/<u>kahr</u>·tohm kreh·dyh·<u>toh</u>·vohm |
| A receipt, please. | **Proszę paragon.** <u>proh</u>·sheh pah·<u>rah</u>·gohn |

Cash is the preferred method of paying in stores. Larger stores and retail chains usually accept major credit cards. Travelers checks and personal checks are rarely accepted in Poland.

## Complaints

| | |
|---|---|
| I'd like... | **Chciałbym♂/Chciałabym♀...** <u>hch'yahw</u>·byhm♂/<u>hch'yah</u>·wah·byhm♀... |
| – to exchange this | – **to wymienić** toh vyh·<u>myeh</u>·n'eech' |
| – to return this | – **to oddać** toh <u>ohd</u>·dahch' |
| – a refund | – **zwrot pieniędzy** zvroht pyeh·<u>n'ehn</u>·dzyh |
| – to see the manager | – **porozmawiać z kierownikiem** poh·rohz·<u>mah</u>·vyahch' skyeh·rohv·<u>n'ee</u>·kyehm |
| Here's the receipt. | **Oto paragon.** oh·toh pah·<u>rah</u>·gohn |

## Souvenirs

| | | |
|---|---|---|
| amber jewelry | **biżuteria z bursztynu** bee·zhuh·<u>teh</u>·ryah zbuhr·<u>shtyh</u>·nuh | |
| box of chocolates | **pudełko czekoladek** puh·<u>dehw</u>·koh cheh·koh·<u>lah</u>·dehk | |
| crystal | **kryształ** <u>kryhsh</u>·tahw | |
| cut glass | **szlifowane szkło** shlee·foh·<u>vah</u>·neh shkwoh | |
| hand-painted eggs | **pisanki** pee·<u>sahn</u>·kee | |
| hand-painted wooden box | **ręcznie malowane drewniane pudełko** <u>rehnch</u>·n'yeh mah·loh·<u>vah</u>·neh drehv·<u>n'yah</u>·neh puh·<u>dehw</u>·koh | |
| key ring | **breloczek na klucze** breh·<u>loh</u>·chehk nah <u>kluh</u>·cheh | |
| Polish vodka | **polska wódka** <u>pohl</u>·skah <u>vuht</u>·kah | |
| postcard | **pocztówka** pohch·<u>tuhf</u>·kah | |
| poster | **plakat** <u>plah</u>·kaht | |
| silver jewelry | **biżuteria ze srebra** bee·zhuh·<u>teh</u>·ryah zeh <u>sreh</u>·brah | |
| tapestry | **kilim** <u>kee</u>·leem | |
| T-shirt | **t-shirt** <u>tee</u>·shehrt | |

| | |
|---|---|
| wood carving | **figurka z drewna** fee·<u>guhr</u>·kah <u>zdrehv</u>·nah |
| Could I see *this/ that*? | **Czy mogę zobaczyć *to/tamto*?** chyh <u>moh</u>·geh zoh·<u>bah</u>·chyhch' *toh/<u>tahm</u>·toh* |
| It's the one in the *window/display case*. | **To ten *na wystawie/w gablocie*.** toh tehn *nah vyhs·<u>tah</u>·vyeh/v gah·<u>bloh</u>·ch'yeh* |
| I'd like... | **Chciałbym♂/Chciałabym♀ ...** hch'yahw·byhm♂/hch'yah·wah·byhm♀... |
| – a battery | – **baterię** bah·<u>teh</u>·ryeh |
| – a bracelet | – **bransoletkę** brahn·soh·<u>leht</u>·keh |
| – a brooch | – **broszkę** <u>brohsh</u>·keh |
| – earrings | – **kolczyki** kohl·<u>chyh</u>·kee |
| – a necklace | – **naszyjnik** nah·<u>shiy</u>·n'eek |
| – a ring | – **pierścionek** pyehr·<u>sh'ch'yoh</u>·nehk |
| – a watch | – **zegarek** zeh·<u>gah</u>·rehk |
| I'd like... | **Chciałbym♂/Chciałabym♀ coś...** hch'yahw·byhm♂/hch'yah·wah·byhm♀ tsohsh'... |
| – amber | – **z bursztynu** zbuhr·<u>shtyh</u>·nuh |
| – copper | – **z miedzi** <u>zmyeh</u>·dj'ee |
| – crystal (quartz) | – **z kryształu** zkryhsh·<u>tah</u>·wuh |
| – diamond | – **z brylantami** zbryh·lahn·<u>tah</u>·mee |
| – enamel | – **z emalii** zeh·<u>mah</u>·lee |
| – *white/yellow* gold | – **z *białego/żółtego* złota** z *byah·<u>weh</u>·goh/ zhuhw·<u>teh</u>·goh* <u>zwoh</u>·tah |
| – pearl | – **z pereł** <u>speh</u>·rehw |
| – pewter | – **z cyny** s·<u>tsyh</u>·nyh |
| – platinum | – **z platyny** splah·<u>tyh</u>·nyh |
| – silver | – **ze srebra** zeh <u>sreh</u>·brah |
| – stainless steel | – **ze stali nierdzewnej** zeh <u>stah</u>·lee n'yeh·<u>rdzehv</u>·ney |

| Is this real? | **Czy to jest prawdziwe?** chyh toh yehst prahv·dj'ee·veh |
| Can you engrave it? | **Można na tym grawerować?** <u>moh</u>·zhnah nah tyhm grah·veh·<u>roh</u>·vach' |

## Antiques

| How old is this? | **Ile to ma lat?** <u>ee</u>·leh toh mah laht |
| Do you have anything from the...period? | **Ma pan coś z okresu...?** mah pahn tsohsh' zoh·<u>kreh</u>·suh... |
| Do I have to fill out any forms? | **Czy muszę wypełniać jakiś formularz?** chyh <u>muh</u>·sheh vyh·<u>pehw</u>·n'yahch' <u>yah</u>·keesh' fohr·<u>muh</u>·lahsh |
| Is there a certificate of authenticity? | **Czy to ma świadectwo autentyczności?** chyh toh mah sh'fyah·<u>dehts</u>·tfoh aw·tehn·tyhch·<u>nohsh</u>·ch'ee |

## Clothing

| I'd like... | **Chciałbym♂/Chciałabym♀...** <u>hch'yahw</u>·byhm♂/<u>hch'yah</u>·wah·byhm♀... |

▶ For clothes and accessories, see page 128.

| Can I try this on? | **Czy mogę to przymierzyć?** chyh <u>moh</u>·geh toh pshyh·<u>myeh</u>·zhyhch' |
| It doesn't fit. | **To nie pasuje.** toh n'yeh pah·<u>suh</u>·yeh |
| It's too... | **To jest za...** toh yehst zah... |
| – big | – **duże** <u>duh</u>·zheh |
| – small | – **małe** <u>mah</u>·weh |
| – short | – **krótkie** <u>kruht</u>·kyeh |
| – long | – **długie** <u>dwuh</u>·gyeh |
| Do you have this in size...? | **Czy jest rozmiar...?** chyh yehst <u>rohz</u>·myahr... |

Do you have this in a *bigger/smaller* size?

**Czy są *większe/mniejsze* rozmiary?** chyh sohm *vyehnk·sheh/mn'yey·sheh* rohz·myah·ryh

▶ For numbers, see page 168.

## You May See...

| | |
|---|---|
| **ODZIEŻ DAMSKA** | men's clothing |
| **ODZIEŻ MĘSKA** | women's clothing |
| **UBRANIA DLA DZIECI** | children's clothing |

### Color

| | |
|---|---|
| I want something... | **Chciałbym♂/Chciałabym♀ coś w kolorze...** hch'yahw·byhm♂/hch'yah·wah·byhm♀ tsohsh' fkoh·loh·zheh... |
| – beige | – **beżowym** beh·zhoh·vyhm |
| – black | – **czarnym** chahr·nyhm |
| – blue | – **niebieskim** n'yeh·byehs·keem |
| – brown | – **brązowym** brohn·zoh·vyhm |
| – gray | – **szarym** shah·ryhm |
| – green | – **zielonym** zh'yeh·loh·nyhm |
| – olive | – **oliwkowym** oh·leef·koh·vyhm |
| – orange | – **pomarańczowym** poh·mah·rahn'·choh·vyhm |
| – pink | – **różowym** ruh·zhoh·vyhm |
| – purple | – **fioletowym** fioh·leh·toh·vyhm |
| – red | – **czerwonym** chehr·voh·nyhm |
| – white | – **białym** byah·wyhm |
| – yellow | – **żółtym** zhuhw·tyhm |

## Clothes and Accessories

| | | |
|---|---|---|
| backpack | **plecak** <u>pleh</u>·tsahk | |
| bag | **torba** <u>tohr</u>·bah | |
| belt | **pasek** <u>pah</u>·sehk | |
| bikini | **bikini** bee·<u>kee</u>·n'ee | |
| blouse | **bluzka** <u>bluhs</u>·kah | |
| bra | **biustonosz** byuhs·<u>toh</u>·nohsh | |
| briefs [underpants] | **majtki** <u>mayt</u>·kee | |
| coat (long/short) | **płaszcz/kurtka** pwahshch/<u>kuhrt</u>·kah | |
| dress | **sukienka** suh·<u>kyehn</u>·kah | |
| hat | **kapelusz** kah·<u>peh</u>·luhsh | |
| jacket | **marynarka♂/żakiet♀** mah·ryh·<u>nahr</u>·kah♂/<u>zhah</u>·kyeht♀ | |
| jeans | **dżinsy** dj'<u>een</u>·syh | |
| pajamas | **piżama** pee·<u>zhah</u>·mah | |
| pants [trousers] | **spodnie** <u>spohd</u>·n'yeh | |
| pantyhose [tights] | **rajstopy** ray·<u>stoh</u>·pyh | |
| purse [handbag] | **torebka** toh·<u>rehp</u>·kah | |
| raincoat | **płaszcz przeciwdeszczowy** pwahshch psheh·ch'eef·dehsh·<u>choh</u>·vyh | |
| scarf | **szalik** <u>shah</u>·leek | |
| shirt | **koszula♂/bluzka♀** koh·<u>shuh</u>·lah♂/<u>bluhs</u>·kah♀ | |
| shorts | **szorty** <u>shohr</u>·tyh | |
| skirt | **spódnica** spuhd·<u>n'ee</u>·tsah | |
| socks | **skarpetki** skahr·<u>peht</u>·kee | |
| stockings | **pończochy** pohn'·<u>choh</u>·hyh | |

| | |
|---|---|
| suit | **garnitur**♂/**kostium**♀ gahr·n'ee·tuhr♂/ kohs·tyuhm♀ |
| sunglasses | **okulary przeciwsłoneczne** oh·kuh·lah·ryh psheh·ch'eef·swoh·nehch·neh |
| sweater | **sweter** sfeh·tehr |
| sweatshirt | **bluza** bluh·zah |
| swimming trunks | **kąpielówki** kohm·pyeh·luhf·kee |
| swimsuit | **kostium kąpielowy** kohs·tyuhm kohm·pyeh·loh·vyh |
| tie | **krawat** krah·vaht |
| T-shirt | **t-shirt** tee·shehrt |
| underwear | **bielizna** byeh·lee·znah |

**Fabric**

| | |
|---|---|
| I'd like... | **Chciałbym**♂/**Chciałabym**♀ **coś...** hch'yahw·byhm♂/hch'yah·wah·byhm♀ tsohsh'... |
| – cotton | **– z bawełny** zbah·vehw·nyh |
| – denim | **– z dżinsu** zdjeen·suh |
| – lace | **– z koronki** skoh·rohn·kee |
| – leather | **– ze skóry** zeh skuh·ryh |
| – linen | **– z lnu** zlnuh |
| – silk | **– z jedwabiu** zyehd·vah·byuh |
| – wool | **– z wełny** zvehw·nyh |
| Is it machine washable? | **Czy można to prać w pralce?** chyh mohzh·nah toh prahch' f prahl·tseh |

## Shoes

| | |
|---|---|
| I'd like... | **Chciałbym♂/Chciałabym ♀...** hch'yahw·byhm♂/hch'yah·wah·byhm ♀... |
| – *high-heeled/flat* shoes | – **buty na obcasie/płaskim obcasie** buh·tyh nah ohp·tsah·sh'yeh/pwahs·keem ohp·tsah·sh'yeh |
| – boots | – **botki** boht·kee |
| – loafers | – **mokasyny** moh·kah·syh·nyh |
| – sandals | – **sandały** sahn·dah·wyh |
| – shoes | – **buty** buh·tyh |
| – slippers | – **kapcie** kahp·ch'yeh |
| – sneakers | – **buty sportowe** buh·tyh spohr·toh·veh |
| In size... | **Rozmiar...** rohz·myahr... |

▶ For numbers, see page 168.

## Sizes

| | |
|---|---|
| extra large (XL) | **bardzo duży/XL** bahr·dzoh duh·zhyh/eeks·ehl |
| large (L) | **duży/L** duh·zhyh/ehl |
| medium (M) | **średni/M** sh'rehd·n'ee/ehm |
| small (S) | **mały/S** mah·wyh/ehs |

## Newsstand and Tobacconist

| | |
|---|---|
| Do you sell English-language newspapers? | **Czy sprzedają państwo gazety anglojęzyczne?** chyh spsheh·dah·yohm pahn'·stfoh gah·zeh·tyh anh·gloh·yehn·zyhch·neh |
| I'd like... | **Poproszę...** poh·proh·sheh... |
| – a cigar | – **cygaro** tsyh·gah·roh |
| – a *pack/carton* of cigarettes | – **paczkę/karton papierosów** pahch·keh/ kahr·tohn pah·pyeh·roh·suhf |

| | |
|---|---|
| – a lighter | – **zapalniczkę** zah·pahl·<u>n'eech</u>·keh |
| – a magazine | – **pismo** <u>pees</u>·moh |
| – matches | – **zapałki** zah·<u>pahw</u>·kee |
| – a newspaper | – **gazetę** gah·<u>zeh</u>·teh |
| – a postcard | – **pocztówkę** pohcz·<u>tuhf</u>·keh |
| – a *road/town* map... | – **mapę** *drogową/miasta*... <u>mah</u>·peh *droh·<u>goh</u>·vohm/<u>myah</u>·stah*... |
| – stamps | – **znaczki** <u>znahch</u>·kee |

## Photography

| | |
|---|---|
| I'm looking for...camera. | **Szukam...aparatu fotograficznego.** <u>shuh</u>·kahm... ah·pah·<u>rah</u>·tuh foh·toh·grah·feech·<u>neh</u>·goh |
| – an automatic | – **automatycznego** ahw·toh·mah·tychn·<u>neh</u>·goh |
| – a digital | – **cyfrowego** tsyhf·roh·<u>veh</u>·goh |
| – a disposable | – **jednorazowego** yehd·noh·rah·zoh·<u>veh</u>·goh |
| I'd like... | **Poproszę...** poh·<u>proh</u>·sheh... |
| – a battery | – **baterię** bah·<u>teh</u>·ryeh |
| – digital prints | – **wydruki zdjęć z aparatu cyfrowego** vyh·<u>druh</u>·kee zdyehnch' zah·pah·<u>rah</u>·tuh tsyhf·roh·<u>veh</u>·goh |
| – a memory card | – **kartę pamięci** <u>kahr</u>·teh pah·<u>myehn</u>'·ch'ee |
| Can I print digital photos here? | **Czy mogę tu wydrukować zdjęcia z aparatu cyfrowego?** chyh <u>moh</u>·geh tuh vyh·druh·<u>koh</u>·vach' <u>zdyehn</u>'·ch'yah zah·pah·<u>rah</u>·tuh tsyhf·roh·<u>veh</u>·goh |
| When will the photos be ready? | **Na kiedy zdjęcia będą gotowe?** nah <u>kyeh</u>·dyh <u>zdyehn</u>'·ch'yah <u>behn</u>·dohm goh·<u>toh</u>·veh |

# Sports and Leisure

## Essential

| | |
|---|---|
| Where's the game? | **Gdzie grają?** gdj'yeh <u>grah</u>·yohm |
| Where's...? | **Gdzie jest...?** gdj'yeh yehst... |
| – the beach | – **plaża** <u>plah</u>·zhah |
| – the park | – **park** pahrk |
| – the pool | – **basen** <u>bah</u>·sehn |
| Is it safe to *swim/ dive* here? | **Można tu bezpiecznie *pływać/skakać?*** <u>mohzh</u>·nah tuh behs·<u>pyehch</u>·n'yeh *<u>pwyh</u>·vahch'/ <u>skah</u>·kahch'* |
| I'd like to rent [hire] golf clubs. | **Chciałbym♂/Chciałabym♀ wypożyczyć kije golfowe.** hch'yahw·byhm♂/hch'yah·wah·byhm♀ vyh·poh·<u>zhyh</u>·chyhch' <u>kee</u>·yeh gohl·<u>foh</u>·veh |
| What's the charge per hour? | **Jaka jest opłata za godzinę?** <u>yah</u>·kah yehst oh·<u>pwah</u>·tah zah goh·<u>dj'ee</u>·neh |
| How far is it to...from here? | **Jak daleko jest stąd do...?** yahk dah·<u>leh</u>·koh yehst stohnt doh... |
| Can you show me on the map? | **Czy może mi pan pokazać na mapie?** chyh <u>mohz</u>·heh mee pahn poh·<u>kah</u>·zahch' nah <u>mah</u>·pyeh |

132

# Spectator Sports

| | |
|---|---|
| When is...? | **Kiedy jest/są...?** <u>kyeh</u>·dyh *yehst/sohm*... |
| – the basketball game | – **mecz koszykówki** mehch koh·shyh·<u>kuhf</u>·kee |
| – the boxing match | – **zawody bokserskie** zah·<u>voh</u>·dyh bohk·<u>sehr</u>·skyeh |
| – the golf tournament | – **zawody golfowe** zah·<u>voh</u>·dyh gohl·<u>foh</u>·veh |
| – the soccer [football] game | – **mecz piłki nożnej** mehch <u>peew</u>·kee <u>nohzh</u>·ney |
| – the tennis match | – **mecz tenisowy** mehch teh·n'ee·<u>soh</u>·vyh |
| Where's...? | **Gdzie jest...?** gdj'yeh yehst... |
| – the horsetrack | – **tor wyścigów konnych** tohr vyhsh'·<u>ch'ee</u>·guhf <u>kohn</u>·nyhh |
| – the racetrack | – **tor wyścigowy** tohr vyhsh'·ch'ee·<u>goh</u>·vyh |
| – the stadium | – **stadion** <u>stah</u>·dyohn |
| Where can I place a bet? | **Gdzie można postawić zakład?** gdj'yeh <u>mohzh</u>·nah pohs·<u>tah</u>·veech' <u>zah</u>·kwaht |

# Participating

| | |
|---|---|
| Where is/are...? | **Gdzie jest/są...?** gdj'yeh yehst/sohm... |
| – the golf course | – **pole golfowe** <u>poh</u>·leh gohl·<u>foh</u>·veh |
| – the gym | – **siłownia** sh'ee·<u>wohv</u>·n'yah |
| – the park | – **park** pahrk |
| – the tennis courts | – **korty tenisowe** <u>kohr</u>·tyh teh·n'ee·<u>soh</u>·veh |
| How much per...? | **Jaka jest stawka za...?** <u>yah</u>·kah yehst <u>stah</u>·fkah zah... |
| – day | – **dzień** dj'yen' |
| – hour | – **godzinę** goh·<u>dj'ee</u>·neh |
| – game | – **mecz** mehch |
| – round | – **turę** <u>tuh</u>·reh |

| Can I rent [hire]...? | **Czy mogę wypożyczyć...?** chyh <u>moh</u>·geh vyh·poh·<u>zhyh</u>·chyhch' |
| - golf clubs | - **kije do golfa** <u>kee</u>·yeh doh <u>gohl</u>·fah |
| - equipment | - **sprzęt** spshehnt |
| - a racket | - **rakietę** rah·<u>kyeh</u>·teh |

## At the Beach/Pool

| Where's the *beach/ pool*? | **Gdzie jest *plaża/basen*?** gdj'yeh yehst <u>plah</u>·zhah/<u>bah</u>·sehn |
| Is there...? | **Czy jest...?** chyh yehst... |
| - a kiddie pool | - **brodzik** <u>broh</u>·dj'eek |
| - an *indoor/ outdoor* pool | - **basen *kryty/odkryty*** <u>bah</u>·sehn <u>kryh</u>·tyh/ oht·<u>kryh</u>·tyh |
| - a lifeguard | - **ratownik** rah·<u>tohv</u>·n'eek |
| Is it safe to *swim/ dive* here? | **Można tu bezpiecznie *pływać/skakać*?** <u>mohzh</u>·nah tuh behs·<u>pyehch</u>·n'yeh <u>pwyh</u>·vach'/ <u>skah</u>·kach' |
| Is it safe for children? | **Czy jest tu bezpiecznie dla dzieci?** chyh yehst tuh behs·<u>pyehch</u>·n'yeh dlah <u>dj'eh</u>·ch'ee |
| I'd like to rent [hire]... | **Chciałbym♂/Chciałabym♀ wypożyczyć...** <u>hch'yahw</u>·byhm♂/<u>hch'yah</u>·wah·byhm♀ vyh·poh·<u>zhyh</u>·chyhch'... |
| - a deck chair | - **leżak** <u>leh</u>·zhahk |
| - diving equipment | - **sprzęt do nurkowania** spshehnt doh nuhr·koh·<u>vah</u>·n'yah |
| - a jet-ski | - **skuter wodny** <u>skuh</u>·tehr <u>vohd</u>·nyh |
| - a motorboat | - **motorówkę** moh·toh·<u>ruhf</u>·keh |
| - a rowboat | - **łódkę wiosłową** <u>wuhd</u>·keh vyohs·<u>woh</u>·vohm |
| - a towel | - **ręcznik** <u>rehn</u>·chn'eek |
| - an umbrella | - **parasol** pah·<u>rah</u>·sohl |

| – waterskis | – **narty wodne** <u>nahr</u>·tyh <u>vohd</u>·neh |
| – a windsurfer | – **deskę windsurfingową** <u>dehs</u>·keh weend·sehr·feen·<u>goh</u>·vohm |
| For...hours. | **Na...godzin.** nah...<u>goh</u>·dj'een |

▶ For travel with children, see page 145.

> *i*
>
> Poland's sandy Baltic coast beaches are very popular during the summer months. Swim only in places that are marked **plaża strzeżona** (supervised beach) and have a **ratownik** (lifeguard); be sure to obey safety notices. The Mazury Lake District in the north-eastern part of Poland and the Greater Poland Lake District in the north-west are popular tourist destinations, especially for water sports lovers (swimming, sailing, windsurfing, fishing, diving and canoeing).

## Winter Sports

| A lift pass for a day/five days, please. | **Poproszę** *jednodniowy/pięciodniowy* **skipass.** poh·<u>proh</u>·sheh *yehd·noh·<u>dn'yoh</u>·vyh/ pyehn'·ch'yoh·<u>dn'yoh</u>·vyh* <u>skee</u>·pahs |
| I'd like to rent [hire]... | **Chciałbym**♂/**Chciałabym** ♀ **wypożyczyć...** <u>hch'yahw</u>·byhm♂/<u>hch'yah</u>·wah·byhm ♀ vyh·poh·<u>zhyh</u>·chich'... |
| – boots | – **buty narciarskie** <u>buh</u>·tyh nahr·<u>ch'yahr</u>·skyeh |
| – cross-country skis | – **biegówki** byeh·<u>guhf</u>·kee |
| – a helmet | – **kask** kahsk |
| – poles | – **kijki** <u>keey</u>·kee |
| – skates | – **łyżwy** <u>wyhzh</u>·vyh |
| – skis | – **narty** <u>nahr</u>·tyh |
| – a snowboard | – **deskę snowboardową** <u>dehs</u>·keh snohw·bohr·<u>doh</u>·vohm |
| – snowshoes | – **rakiety śnieżne** rah·<u>kyeh</u>·tyh <u>sh'n'yehzh</u>·neh |

| These are too big/small. | **Te są za** *duże/małe.* teh sohm zah <u>duh</u>·zheh/<u>mah</u>·weh |
|---|---|
| Are there ski/snowboard lessons? | **Czy jest nauka jazdy na** *nartach/ snowboardzie?* chyh yehst nah·<u>uh</u>·kah <u>yahz</u>·dyh nah <u>nahr</u>·tahh/snohw·<u>bohr</u>·dj'yeh |
| I'm a beginner. | **Jestem początkujący**♂**/początkująca**♀. <u>yehs</u>·tehm poh·chohn·tkuh·<u>yohn</u>·tsyh♂/ poh·chohn·tkuh·<u>yohn</u>·tsah♀ |
| I'm experienced. | **Jestem zaawansowany**♂**/zaawansowana**♀. <u>yehs</u>·tehm zah·ah·vahn·soh·<u>vah</u>·nyh♂/zah· ah·vahn·soh·<u>vah</u>·nah♀ |
| A trail [piste] map, please. | **Poproszę mapę tras.** poh·<u>proh</u>·sheh <u>mah</u>·peh trahs |

There are many ski resorts in the southern part of Poland, the most popular being Zakopane, Szczyrk and Wisła. The high Tatra Mountains offer excellent downhill skiing, and there are plenty of skiing opportunities on the lower slopes of many other mountains.

## You May See...

| WYCIĄG | drag lift |
|---|---|
| KOLEJKA LINOWA/GONDOLA | cable car/gondola |
| WYCIĄG KRZESEŁKOWY | chair lift |
| TRASA ŁATWA | novice |
| TRASA TRUDNA | intermediate |
| TRASA BARDZO TRUDNA | expert |
| TRASA ZAMKNIĘTA | trail [piste] closed |
| UWAGA LAWINY | caution, avalanches |

# In the Countryside

| | |
|---|---|
| I'd like a map of... | **Poproszę mapę...** poh·<u>proh</u>·sheh <u>mah</u>·peh... |
| - this region | - **tego regionu** teh·goh reh·<u>gyoh</u>·nuh |
| - the bike routes | - **szlaków rowerowych** <u>shlah</u>·kuhf roh·veh·<u>roh</u>·vyhh |
| - the trails | - **szlaków** <u>shlah</u>·kuhf |
| Is it far? | **Czy to daleko?** chyh toh dah·<u>leh</u>·koh |
| Is it steep? | **Jest stromo?** yehst <u>stroh</u>·moh |
| I'm lost. | **Zgubiłem♂/Zgubiłam♀ się.** zguh·<u>bee</u>·wehm♂/zguh·<u>bee</u>·wahm♀ sh'yeh |
| Where's...? | **Gdzie jest...?** gdj'yeh yehst... |
| - the bridge | - **most** mohst |
| - the cave | - **jaskinia** yahs·<u>kee</u>·n'yah |
| - the cliff | - **klif** kleef |
| - the forest | - **las** lahs |
| - the lake | - **jezioro** yeh·<u>zh'yoh</u>·roh |
| - the mountain | - **góra** <u>guh</u>·rah |
| - the national park | - **park narodowy** pahrk nah·roh·<u>doh</u>·vyh |
| - the nature reserve | - **rezerwat przyrody** reh·<u>zehr</u>·vaht pshyh·<u>roh</u>·dyh |
| - the overlook [viewpoint] | - **punkt widokowy** puhnkt vee·doh·<u>koh</u>·vyh |
| - the park | - **park** pahrk |
| - the path | - **ścieżka** <u>sh'ch'yesh</u>·kah |
| - the peak | - **szczyt** sh·chyht |
| - the picnic area | - **pole piknikowe** <u>poh</u>·leh peek·n'ee·<u>koh</u>·veh |
| - the river | - **rzeka** <u>zheh</u>·kah |
| - the (thermal) spring | - **(gorące) źródło** (goh·<u>rohn</u>·tseh) <u>zh'ruhd</u>·woh |
| - the stream | - **strumień** <u>struh</u>·myehn' |
| - the waterfall | - **wodospad** voh·<u>dohs</u>·paht |

# Culture and Nightlife

## Essential

| | |
|---|---|
| What is there to do at night? | **Co można robić wieczorami?** tsoh <u>mohzh</u>·nah <u>roh</u>·beech' vyeh·choh·<u>rah</u>·mee |
| Do you have a program of events? | **Czy jest program imprez?** chyh yehst <u>proh</u>·grahm <u>eem</u>·prehs |
| What's playing at the movies [cinema] today? | **Co dzisiaj grają w kinie?** tsoh <u>dj'ee</u>·sh'yay <u>grah</u>·yohm <u>fkee</u>·n'yeh |
| Where's...? | **Gdzie jest...?** gdj'yeh yehst... |
| – the downtown area | – **centrum** <u>tsehn</u>·truhm |
| – the bar | – **bar** bahr |
| – the dance club | – **dyskoteka** dyhs·koh·<u>teh</u>·kah |

---

*i* While visiting Poland, tourists can enjoy arts and culture throughout the year. Classical music enthusiasts should visit Chopin's birthplace, Żelazowa Wola, during the summer for free outdoors concerts. Historic Cracow features many art galleries and museums, including **Muzeum Narodowe** (National Museum) and **Muzeum Czartoryskich** (Cartoryski Museum). Warsaw, Poland's capital, is home to numerous renowned theaters and concert halls, as well as one of Europe's most beautiful city parks, **Łazienki Królewskie**. During August, the beach town of Sopot entertains music lovers with its International Pop Festival.

# Entertainment

| Can you recommend...? | **Czy może pan polecić...?** chyh <u>moh</u>·zheh pahn poh·<u>leh</u>·ch'eech'... |
|---|---|
| – a concert | – **koncert** <u>kohn</u>·tsehrt |
| – a movie | – **film** feelm |
| – an opera | – **operę** oh·<u>peh</u>·reh |
| – a play | – **sztukę** <u>shtuh</u>·keh |
| When does it *start/end*? | **Kiedy to się *zaczyna/kończy*?** <u>kyeh</u>·dyh toh sh'yeh zah·<u>chyh</u>·nah/<u>kohn'</u>·chyh |
| What's the dress code? | **Jaki strój obowiązuje?** <u>yah</u>·kee struy oh·boh·vyohn·<u>zuh</u>·yeh |
| I like... | **Lubię...** <u>luh</u>·byeh... |
| – classical music | – **muzykę poważną** muh·<u>zyh</u>·keh poh·<u>vahzh</u>·nohm |
| – folk music | – **muzykę ludową** muh·<u>zyh</u>·keh luh·<u>doh</u>·vohm |
| – jazz | – **jazz** djehz |
| – pop music | – **pop** pohp |
| – rap | – **rap** rahp |

► For ticketing, see page 19.

Most hotels will have some information available in English about events around town. There are also culture magazines, such as **Kalejdoskop Kulturalny** (Cultural Kaleidoscope), which have weekly events listings, often provided in Polish and English. These are available at newsstands and bookstores.

Prosimy o wyłączenie telefonów komórkowych. **Turn off your cell**
proh·sh'ee·myh oh vyh·wohn·cheh·n'yeh **[mobile] phones,**
teh·leh·foh·nuhf koh·muhr·koh·vyhh **please.**

## Nightlife

| | |
|---|---|
| What is there to do at night? | **Co można robić wieczorami?** tsoh <u>mohzh</u>·nah <u>roh</u>·beech' vyeh·choh·<u>rah</u>·mee |
| Can you recommend...? | **Czy może pan polecić...?** chyh <u>moh</u>·zheh pahn poh·<u>leh</u>·ch'eech'... |
| – a bar | – **bar** bahr |
| – a casino | – **kasyno** kah·<u>syh</u>·noh |
| – a dance club | – **dyskotekę** dyhs·koh·<u>teh</u>·keh |
| – a gay club | – **klub dla gejów** kluhp dlah <u>geh</u>·yuhf |
| – a jazz club | – **klub jazzowy** kluhp djeh·<u>zoh</u>·vyh |
| – a club with Polish music | – **klub z polską muzyką** kluhp <u>spohls</u>·kohm muh·<u>zyh</u>·kohm |
| Is there live music? | **Czy grają muzykę na żywo?** chyh grah·yohm muh·<u>zyh</u>·keh nah <u>zhyh</u>·voh |
| How do I get there? | **Jak tam dotrzeć?** yahk tahm <u>doh</u>·t·shehch' |
| Let's go dancing. | **Chodźmy potańczyć.** <u>hohch</u>'·myh poh·<u>tahn</u>'·chyhch' |

**Dyskoteki** (dance clubs) are popular throughout Poland.
These feature a variety of music: dance, jazz, pop, etc.
Prices are reasonable and many venues offer student
discounts. At popular dance clubs you may need to make
a reservation in advance.

# Special Needs

# Business Travel

## Essential

| | |
|---|---|
| I'm here on business. | **Przyjechałem♂/Przyjechałam♀ tutaj służbowo.** pshyh·yeh·<u>hah</u>·wehm♂/ pshyh·yeh·<u>hah</u>·wahm♀ tuh·tay swuhzh·<u>boh</u>·voh |
| Here's my business card. | **To moja wizytówka.** toh <u>moh</u>·yah vee·zyh·<u>tuhf</u>·kah |
| Can I have your card? | **Mogę prosić o pana wizytówkę?** <u>moh</u>·geh <u>proh</u>·sh'eech' oh <u>pah</u>·nah vee·zyh·<u>tuhf</u>·keh |
| I have a meeting with... | **Mam spotkanie z...** mahm spoht·<u>kah</u>·n'yeh z... |
| Where's...? | **Gdzie jest...?** gdj'yeh yehst... |
| – the business center | – **centrum biznesowe** <u>tsehn</u>·truhm beez·neh·<u>soh</u>·veh |
| – the convention hall | – **sala konferencyjna** <u>sah</u>·lah kohn·feh·rehn·<u>tsiy</u>·nah |
| – the meeting room | – **sala spotkań** <u>sah</u>·lah <u>spoht</u>·kahn' |

## Business Communication

| | |
|---|---|
| I'm here to attend... | **Przyjechałem♂/Przyjechałam♀ na...** pshyh·yeh·<u>hah</u>·wehm♂/pshyh·yeh·<u>hah</u>·wahm♀ nah... |
| – a seminar | – **seminarium** seh·mee·<u>nah</u>·ryuhm |
| – a conference | – **konferencję** kohn·feh·<u>rehn</u>·tsyeh |
| – a meeting | – **spotkanie** spoht·<u>kah</u>·n'yeh |
| My name is... | **Nazywam się...** nah·<u>zyh</u>·vahm sh'yeh... |
| May I introduce my colleague... | **Proszę pozwolić mi przedstawić kolegę...** <u>proh</u>·sheh pohz·<u>voh</u>·leech' mee pshet·<u>stah</u>·veech' koh·<u>leh</u>·geh... |

| | |
|---|---|
| Nice to meet you. | **Miło mi pana poznać.** <u>mee</u>·woh mee <u>pah</u>·nah <u>pohz</u>·nahch' |
| I have a meeting with... | **Mam spotkanie z...** mahm spoht·<u>kah</u>·n'yeh z... |
| I have an appointment with... | **Jestem umówiony z...** <u>yehs</u>·tehm uh·muh·<u>vyoh</u>·nyh z... |
| I'm sorry I'm late. | **Przepraszam za spóźnienie.** psheh·<u>prah</u>·shahm zah spuhzh'·<u>n'yeh</u>·n'yeh |
| I'd like an interpreter. | **Proszę o tłumacza.** <u>proh</u>·sheh oh twuh·<u>mah</u>·chah |
| You can reach me at the...Hotel. | **Można się ze mną kontaktować w hotelu...** <u>moh</u>·zhnah sh'yeh zeh mnohm kohn·tahk·<u>toh</u>·vach' f hoh·<u>teh</u>·luh... |
| I'm here until... | **Zostaję tu do...** zohs·<u>tah</u>·yeh tuh doh... |

*i*

Business people who meet for the first time shake hands and share their first names and surnames. Avoid clasping the hand of your partner with both hands. It is an accepted custom to exchange business cards at the first meeting. For subsequent meetings simply say: **dzień dobry/dobry wieczór** (hello/good evening) and shake hands.

If a woman and a man meet, she is supposed to reach out her hand first. However, if two business people occupy different positions, it is always the senior one who reaches out his/her hand first.

| I need to... | **Muszę...** <u>muh</u>·sheh... |
|---|---|
| – make a call | – **zadzwonić** zah·<u>dzvoh</u>·n'eech' |
| – make a photocopy | – **zrobić ksero** <u>zroh</u>·beech' <u>kseh</u>·roh |
| – send an e-mail | – **wysłać e-mail** <u>vyh</u>·swahch' <u>ee</u>·meyl |
| – send a fax | – **wysłać fax** <u>vyh</u>·swahch' fahks |
| – send a package (overnight) | – **wysłać paczkę (pocztą kurierską)** <u>vyh</u>·swahch' <u>pahch</u>·keh (<u>pohch</u>·tohm kuhr·<u>yehr</u>·skohm) |

▶ For internet and communications, see page 46.

## You May Hear...

| **Czy jest pan umówiony na spotkanie?** chyh yehst pahn uh·muh·<u>vyoh</u>·nyh nah spoht·<u>kah</u>·n'yeh | Do you have an appointment? |
|---|---|
| **Z kim?** skeem | With whom? |
| **Jest na zebraniu.** yehst nah zehb·<u>rah</u>·n'yuh | He/She is in a meeting. |
| **Proszę chwilę poczekać.** <u>proh</u>·sheh hvee·leh poh·<u>cheh</u>·kahch' | One moment, please. |
| **Proszę usiąść.** <u>proh</u>·sheh uh·sh'ohn'sh'ch' | Have a seat. |
| **Dziękuję za przybycie.** dj'yehn·<u>kuh</u>·yeh zah pshyh·<u>byh</u>·ch'yeh | Thank you for coming. |

## Essential

| | |
|---|---|
| Is there a discount for children? | **Czy jest zniżka dla dzieci?** chyh yehst <u>zn'eezh</u>·kah dlah dj'yeh·ch'ee |
| Can you recommend a babysitter? | **Czy może pan polecić opiekunkę do dzieci?** chyh <u>moh</u>·zheh pahn poh·<u>leh</u>·ch'eech' oh·pyeh·<u>kuhn</u>·keh doh <u>dj'yeh</u>·ch'ee |
| Do you have a child's seat/highchair? | **Mają państwo *krzesełko dla dziecka/ wysokie krzesełko*?** <u>mah</u>·yohm <u>pahn'</u>·stfoh ksheh·<u>seh</u>·wkoh dlah <u>dj'yeh</u>·tskah/vyh·soh·kyeh ksheh·<u>sehw</u>·koh |
| Where can I change the baby? | **Gdzie mogę przewinąć dziecko?** gdj'yeh <u>moh</u>·geh psheh·<u>vee</u>·nohn'ch' <u>dj'yehts</u>·koh |

## Fun with Kids ─────────

| | |
|---|---|
| Can you recommend something for kids? | **Czy może pan polecić coś dla dzieci?** chyh <u>moh</u>·zheh pahn poh·<u>leh</u>·ch'eech' tsohsh' dlah <u>dj'yeh</u>·ch'ee |
| Where's...? | **Gdzie jest...?** gdj'yeh yehst... |
| – the amusement park | – **wesołe miasteczko** veh·<u>soh</u>·weh myahs·<u>teh</u>·chkoh |
| – the arcade | – **salon gier** <u>sah</u>·lohn gyehr |
| – the kiddie [paddling] pool | – **brodzik** <u>broh</u>·dj'eek |
| – the park | – **park** pahrk |
| – the playground | – **plac zabaw** plahts <u>zah</u>·bahf |
| – the zoo | – **zoo** zoh·oh |

| Are children allowed? | **Czy można wchodzić z dziećmi?** chyh <u>mohzh</u>·nah <u>fhoh</u>·dj'eech' <u>zdj'yehch'</u>·mee |
| Is it safe for kids? | **Czy to jest bezpieczne dla dzieci?** chyh toh yehst behs·<u>pyehch</u>·n'yeh dlah <u>dj'yeh</u>·ch'ee |
| Is it suitable for...year olds? | **Czy to jest odpowiednie dla...-latków?** chyh toh yehst oht·poh·<u>vyehd</u>·n'yeh dlah...<u>laht</u>·kuhf |

▶ For numbers, see page 168.

## You May Hear...

| Jakie słodkie! <u>yah</u>·kyeh <u>swoht</u>·kyeh | How cute! |
| Jak ma na imię? yahk mah nah <u>ee</u>·myeh | What's his/her name? |
| Ile ma lat? <u>ee</u>·leh mah laht | How old is he/she? |

146

# Basic Needs for Kids

| Do you have...? | **Czy mają państwo...?** chyh <u>mah</u>·yohm pahn'·stfoh... |
|---|---|
| - a baby bottle | - **butelkę ze smoczkiem** buh·<u>tehl</u>·keh zeh <u>smohch</u>·kyehm |
| - baby wipes | - **wilgotne chusteczki pielęgnacyjne** veel·<u>goht</u>·neh huhsh·<u>tehch</u>·kee pyeh·lehn·gnah·<u>tsiy</u>·neh |
| - a car seat | - **fotelik samochodowy** foh·<u>teh</u>·leek sah·moh·hoh·<u>doh</u>·vyh |
| - a child's seat/ highchair | - **krzesełko dla dziecka/wysokie krzesełko** ksheh·<u>seh</u>·wkoh dlah <u>dj'yeh</u>·tskah/ vyh·soh·kyeh ksheh·<u>seh</u>·wkoh |
| - a crib/cot | - **łóżko składane/łóżeczko dziecinne** wuh·shkoh skwah·dah·neh/wuh·<u>zhehch</u>·koh dj'yeh·<u>ch'een</u>·neh |
| - diapers [nappies] | - **pieluszki** pyeh·<u>luhsh</u>·kee |
| - a pacifier [soother] | - **smoczek** <u>smoh</u>·chehk |
| - a playpen | - **kojec** <u>koh</u>·yehts |
| - a stroller [pushchair] | - **wózek spacerowy** <u>vuh</u>·zehk spah·tseh·<u>roh</u>·vyh |
| Can I breastfeed the baby here? | **Czy mogę tutaj karmić dziecko piersią?** chyh <u>moh</u>·geh <u>tuh</u>·tay <u>kahr</u>·meech' <u>dj'yehts</u>·koh pyehr·sh'yohm |
| Where can I change the baby? | **Gdzie mogę przewinąć dziecko?** gdj'yeh <u>moh</u>·geh psheh·<u>vee</u>·nohn'ch' <u>dj'yehts</u>·koh |

▶ For dining with kids, see page 60.

# Babysitting

| Can you recommend a babysitter? | **Czy może pan polecić opiekunkę do dzieci?** chyh <u>moh</u>·zheh pahn poh·<u>leh</u>·ch'eech' oh·pyeh·<u>kuhn</u>·keh doh <u>dj'yeh</u>·ch'ee |
|---|---|

| What's the charge? | **Jaka jest opłata?** yah·kah yehst oh·<u>pwah</u>·tah |
| I'll be back by... | **Przyjdę za...** <u>pshiy</u>·deh zah... |

▶ For time, see page 170.

| I can be reached at... | **Można do mnie dzwonić na numer...** moh-zhnah doh mn'yeh <u>dzvoh</u>·n'eech' nah <u>nuh</u>·mehr... |

## Health and Emergency

| Can you recommend a pediatrician? | **Czy może pan polecić pediatrę?** chyh <u>moh</u>·zheh pahn poh·<u>leh</u>·ch'eech' peh·<u>dyaht</u>·reh |
| My child is allergic to... | **Moje dziecko ma uczulenie na...** moh·yeh <u>dj'yeh</u>·tskoh mah uh·chuh·<u>leh</u>·n'yeh nah... |
| My child is missing. | **Moje dziecko się zgubiło.** <u>moh</u>·yeh <u>dj'yeh</u>·tskoh sh'yeh zguh·<u>bee</u>·woh |
| Have you seen a *boy/girl*? | **Czy widział pan *chłopca/dziewczynkę*?** chyh <u>vee</u>·dj'yahw pahn <u>hwohp</u>·tsah/ dj'yehv·<u>chyhn</u>·keh |

▶ For food items, see page 81.

▶ For health, see page 154.

▶ For police, see page 151.

## For the Disabled

## Essential

| Is there...? | **Czy jest...?** chyh yehst... |
| - access for the disabled | - **dostęp dla niepełnosprawnych** <u>dohs</u>·tehmp dlah n'yeh·pehw·noh·<u>sprahv</u>·nyhh |
| - a wheelchair ramp | - **podjazd dla wózków inwalidzkich** <u>pohd</u>·yahst dlah <u>vuhs</u>·kuhf een·vah·<u>leedz</u>·keeh |

| – a handicapped-<br>[disabled-]<br>accessible toilet | – **toaleta dla niepełnosprawnych**<br>toh·ah·<u>leh</u>·tah dlah<br>n'yeh·pew·noh·<u>sprahv</u>·nyhh |
|---|---|
| I need... | **Potrzebuję...** poh·tsheh·<u>buh</u>·yeh... |
| – assistance | – **pomocy** poh·<u>moh</u>·tsyh |
| – an elevator [lift] | – **windy** <u>veen</u>·dyh |
| – a ground-floor<br>room | – **pokoju na parterze** poh·<u>koh</u>·yuh nah<br>pahr·<u>teh</u>·zheh |

## Getting Help

| I'm disabled. | **Jestem nepełnosprawny**♂/**niepełnosprawna**♀.<br><u>yehs</u>·tehm n'yeh·pehw·noh·<u>sprahv</u>·nyh♂/<br>n'yeh·pehw·noh·<u>sprahv</u>·nah♀ |
|---|---|
| I'm deaf. | **Jestem głuchy**♂/**głucha**♀. <u>yehs</u>·tehm<br><u>gwuh</u>·hyh♂/<u>gwuh</u>·hah♀ |
| I'm *visually/<br>hearing* impaired. | **Niedowidzę./Niedosłyszę.**<br>n'yeh·doh·<u>vee</u>·dzeh/n'yeh·doh·<u>swyh</u>·sheh |
| I'm unable to *walk<br>far/use the stairs*. | **Nie mogę *dużo chodzić/chodzić po<br>schodach*.** n'yeh <u>moh</u>·geh <u>duh</u>·zhoh<br><u>hoh</u>·dj'eech'/<u>hoh</u>·dj'eech' poh s·<u>hoh</u>·dahh |
| Can I bring my<br>wheelchair? | **Czy mogę być na wózku inwalidzkim?** chyh<br><u>moh</u>·geh byhch' nah <u>vuhs</u>·kuh een·vah·<u>leedz</u>·keem |
| Are guide dogs<br>permitted? | **Czy mogę być z psem przewodnikiem?** chyh<br><u>moh</u>·geh byhch' spsehm psheh·vohd·<u>n'ee</u>·kyem |
| Can you help me? | **Czy może mi pan pomóc?** chyh <u>moh</u>·zheh mee<br>pahn <u>poh</u>·muhts |
| Please *open/hold*<br>the door. | **Proszę *otworzyć/przytrzymać* drzwi.** <u>proh</u>·sheh<br>oht·<u>foh</u>·zhyhch'/pshyh·<u>tshyh</u>·mahch' djvee |

# ▼ Resources

# Emergencies

## Essential

| | |
|---|---|
| Help! | **Pomocy!** poh·<u>moh</u>·tsih |
| Go away! | **Proszę odejść!** <u>proh</u>·sheh <u>oh</u>·deysh'ch' |
| Leave me alone! | **Zostaw mnie w spokoju!** <u>zoh</u>·stahf mn'yeh f spoh·<u>koh</u>·yuh |
| Stop thief! | **Łapać złodzieja!** <u>wah</u>·pach' zwoh·<u>dj'yeh</u>·yah |
| Get a doctor! | **Wezwijcie lekarza!** vez·<u>veey</u>·ch'yeh leh·<u>kah</u>·zhah |
| Fire! | **Pali się!** <u>pah</u>·lee sh'yeh |
| I'm lost. | **Zgubiłem się.** zguh·<u>bee</u>·wehm sh'yeh |
| Can you help me? | **Czy może mi pan pomóc?** chyh <u>moh</u>·zheh mee pahn <u>poh</u>·muhts |

# Police

## Essential

| | |
|---|---|
| Call the police! | **Wezwijcie policję!** vez·<u>veey</u>·ch'yeh poh·<u>leets</u>·yeh |
| Where's the police station? | **Gdzie jest komisariat?** gdj'yeh yehst koh·mee·<u>sahr</u>·yaht |
| There has been an *accident/attack*. | **Zdarzył się *wypadek/napad*.** <u>zdah</u>·zhiw sh'yeh vyh·<u>pah</u>·dehk/<u>nah</u>·paht |
| My child is missing. | **Moje dziecko się zgubiło.** <u>moh</u>·yeh <u>dj'yeh</u>·tskoh sh'yeh zguh·<u>bee</u>·woh |

| I need... | Potrzebuję... poht·sh'eh·<u>buh</u>·yeh... |
|---|---|
| – an interpreter | – tłumacza twuh·<u>mah</u>·chah |
| – to contact my lawyer | – skontaktować się z moim prawnikiem skohn·tah·<u>ktoh</u>·vahch' sh'yeh <u>zmoh</u>·eem prah·<u>vneeh</u>·kee'ehm |
| – to make a phone call | – zatelefonować zah·teh·leh·foh·<u>noh</u>·vach' |
| I'm innocent. | Jestem niewinny♂/niewinna♀. <u>yeh</u>·stehm n'yeh·<u>veen</u>·nyh♂/n'yeh·<u>veen</u>·nah♀ |
| It was an accident. | To był wypadek. toh byhw vyh·<u>pah</u>·dehk |

## You May Hear...

| | |
|---|---|
| Proszę wypełnić ten formularz. <u>proh</u>·sheh vyh·<u>pehw</u>·n'eech' tehn fohr·<u>muh</u>·lash' | Please fill out this form. |
| Poproszę dowód tożsamości. poh·<u>proh</u>·sheh <u>doh</u>·vuht tohsh'·sah·<u>mohsh</u>'·ch'ee | Your identification, please. |
| *Gdzie/Kiedy* to się stało? gdj'eh/<u>kee</u>'eh·dyh toh sh'yeh <u>stah</u>·woh | *When/Where* did it happen? |
| Jak *on/ona* wygląda? yahk *ohn/<u>oh</u>·nah* vyh·<u>glohn</u>·dah | What does *he/she* look like? |
| Proszę tu poczekać. <u>proh</u>·sheh tuh poh·<u>ch'eh</u>·kahch' | Please wait here. |
| Jak można się z panem skontaktować? yahk <u>moh</u>·znah sh'yeh z <u>pah</u>·nehm skohn·tahk·<u>toh</u>·vahch' | How may we contact you? |

## Lost Property and Theft

| I want to report... | Chcę zgłosić... htseh <u>zgwoh</u>·sh'eech'... |
|---|---|
| – a mugging | – napad <u>nah</u>·paht |
| – a rape | – gwałt gvahwt |
| – a theft | – kradzież <u>krah</u>·djyesh |

| I've been *robbed/ mugged*. | *Okradli/Napadli* mnie. oh·_krah_·dlee/ nah·_pah_·dlee mn'yeh |
|---|---|
| I've lost my... | **Zgubiłem...** zguh·_bee_·wehm... |
| My...has been stolen. | **Ukradli mi...** uh·_krah_·dlee mee... |
| - luggage | - **bagaż** _bah_·gahsh |
| - backpack [rucksack] | - **plecak** _pleh_·tsahk |
| - bicycle | - **rower** roh·vehr |
| - camera | - **aparat fotograficzny** ah·_pah_·raht foh·toh·grah·_feech_·nyh |
| - video camera | - **kamerę** kah·_meh_·reh |
| - (rental [hire]) car | - **(wynajęty) samochód** (vyh·nah·_yen_·tyh) sah·_moh_·huht |
| - laptop | - **laptop** _lahp_·tohp |
| - credit card | - **kartę kredytową** _kahr_·teh kreh·dyh·_toh_·vohm |
| - cell [mobile] phone | - **komórkę** koh·_muhr_·keh |
| - jewelry | - **biżuterię** bee·zhuh·_tehr_·yeh |
| - money | - **pieniądze** pyeh·_n'yohn_·dzeh |
| - passport | - **paszport** _pahsh_·pohrt |
| - purse [handbag] | - **torebkę** toh·_rehp_·keh |
| - travelers checks [cheques] | - **czeki podróżne** _cheh_·kee pohd·_ruhzh_·neh |
| - wallet | - **portfel** _pohrt_·fehl |
| I need a police report. | **Muszę mieć raport z policji.** _muh_·sheh myehch' _rah_·pohrt spoh·_leets_·yee |

# Health

## Essential

| | |
|---|---|
| I'm sick [ill]. | **Jestem chory♂/chora♀.** yeh·stehm <u>hoh</u>·ryh♂/<u>hoh</u>·rah♀ |
| I don't feel well. | **Źle się czuję.** zh'leh sh'yeh <u>chuh</u>·yeh |
| Is there an English-speaking doctor? | **Czy jest tu lekarz mówiący po angielsku?** chyh yehst tuh <u>leh</u>·kahsh muh·<u>vyohn</u>·tsyh poh ahn·<u>gyehls</u>·kuh |
| It hurts here. | **Boli mnie tutaj.** <u>boh</u>·lee mn'yeh <u>tuh</u>·tay |
| I have a stomachache. | **Boli mnie brzuch.** <u>boh</u>·lee mn'yeh bzhuhh |

## Finding a Doctor

| | |
|---|---|
| Can you recommend a *doctor/dentist*? | **Czy może pan polecić *lekarza/dentystę*?** chyh <u>moh</u>·zheh pahn poh·<u>leh</u>·ch'eech' leh·<u>kah</u>·zhah/dehn·<u>tyh</u>·steh |
| Could the doctor come to see me here? | **Czy lekarz może przyjść mnie zbadać tutaj?** chyh <u>leh</u>·kash <u>moh</u>·zheh pshiysh'ch' mn'yeh <u>zbah</u>·dach' <u>tuh</u>·tay |
| I need an English-speaking doctor. | **Potrzebuję lekarza mówiącego po angielsku.** poht·sheh·<u>buh</u>·yeh leh·<u>kah</u>·zhah muh·vyohn·<u>tseh</u>·goh poh ahn·<u>gyehls</u>·kuh |
| What are the office [surgery] hours? | **Jakie są godziny przyjęć?** <u>yahk</u>·yeh sohm goh·<u>djee</u>·nyh <u>pshyh</u>·yehnch' |
| Can I make an appointment...? | **Czy mogę zamówić wizytę...?** chyh <u>moh</u>·geh zah·<u>muh</u>·veech' vee·<u>zyh</u>·teh... |
| – for today | – **na dzisiaj** nah <u>dj'ee</u>·sh'yay |
| – for tomorrow | – **na jutro** nah <u>yuh</u>·troh |
| – as soon as possible | – **na jak najbliższy termin** nah yahk nay·<u>bleesh</u>·shih <u>tehr</u>·meen |

| It's urgent. | **To jest pilne.** toh yest <u>peel</u>·neh |
| It's an emergency. | **To nagły wypadek.** toh <u>nah</u>·gwih vih·<u>pah</u>·dehk |

## Symptoms

| I'm... | **Mam...** mahm... |
| – bleeding | – **krwotok** <u>krfoh</u>·tohk |
| – constipated | – **zaparcie** zah·<u>pahr</u>·ch'yeh |
| – dizzy | – **zawroty głowy** zah·<u>vroh</u>·tih <u>gwoh</u>·vih |
| – nauseous | – **mdłości** <u>mdwosh'</u>·ch'ee |
| I'm vomiting. | **Wymiotuję.** vih·myoh·<u>tuh</u>·yeh |
| It hurts here. | **Boli mnie tutaj.** <u>boh</u>·lee mn'yeh <u>tuh</u>·tay |
| I have... | **Mam...** mahm... |
| – an allergic reaction | – **reakcję alergiczną** reh·<u>ahk</u>·tsyeh ah·lehr·<u>geech</u>·nohm |
| – chest pain | – **bóle w klatce piersiowej** <u>buh</u>·leh f <u>klaht</u>·tseh pyehr·<u>sh'yoh</u>·vey |
| – a fever | – **gorączkę** goh·<u>rohnch</u>·keh |
| – pain | – **bóle** <u>buh</u>·leh |
| – a rash | – **wysypkę** vih·<u>syhp</u>·keh |
| – a sprain | – **zwichnięcie** zvee·<u>hn'yehn'</u>·ch'yeh |
| – some swelling | – **opuchliznę** oh·puh·<u>hleez</u>·neh |
| – sunstroke | – **udar słoneczny** <u>uh</u>·dahr swoh·<u>nehch</u>·nih |
| I have... | **Boli mnie...** <u>boh</u>·lee mn'yeh... |
| – an earache | – **ucho** <u>uh</u>·hoh |
| – a stomachache | – **brzuch** bzhuhh |
| – a headache | – **głowa** <u>gwoh</u>·vah |
| I've been sick [ill] for...days. | **Źle się czuję od...dni.** zh'leh sh'yeh <u>chuh</u>·yeh oht...dn'yee |

▶ For numbers, see page 168.

## Health Conditions

| I'm... | Mam... mahm... |
|---|---|
| – anemic | – anemię ah·<u>neh</u>·myeh |
| – diabetic | – cukrzycę tsuhk·<u>shyh</u>·tseh |
| – asthmatic | – astmę <u>ahst</u>·mehm |
| I'm allergic to *antibiotics/ penicillin.* | Mam uczulenie na *antybiotyki/ penicylinę.* Mahm uh·chuh·<u>leh</u>·n'yeh nah ahn·tih·<u>byoh</u>·tih·kee/peh·nee·tsih·<u>lee</u>·neh |

▶ For food items, see page 81.

| I have arthritis. | Mam artretyzm. mahm ahr·<u>treh</u>·tihsm |
|---|---|
| I have *high/low* blood pressure. | Mam *wysokie/niskie* ciśnienie. mahm vih·<u>soh</u>·kyeh/<u>nees</u>·kyeh ch'eesh·<u>n'yeh</u>·n'yeh |
| I have a heart condition. | Choruję na serce. hoh·<u>ruh</u>·yeh na <u>sehr</u>·tseh |
| I'm on... | Zażywam... zah·<u>zhyh</u>·vahm... |

## You May Hear...

| | |
|---|---|
| W czym problem? fchihm <u>proh</u>·blehm | What's wrong? |
| Gdzie boli? gdj'yeh <u>boh</u>·lee | Where does it hurt? |
| Czy boli tutaj? chih <u>boh</u>·lee <u>tuh</u>·tay | Does it hurt here? |
| Czy przyjmuje pan regularnie leki? chih pshiy·<u>muh</u>·yeh pahn reh·guh·<u>lahr</u>·n'yeh <u>leh</u>·kee | Are you on medication? |
| Czy jest pan na coś uczulony? chih yehst pahn nah tsosh' uh·chuh·<u>loh</u>·nih | Are you allergic to anything? |
| Proszę otworzyć usta. <u>proh</u>·sheh oht·<u>foh</u>·zhich' <u>uh</u>·stah | Please open your mouth. |
| Oddychać głęboko. ohd·<u>dyh</u>·hach' gwehm·<u>boh</u>·koh | Breathe deeply. |

| Pójdzie pan do szpitala. <u>puy</u>·dj'yeh pahn doh shpee·<u>tah</u>·lah | You must go to the hospital. |

## Hospital

| Please notify my family. | Proszę zawiadomić moją rodzinę. <u>proh</u>·sheh zah·vyah·<u>doh</u>·meech' <u>moh</u>·yohm roh·<u>dj'ee</u>·neh |
| I'm in pain. | Boli mnie. <u>boh</u>·lee mn'yeh |
| I need a *doctor/ nurse*. | Potrzebuję *lekarza/pielęgniarki*. poh·tsheh·<u>buh</u>·yeh leh·<u>kah</u>·zhah/ pyeh·lehng·<u>n'yahr</u>·kee |
| When are visiting hours? | Jakie są godziny odwiedzin? <u>yah</u>·kyeh sohm goh·<u>dj'ee</u>·nyh ohd·<u>vyeh</u>·dj'een |
| I'm visiting... | Odwiedzam... ohd·<u>vyeh</u>·dzahm... |

## You May Hear...

| Musimy zrobić rentgen. muh·<u>sh'ee</u>·mih <u>zroh</u>·beech' <u>rehnt</u>·gehn | We must X-ray you. |
| Proszę podpisać zgodę na operację. <u>proh</u>·sheh poht·<u>pee</u>·sahch' <u>zgoh</u>·deh nah oh·peh·<u>rah</u>·tsyeh | Please sign the consent for surgery. |

## Dentist

| I've lost a filling. | Wypadła mi plomba. vih·<u>pahd</u>·wah mee <u>plohm</u>·bah |
| I've lost a tooth. | Wypadł mi ząb. <u>vyh</u>·pahdw mee zohmp |
| I have a toothache. | Boli mnie ząb. <u>boh</u>·lee mn'yeh zohmp |
| Can you fix this denture? | Czy da się naprawić tę protezę? chih dah sh'yeh nah·<u>prah</u>·veech' teh proh·<u>teh</u>·zeh |

| I'd like an anesthetic. | **Poproszę znieczulenie.** poh·<u>proh</u>·sheh zn'yeh·chuh·<u>leh</u>·n'yeh |
| --- | --- |

## Gynecologist

| I have *menstrual cramps/a vaginal infection.* | **Mam *bóle miesiączkowe/infekcję pochwy.*** mahm <u>buh</u>·leh myeh·sh'yohn·ch<u>koh</u>·veh/ een·<u>fehk</u>·tsyeh poh·hfih |
| --- | --- |
| I missed my period. | **Spóźnia mi się okres.** <u>spuh</u>·zh'n'yah mee sh'yeh <u>ohk</u>·rehs |
| I'm on the pill. | **Biorę pigułki antykoncepcyjne.** <u>byoh</u>·reh pee·<u>guhw</u>·kee ahn·tih·kohn·tsep·<u>tsiy</u>·neh |
| I'm (not) pregnant. | **(Nie) Jestem w ciąży.** (n'yeh) <u>yehs</u>·tehm <u>fch'yohn</u>·zhih |
| I haven't had my period for...months. | **Nie miałam okresu od...miesięcy.** n'yeh <u>myah</u>·wahm oh·<u>kreh</u>·suh oht...myeh·<u>sh'yen</u>·tsih |

## Optician

| I've lost... | **Zgubiłem♂/Zgubiłam♀ ...** zguh·<u>bee</u>·wehm♂/ zguh·<u>bee</u>·wahm♀... |
| --- | --- |
| – a contact lens | **– soczewkę kontaktową** soh·<u>chehf</u>·keh kohn·tahk·<u>toh</u>·vohm |
| – my glasses | **– okulary** oh·kuh·<u>lah</u>·rih |
| – a lens | **– soczewkę** soh·<u>chef</u>·keh |

## Payment and Insurance

| How much? | **Ile to kosztuje?** <u>ee</u>·leh toh kohsh·<u>tuh</u>·yeh |
| --- | --- |
| Can I pay by credit card? | **Czy mogę zapłacić kartą kredytową?** chih <u>moh</u>·geh zah·<u>pwah</u>·ch'eech' <u>kahr</u>·tohm kreh·dih·<u>toh</u>·vohm |
| I have insurance. | **Mam ubezpieczenie.** mam uh·behs·pyeh·<u>che</u>·n'yeh |

| | |
|---|---|
| Can I have a receipt for my insurance? | **Czy mogę dostać pokwitowanie dla mojego ubezpieczenia?** chih <u>moh</u>·geh dohs·tach' poh·kfee·toh·<u>vah</u>·n'yeh dlah moh·<u>yeh</u>·goh uh·behs·pyeh·<u>cheh</u>·n'yah |

## Pharmacy [Chemist]

### Essential

| | |
|---|---|
| Where's the nearest (24-hour) pharmacy? | **Gdzie jest najbliższa apteka (całodobowa)?** gdj'yeh yest nay·<u>bleesh</u>·sha ah·<u>pteh</u>·kah (tsah·woh·doh·<u>boh</u>·vah) |
| What time does the pharmacy *open/close*? | **O której *otwierają/zamykają* aptekę?** oh <u>ktuh</u>·rey oht·fyeh·<u>rah</u>·yohm/zah·myh·<u>kah</u>· yohm ah·<u>pteh</u>·keh |
| What would you recommend for...? | **Co może mi pan polecić na...?** tsoh <u>moh</u>·zheh mee pahn poh·<u>leh</u>·ch'eech' nah... |
| How much should I take? | **Ile mam brać?** eeleh mahm brahch' |
| Can you fill [make up] this prescription? | **Czy możecie zrealizować tę receptę?** chih moh·<u>zheh</u>·ch'yeh zreh·ah·lee·<u>zoh</u>·vach' teh reh·<u>tsehp</u>·teh |
| I'm allergic to... | **Mam uczulenie na...** mahm uh·chuh·<u>leh</u>·n'yeh nah... |

 Pharmacies in Poland are easily identifiable by the sign **APTEKA** and a cross. Hours are generally from 9:00 a.m. to 6:00 p.m.; some operate around the clock. The names and locations of these 24-hour pharmacies are posted on the doors and windows of other pharmacies. You will need a prescription for drugs not available over the counter. Most pharmacies nowadays sell toiletries and cosmetics, too.

### Dosage Instructions

| | |
|---|---|
| How much should I take? | **Ile mam wziąć?** <u>ee</u>·leh mahm vzh'yonch' |
| How often should I take it? | **Jak często mam to brać?** yahk chehn·stoh mahm toh brahch' |
| Is it suitable for children? | **Czy to jest odpowiednie dla dzieci?** chih toh yest oht·poh·<u>vyehd</u>·n'yeh dlah <u>dj'yeh</u>·ch'ee |
| I'm on... | **Biorę...** <u>byoh</u>·reh... |
| Are there side effects? | **Czy są jakieś efekty uboczne?** chih sohm <u>yah</u>·kyesh' eh·<u>fek</u>·tih uh·<u>bohch</u>·neh |

## You May See...

| | |
|---|---|
| *RAZ/TRZY RAZY DZIENNIE* | *once/three times a day* |
| **TABLETKA** | tablet |
| **KROPLA** | drop |
| **ŁYŻECZKA** | teaspoon |
| **PRZED POSIŁKIEM** | before meals |
| *PO/W TRAKCIE POSIŁKU* | *after/with meals* |

| | |
|---|---|
| NA CZCZO | on an empty stomach |
| POŁYKAĆ W CAŁOŚCI | swallow whole |
| MOŻE POWODOWAĆ SENNOŚĆ | may cause drowsiness |
| WYŁĄCZNIE DO UŻYTKU ZEWNĘTRZNEGO | for external use only |

## Health Problems

I'd like some medicine for...
**Poproszę lekarstwo na...** poh·<u>proh</u>·sheh leh·<u>kahrs</u>·tfoh nah...

- a cold
  – **przeziębienie** psheh·<u>zh'yehm</u>·byeh·n'yeh
- a cough
  – **kaszel** <u>kah</u>·shehl
- diarrhea
  – **biegunkę** byeh·<u>guhn</u>·keh
- the flu
  – **grypę** grih·peh
- motion [travel] sickness
  – **chorobę lokomocyjną** hoh·<u>roh</u>·beh loh·koh·moh·<u>tsiy</u>·nohm
- a sore throat
  – **ból gardła** buhl <u>gahr</u>·dwah
- an upset stomach
  – **rozstrój żołądka** <u>rohs</u>·struy zhoh·<u>wohnt</u>·kah

## Basic Needs

I'd like...
**Poproszę...** poh·<u>proh</u>·sheh...

- acetaminophen [paracetamol]
  – **paracetamol** pah·rah·tseh·<u>tah</u>·mohl
- antiseptic cream
  – **krem aseptyczny** krehm ah·sep·<u>tyhch</u>·nih
- aspirin
  – **aspirynę** ah·spee·<u>ryh</u>·neh
- a bandage
  – **bandaż** <u>bahn</u>·dahzh
- a comb
  – **grzebień** <u>gzheh</u>·byen'
- condoms
  – **prezerwatywy** preh·zehr·vah·<u>tyh</u>·vyh
- contact lens solution
  – **płyn do soczewek kontaktowych** pwihn doh soh·<u>cheh</u>·vehk kohn·tahk·<u>toh</u>·vih

| I'd like... | Poproszę... poh·_proh_·sheh... |
|---|---|
| – deodorant | – **dezodorant** deh·zoh·_doh_·rahnt |
| – a hairbrush | – **szczotkę do włosów** shchoht·keh doh _vwoh_·suhf |
| – hair spray | – **lakier do włosów** _lah_·kyehr doh _vwoh_·suhf |
| – ibuprofen | – **ibuprofen** ee·buh·_proh_·fehn |
| – insect repellent | – **środek na owady** sh'roh·dehk nah oh·_vah_·dih |
| – lotion | – **balsam** _bahl_·sahm |
| – a nail file | – **pilnik do paznokci** _peel_·n'eek doh pahz·_nohk_·ch'ee |
| – painkillers | – **środki przeciwbólowe** sh'roht·kee psheh·ch'eef·buh·_loh_·veh |
| – a (disposable) razor | – **(jednorazową) maszynkę do golenia** (yehd·noh·rah·_zoh_·vohm) mah·_shyhn_·keh doh goh·_leh_·n'yah |
| – razor blades | – **żyletki** zhih·_leht_·kee |
| – sanitary napkins [pads] | – **podpaski** poht·_pahs_·kee |
| – shampoo/ conditioner | – **szampon/odżywkę** _shahm_·pohn/ ohd·_zhyhf_·keh |
| – soap | – **mydło** _myh_·dwoh |
| – sunscreen | – **krem do opalania** krehm doh oh·pah·_lah_·n'yah |
| – tampons | – **tampony** tahm·_poh_·nih |
| – tissues | – **chusteczki papierowe** huhs·_tech_·kee pahp·yeh·_roh_·veh |
| – toilet paper | – **papier toaletowy** _pah_·pyehr toh·ah·leh·_toh_·vih |
| – a toothbrush | – **szczoteczkę do zębów** shchoh·_tech_·keh doh _zehm_·buhf |
| – toothpaste | – **pastę do zębów** _pah_·steh doh _zehm_·buhf |

▶ For baby products, see page 146.

# Reference

In Polish, there are two forms for you: **ty** (singular) and **wy** (plural). These are used when talking to relatives, close friends and children as well as among young people. When addressing someone in a formal situation use **pan** (Mr/sir), **pani** (Mrs/Ms/ma'am [madam]) or **państwo** (for groups).

## Grammar

### Regular Verbs

Polish verbs are conjugated based on person, number, tense and gender. Following are the present, past and future forms of the verbs **robić** (to do) and **mieć** (to have).

| ROBIĆ | | PRESENT | PAST | FUTURE |
|---|---|---|---|---|
| I | ja | robię | robiłem♂ <br> robiłam♀ | będę robić |
| you | ty | robisz | robiłeś♂ <br> robiłaś♀ | będziesz robić |
| he/sir | on/pan | robi | robił♂ | będzie robić |
| she/madam | ona/pani | robi | robiła♀ | będzie robić |
| it | ono | robi | robiło | będzie robić |
| we | my | robimy | robiliśmy♂ <br> robiłyśmy♀ | będziemy robić |
| you | wy | robicie | robiliście♂ <br> robiłyście♀ | będziecie robić |
| they <br> (pl. fml.) | oni♂/one♀/ <br> państwo | robią | robili♂ <br> robiły♀ | będą robić |

pl. = plural;    fml. = formal

| MIEĆ | | PRESENT | PAST | FUTURE |
|---|---|---|---|---|
| I | ja | mam | miałem♂ miałam♀ | będę mieć |
| you | ty | masz | miałeś♂ miałaś♀ | będziesz mieć |
| he/sir | on/pan | ma | miał♂ | będzie mieć |
| she/madam | ona/pani | ma | miała♀ | będzie mieć |
| it | ono | ma | miało | będzie mieć |
| we | my | mamy | mieliśmy♂ miałyśmy♀ | będziemy mieć |
| you | wy | macie | mieliście♂ miałyście♀ | będziecie mieć |
| they (pl. fml.) | oni♂/one♀/ państwo | mają | mieli♂ miały♀ | będą mieć |

## Irregular Verbs

Irregular verbs are not conjugated by following the normal rules. Following are two common irregular verbs, **być** (to be) and **iść** (to go):

| BYĆ | | PRESENT | PAST | FUTURE |
|---|---|---|---|---|
| I | ja | jestem | byłem♂ byłam♀ | będę |
| you | ty | jesteś | byłeś♂ byłaś♀ | będziesz |
| he/sir | on/pan | jest | był♂ | będzie |
| she/madam | ona/pani | jest | była♀ | będzie |
| it | ono | jest | było | będzie |
| we | my | jesteśmy | byliśmy♂ byłyśmy♀ | będziemy |
| you | wy | jesteście | byliście♂ byłyście♀ | będziecie |
| they (pl. fml.) | oni♂/one♀ państwo | są | byli♂ były♀ | będą |

| IŚĆ | | PRESENT | PAST | FUTURE |
|---|---|---|---|---|
| I | ja | idę | szedłem♂<br>szłam♀ | będę iść |
| you | ty | idziesz | szedłeś♂<br>szłaś♀ | będziesz iść |
| he/sir | on/pan | idzie | szedł♂ | będzie iść |
| she/madam | ona/pani | idzie | szła♀ | będzie iść |
| it | ono | idzie | szło | będzie iść |
| we | my | idziemy | szliśmy♂<br>szłyśmy♀ | będziemy iść |
| you | wy | idziecie | szliście♂<br>szłyście♀ | będziecie iść |
| they<br>(pl. fml.) | oni♂/one♀/<br>państwo | idą | szli♂<br>szły♀ | będą iść |

## Nouns

Nouns in Polish are either masculine, feminine or neuter. Masculine nouns usually end in a consonant. Feminine nouns usually end in –a or, less often, –i. Neuter nouns end in –ę or –o. Most masculine and feminine nouns, when plural, end in –y or in –i; most neuter nouns in –a. The endings of nouns vary according to their role in the sentence. There are seven different cases (roles) in both the singular and plural. There are no articles (a, an, the) in Polish.

## Word Order

Word order in Polish is usually as in English, i.e., subject-verb-object. However, word order can be more flexible, because the word endings indicate the role of each word in the sentence.

Example:  **Ania dała książkę Markowi. = Ania dała Markowi książkę. = Ania Markowi dała książkę.** (Ania gave Marek a book.)

To ask a question in Polish:

1. use **czy**

Example:     **Czy to pan Kowalski?** Is it Mr. Kowalski?

2. add rising intonation to an affirmative statement

Example:     **Pan Kowalski?** Mr. Kowalski?

3. use question words

**gdzie, kiedy, kto, co** where, when, who, what

Example:     **Gdzie jesteś?** Where are you?
             **Kiedy wrócisz?** When are you coming back?
             **Co będziemy robić?** What are we going to do?

## Negation

To form a negative sentence, add **nie** (not) before the verb. Note that noun endings may change.

Example:     **Mam bilet.** I have a ticket.
             **Nie mam biletu.** I don't have a ticket.

## Imperatives

Imperative sentences are formed by adding the appropriate ending to the verb stem.

Example: Go!

| you | ty | Idź! |
|---|---|---|
| he/sir | on/pan | Niech idzie! |
| she/madam | ona/pani | Niech idzie! |
| it | ono | Niech idzie! |
| we | my | Idźmy! |
| you | wy | Idźcie! |
| they (pl. fml.) | oni♂/one♀ | Niech idą!<br>Niech państwo idą! |

## Adjectives

Adjectives must agree in gender, number and case with the nouns they modify. Masculine adjectives usually end in –y or –i. The feminine and neuter endings are –a and –e, respectively.

Example:  To duży♂ dom♂. This is a big house.

To duża♀ szkoła♀. This is a big school.

To duże dziecko. This is a big child.

## Comparative and Superlative

The comparative is usually formed by adding –szy♂/–sza♀/–sze (neuter) and the superlative by adding naj...–szy♂/–sza♀/–sze (neuter).

Example:

| tani (cheap) | tańszy | najtańszy |
|---|---|---|

Less common adjectives often use the complex comparative and superlative form:

comparative = bardziej (more) + adjective
superlative = najbardziej (the most) + adjective

Example:

| tradycyjny (traditional) | bardziej tradycyjny | najbardziej tradycyjny |
|---|---|---|

## Adverbs

Some adverbs in Polish are formed from adjectives by adding the ending –o, but there is no fixed rule.

Example:  To <u>szybki</u> samochód. This is a <u>fast</u> car. (adjective)

Robert jeździ <u>szybko</u> samochodem. Robert drives his car <u>fast</u>. (adverb)

# Numbers

## Essential

| | | |
|---|---|---|
| 0 | **zero** | zeh·roh |
| 1 | **jeden** | yeh·dehn |
| 2 | **dwa** | dvah |
| 3 | **trzy** | tshyh |
| 4 | **cztery** | chteh·ryh |
| 5 | **pięć** | pyehn'ch' |
| 6 | **sześć** | shehsh·ch' |
| 7 | **siedem** | sh'yeh·dehm |
| 8 | **osiem** | oh·sh'yehm |
| 9 | **dziewięć** | dj'yeh·vyehn'ch' |
| 10 | **dziesięć** | dj'yeh·sh'yehn'ch' |
| 11 | **jedenaście** | yeh·deh·nahsh'·ch'yeh |
| 12 | **dwanaście** | dvah·nahsh'·ch'yeh |
| 13 | **trzynaście** | tshyh·nahsh'·ch'yeh |
| 14 | **czternaście** | chtehr·nahsh'·ch'yeh |
| 15 | **piętnaście** | pyeht nahsh'·ch'yeh |
| 16 | **szesnaście** | shehs·nahsh'·ch'yeh |
| 17 | **siedemnaście** | sh'yehdehm nahsh'·ch'yeh |
| 18 | **osiemnaście** | oh·sh'yehm·nahsh'·ch'yeh |
| 19 | **dziewiętnaście** | dj'yeh·vyeht·nahsh'·ch'yeh |
| 20 | **dwadzieścia** | dvah·dj'yehsh'·ch'yah |
| 21 | **dwadzieścia jeden** | dvah·dj'yehsh'·ch'yah yeh·dehn |
| 22 | **dwadzieścia dwa** | dvah·dj'yehsh'·ch'yah dvah |
| 30 | **trzydzieści** | tshyh·dj'yehsh'·ch'ee |

| 40 | **czterdzieści** chtehr· <u>dj'yehsh'</u>·ch'ee |
| 50 | **pięćdziesiąt** pyehn'· <u>dj'yeh</u>·sh'yohnt |
| 60 | **sześćdziesiąt** shehsh'· <u>dj'yeh</u>·sh'yont |
| 70 | **siedemdziesiąt** sh'yeh·dehm· <u>dj'yeh</u>·sh'yohnt |
| 80 | **osiemdziesiąt** oh·sh'yehm· <u>dj'yeh</u>·sh'yohnt |
| 90 | **dziewięćdziesiąt** dj'eh·vyen'· <u>dj'yeh</u>·sh'ohnt |
| 100 | **sto** stoh |
| 101 | **sto jeden** stoh· <u>yeh</u>·dehn |
| 200 | **dwieście** <u>dvyehsh'</u>·ch'yeh |
| 500 | **pięćset** <u>pyehn'</u>·seht |
| 1,000 | **tysiąc** <u>tyh</u>·sh'yohnts |
| 10,000 | **dziesięć tysięcy** <u>dj'yeh</u>·sh'yehn'ch' tyh· <u>sh'yen</u>·tsyh |
| 1,000,000 | **milion** <u>meel</u>·yohn |

## Ordinal Numbers

| first | **pierwszy** <u>pyehr</u>·vshyh |
| second | **drugi** <u>druh</u>·gee |
| third | **trzeci** <u>tsheh</u>·ch'ee |
| fourth | **czwarty** <u>chfahr</u>·tyh |
| fifth | **piąty** <u>pyohn</u>·tyh |
| once | **raz** rahs |
| twice | **dwa razy** dvah <u>rah</u>·zyh |
| three times | **trzy razy** tshyh <u>rah</u>·zyh |

> In Polish, as in the majority of European countries, a comma is used in place of a decimal point, and gaps are used in long numbers in place of commas. Example: **1 234 567,89 jeden milion, dwieście trzydzieści cztery tysiące, pięćset sześćdziesiąt siedem, osiemdziesiąt dziewięć.**

## Time

### Essential

| | |
|---|---|
| What time is it? | **Czy może mi pan powiedzieć, która godzina?** chyh <u>moh</u>·zheh mee pahn poh·<u>vyeh</u>·dj'yehch' <u>ktuh</u>·rah goh·<u>dj'ee</u>·nah |
| five after [past] five | **pięć po piątej** pyehn'ch' poh <u>pyohn</u>·tehy |
| quarter to nine | **za piętnaście dziewiąta** zah pyeht·<u>nahsh'</u>·ch'yeh dj'yeh·<u>vyohn</u>·tah |
| ten to seven | **za dziesięć siódma** zah <u>dj'yeh</u>·sh'yehn'ch' <u>sh'yuhd</u>·mah |
| 5:30 *a.m./p.m.* | **piąta trzydzieści rano/siedemnasta trzydzieści** <u>pyohn</u>·tah tshyh·<u>dj'yehsh'</u>·ch'ee rah·noh/ sh'yeh·dehm·<u>nahs</u>·tah tshyh·<u>dj'yehsh'</u>·ch'ee |
| It's noon [midday]. | **Jest południe.** yehst poh·<u>wuhd</u>·n'yeh |
| It's midnight. | **Jest północ.** yehst <u>puhw</u>·nohts |

*i* The Poles use the 24-hour clock. However, in ordinary conversation, time is usually expressed using numbers 1-12 with the addition of **rano** (morning), **po południu** (afternoon) or **wieczorem** (evening).

## Days

### Essential

| Monday | **poniedziałek** poh·n'yeh·<u>dj'yah'</u>·wehk |
| Tuesday | **wtorek** <u>ftoh</u>·rehk |
| Wednesday | **środa** <u>sh'roh</u>·dah |
| Thursday | **czwartek** <u>chfahr</u>·tehk |
| Friday | **piątek** <u>pyohn</u>·tehk |
| Saturday | **sobota** soh·<u>boh</u>·tah |
| Sunday | **niedziela** n'yeh·<u>dj'yeh</u>·lah |

## Dates

| yesterday | **wczoraj** <u>fchoh</u>·rahy |
| today | **dzisiaj** <u>dj'ee</u>·sh'yahy |
| tomorrow | **jutro** <u>yuht</u>·roh |
| day | **dzień** dj'yehn' |
| week | **tydzień** <u>tyh</u>·dj'yehn' |
| month | **miesiąc** <u>myeh</u>·sh'ohnts |
| year | **rok** rohk |

## Months

| January | **styczeń** <u>styh</u>·chehn' |
| February | **luty** <u>luh</u>·tyh |
| March | **marzec** <u>mah</u>·zhehts |

| April | **kwiecień** <u>kfyeh</u>·ch'yehn' |
| May | **maj** mahy |
| June | **czerwiec** <u>chehr</u>·vyehts |
| July | **lipiec** <u>lee</u>·pyehts |
| August | **sierpień** <u>sh'yehr</u>·pyehn' |
| September | **wrzesień** <u>vzheh</u>·sh'yehn' |
| October | **paędziernik** pahzh'·<u>dj'yehr</u>·n'eek |
| November | **listopad** lees·<u>toh</u>·paht |
| December | **grudzień** <u>gruh</u>·dj'yehn' |

## Seasons

| spring | **wiosna** <u>vyohs</u>·nah |
| summer | **lato** <u>lah</u>·toh |
| fall [autumn] | **jesień** <u>yeh</u>·sh'yehn' |
| winter | **zima** <u>zh'ee</u>·mah |

## Holidays

| January 1 | **Nowy Rok** New Year's Day |
| January 6 | **Trzech Króli** Epiphany |
| March/April (moveable) | **Wielkanoc** Easter |
| May 1 | **Święto 1 Maja** Labor Day |
| May 3 | **Konstytucja 3 Maja** Constitution Day |
| Thursday in May/June (moveable) | **Boże Ciało** Corpus Christi |
| August 15 | **Wniebowzięcie** Assumption Day |
| November 1 | **Wszystkich Świętych** All Saints' Day |
| November 11 | **Święto Niepodległości** Independence Day |
| December 25 & 26 | **Boże Narodzenie** Christmas |

# Conversion Tables ——————————————

## Mileage

| | |
|---|---|
| 1 km – 0.62 mi | 20 km – 12.4 mi |
| 5 km – 3.10 mi | 50 km – 31.0 mi |
| 10 km – 6.20 mi | 100 km – 61.0 mi |

## Measurement

| | | |
|---|---|---|
| 1 gram | **gram** grahm | = 0.035 oz. |
| 1 kilogram (kg) | **kilo** <u>kee</u>·loh | = 2.2 lb |
| 1 liter (l) | **litr** leetr | = 1.06 U.S./0.88 Brit. quarts |
| 1 centimeter (cm) | **centymetr** tsehn·<u>tyh</u>·mehtr | = 0.4 inch |
| 1 meter (m) | **metr** mehtr | = 3.28 feet |
| 1 kilometer (km) | **kilometr** kee·<u>loh</u>·mehtr | = 0.62 mile |

## Temperature

| | | |
|---|---|---|
| -40° C – -40° F | -1° C – 30° F | 20° C – 68° F |
| -30° C – -22° F | 0° C – 32° F | 25° C – 77° F |
| -20° C – -4° F | 5° C – 41° F | 30° C – 86° F |
| -10° C – 14° F | 10° C – 50° F | 35° C – 95° F |
| -5° C – 23° F | 15° C – 59° F | |

## Oven Temperature

| | |
|---|---|
| 100° C – 212° F | 177° C – 350° F |
| 121° C – 250° F | 204° C – 400° F |
| 149° C – 300° F | 260° C – 500° F |

## Useful Websites

www.poland.pl
*General information about Poland*

www.polandtour.org
*Polish National Tourist Office*

www.lot.com
*Polish airlines (LOT)*

www.gwardak.com.pl/pex.html
*Bus network (POLSKI EXPRESS) (only in Polish)*

rozklad.pkp.pl/bin/query.exe/pn
*National train network (PKP)*

www.pks.pl
*Bus transport (PKS)*

www.um.warszawa.pl
*Warsaw webpage*

www.cracowonline.com
*Cracow webpage*

www.gdansk-online.eu
*Gdansk webpage*

www.tsa.gov
*U.S. Transportation Security Administration (TSA)*

www.caa.co.uk
*UK Civil Aviation Authority (CAA)*

www.hihostels.com
*Hostelling International website*

# English–Polish Dictionary

## A

a little trochę
a lot dużo
a.m. przed południem
accept *v* zaakceptować
accident (road) wypadek
accidentally przypadkowo
across przez
acrylic *adj* akrylowy; *n* akryl
actor aktor
adapter przejściówka
address adres
admission charge opłata za wstęp
adult *n* dorosły
afraid przestraszony
after (time) po; (place) za
afternoon popołudnie
aftershave płyn po goleniu
ago temu
agree zgadzać się
air conditioner klimatyzator
air conditioning klimatyzacja
air mattress materac nadmuchiwany

air pump kompresor
airline linia lotnicza
airmail poczta lotnicza
airport lotnisko
air-sickness bag torebka na chorobę lotniczą
aisle seat miejsce przy przejściu
alarm clock budzik
allergic uczulony
allergy uczulenie
allowance ilość
almost prawie
alone sam
already już
also również
alter poprawić
aluminum foil folia aluminiowa
always zawsze
amazing zdumiewający
ambassador ambasador
ambulance karetka
American *adj* amerykański; *n* Amerykanin
amount (money) kwota
and i
anesthetia znieczulenie
animal zwierzę
another inny

---

adj adjective     BE British English     n noun     v verb

**antacid** środek neutralizujący kwas
**antibiotics** antybiotyk
**antique** *n* antyk
**antiseptic** aseptyczny
**antiseptic cream** krem aseptyczny
**any** jakiś
**anyone** ktoś
**apartment** mieszkanie
**apologize** przepraszać
**appendix** wyrostek robaczkowy
**appetite** apetyt
**appetizer** przekąska
**appointment (business)** spotkanie; **(doctor)** wizyta
**approximately** około
**arcade** salon gier
**area code** numer kierunkowy
**arm (body part)** ramię
**around (time)** około; **(place)** po
**arrive (car, train)** przyjeżdżać; **(plane)** lądować
**art gallery** galeria sztuki
**artist** artysta
**ashtray** popielniczka
**ask (question)** pytać; **(request)** prosić
**aspirin** aspiryna
**asthma** astma

**at (time)** o; **(place)** na
**ATM** bankomat
**attack** atak
**attractive** atrakcyjny
**audioguide** przewodnik dźwiękowy
**Australia** Australia
**authenticity** autentyczność
**automatic trasmission** automatycza skrzynia biegów
**autumn [BE]** jesień
**available (free)** wolne
**avalanche** lawina

# B

**baby** dziecko
**baby food** jedzenie dla dzieci
**baby wipe** wilgotne chusteczki pielęgnacyjne
**babysitter** opiekunka
**back (head)** tył; **(body)** grzbiet
**backache** ból grzbietu
**backpack** *n* plecak; *v* wędrować z plecakiem
**bad** zły
**bag** torba
**baggage [BE]** bagaż
**baggage room** przechowalnia bagażu
**bakery** piekarnia

**balcony** balkon
**ball** piłka
**ballet** balet
**band (music)** zespół
**bandage** bandaż
**bank** bank
**bar** bar
**barber** fryzjer męski
**basement** piwnica
**basketball** koszykówka
**bath** *n* wanna; *v* kąpiel
**bathroom** łazienka
**battery** bateria; **(car)** akumulator
**battle site** pole bitwy
**be** być
**beach** plaża
**beautiful** piękny
**because** ponieważ
**bed** łóżko
**bedding** pościel
**bedroom** sypialnia
**before (time)** przed
**begin** zaczynać
**beginner** początkujący
**behind** za
**belong** należeć
**belt** pasek
**berth (ship)** koja; **(train)** kuszetka
**best** najlepszy
**better** lepszy

**between** pomiędzy
**bib** śliniaczek
**bicycle** rower
**bicycle route** szlak rowerowy
**big** duży
**bikini** bikini
**bill (restaurant)** rachunek
**binoculars** lornetka
**bird** ptak
**birthday** urodziny
**bite** *n* ugryzienie
**bitter** gorzki
**bizarre** dziwaczny
**black** czarny
**bladder** pęcherz moczowy
**bland** mdły
**blanket** koc
**bleach** wybielacz
**bleed** krwawić
**bleeding** krwotok
**blister** pęcherz
**block** *v* blokować
**blood** krew
**blood pressure** ciśnienie krwi
**blouse** bluzka
**blow-dry** suszenie z modelowaniem
**blue** niebieski
**board** pokład
**boarding card** karta pokładowa
**boat trip** przejażdżka statkiem

**boil** v gotować
**boiler** boiler
**bone** kość
**book** książka
**bookstore** księgarnia
**boots** botki
**boring** nudny
**born** v urodzić się
**borrow** pożyczyć
**botanical garden** ogród botaniczny
**bottle** butelka
**bottle opener** otwieracz do butelek
**bowl** miska
**box (container)** pudełko
**boy** chłopiec
**boyfriend** chłopak
**bra** biustonosz
**bracelet** bransoletka
**brake** hamulec
**break (destroy)** zepsuć; **(body part)** złamać
**break down (go wrong)** zepsuć się
**breakfast** śniadanie
**breast (body)** pierś
**breathe** oddychać
**bridge** most
**briefs (clothing)** majtki
**bring** przenieść
**Britain** Wielka Brytania

**British** adj brytyjski; n Brytyjczyk
**brochure** broszura
**broken** zepsuty
**bronchitis** bronchit
**brooch** broszka
**brother** brat
**browse** patrzeć
**bruise** siniak
**bucket** wiaderko
**bug** robak
**build** budować
**building** budynek
**bulletin board** tablica informacyjna
**burn** n oparzenie
**bus** autobus
**bus route** trasa autobusowa
**bus station** dworzec autobusowy
**bus stop** przystanek autobusowy
**business** biznes
**business class** klasa biznes
**busy** zajęty
**but** ale
**butane gas** butan
**butcher (store)** rzeźnik
**button** guzik
**buy** kupić

# C

cabaret kabaret
café kawiarnia
call (ambulance) wezwać;
  (telephone) zadzwonić
camera aparat fotograficzny
camera case futerał na aparat
camp *n* obóz; *v* obozować
campfire ognisko
campsite pole namiotowe
can *n* puszka; *v* móc
can opener otwieracz do
  puszek
Canada Kanada
canal kanał
cancel odwołać
cancer rak
cap (dental) koronka;
  (clothing) czapka
car samochód; (train) wagon
car hire [BE] wynajem
  samochodów
car insurance ubezpiecznie
  samochodowe
car park parking
car rental wynajem samochodów
car seat fotelik dziecięcy
carafe karafka
card karta
careful ostrożny
carpet dywan

carry-on (luggage) bagaż
  podręczny
cart wózek
carton karton
cash (money) gotówka;
  *v* zrealizować
cashier kasjer
casino kasyno
castle zamek
catch (bus) złapać
cathedral katedra
cave jaskinia
CD płyta
CD player odtwarzacz płyt
  kompaktowych
cell phone telefon komórkowy
cemetery cmentarz
ceramics ceramika
certificate certyfikat
chain łańcuszek
change *n* (small coins)
  drobne; (in shop) reszta;
  *v* (bus, train) przesiadać się;
  (baby) przewinąć; (money)
  wymieniać; (reservation)
  zmienić, (clothes) przebrać
  się
changing room przebieralnia
charcoal węgiel drzewny
charge opłata
cheap tani
check *n* czek

check in n odprawa

check out (hotel) wyrejestrować się

checkbook książeczka czekowa

check-in desk stanowisko odprawy

chemical toilet chemiczna toaleta

chemist [BE] apteka

cheque [BE] czek

chess szachy

chest (body) klatka persiowa

child dziecko

child's cot łóżeczko dziecięce

child's seat krzesełko dla dziecka

church kościół

cigar cygaro

cigarette papieros

clamp założyć blokadę na koła

clean adj czysty; v wyczyścić

cliff klif

cling film [BE] folia do żywności

clinic klinika

clock zegar

close (near) niedaleko; (store) zamykać

clothing store sklep odzieżowy

cloudy pochmurno

coach [BE] (long-distance bus) autokar

coat płaszcz

coat check szatnia

coat hanger wieszak

cockroach karaluch

coin moneta

cold adj zimny; adv zimno; n (illness) przeziębienie

collapse upaść

collect zebrać

collect call rozmowa na koszt rozmówcy

color kolor

color film film kolorowy

comb grzebień

come przyjść

come back (return) wrócić

commission prowizja

company (companionship) towarzystwo; (business) firma

compartment (train) przedział

composer kompozytor

computer komputer

concert koncert

concert hall sala koncertowa

concession koncesja

concussion wstrząs mózgu

conditioner odżywka

condom prezerwatywa

**conductor** dyrygent
**confirm** potwierdzić
**confirmation** potwierdzenie
**connect (internet)** połączyć się z siecią
**connection (train)** połączenie
**conscious (awake)** przytomny
**constant** ciągły
**constipation** zaparcie
**consulate** konsulat
**consult** skonsultować się
**contact** skontaktować się
**contact lens** szkło kontaktowe
**contagious** zakaźny
**contain** zawierać
**contraceptive** środek antykoncepcyjny
**convenience store** sklep osiedlowy
**cook** *v* gotować; *n* kucharz
**cooker [BE]** kuchenka
**cooking (cuisine)** kuchnia
**cooking facilities** możliwość gotowania
**copper** miedź
**copy** kopia
**corkscrew** korkociąg
**correct** prawidłowy
**cosmetics** kosmetyki
**cost** *v* kosztować
**cot** rozkładane łóżko
**cottage** domek

**cotton (material)** bawełna
**cough** *n* kaszel; *v* kaszleć
**country** kraj
**country code** numer kierunkowy
**country music** muzyka country
**course (meal)** danie; **(path)** droga
**cousin** kuzyn
**cramp** skurcz
**credit card** karta kredytowa
**credit card number** numer karty kredytowej
**crib** łóżeczko dziecięce
**cross** *v* przejść
**cross-country skis** biegówki
**crowd** tłok
**crowded** zatłoczony
**crown (dental)** koronka; **(royal)** korona
**cruise** *n* rejs
**crystal (quartz)** kryształ
**cup** filiżanka
**cupboard** szafka kuchenna
**currency** waluta
**currency exchange office** kantor
**currency exchange rate** kurs wymiany
**curtain** zasłona
**customs** urząd celny

**customs declaration**
deklaracja celna
**cut (hair)** strzyżenie; **(wound)**
rana cięta
**cut glass** cięte szkło
**cutlery** sztućce
**cycling** kolarstwo

## D

**daily** *adj* codzienny; *adv*
codziennie
**damaged** zniszczony
**damp** *adj* wilgotny
**dance** *n* taniec; *v* tańczyć
**dance club** dyskoteka
**dangerous** niebezpieczny
**dark** ciemny
**daughter** córka
**dawn** świt
**day** dzień
**day charge** opłata za dzień
**day ticket** bilet jednodniowy
**day trip** wycieczka
jednodniowa
**dead (battery)** wyczerpany
**deaf** głuchy
**deck chair** leżak
**declare** zadeklarować
**deduct** odejmować
**deep** głęboki
**defrost** rozmrozić

**degree (temperature)**
stopień
**delay** opóźnienie
**delayed** opóźniony
**delicatessen** delikatesy
**delicious** smaczny
**deliver** dostarczyć
**delivery** dostawa
**denim** drelich
**dental floss** nić dentystyczna
**dentist** dentysta
**denture** proteza dentystyczna
**deodorant** dezodorant
**depart (train, bus)** odjeżdżać;
**(plane)** startować
**department store** dom
towarowy
**departure lounge** poczekalnia
**departures (airport)** hala
odlotów
**deposit (security)** kaucja
**describe** opisać
**description** opis
**destination (travel)** cel
podróży
**detail** szczegół
**detergent** środek czystości
**develop (photos)** wywołać
**diabetes** cukrzyca
**diabetic** *n* cukrzyk
**dialing code** numer
kierunkowy

**diamond** brylant
**diaper** pieluszka
**diarrhea** biegunka
**dice** kostka do gry
**dictionary** słownik
**diesel** diesel
**diet** dieta
**difficult** trudny
**dining car** wagon restauracyjny
**dining room** jadalnia
**dinner** kolacja
**direct** *adj* (train, journey) bezpośredni; *v* (to a place) wskazać kierunek
**direction** kierunek
**director** (company) dyrektor
**directory** (telephone) książka telefoniczna
**dirty** brudny
**disabled** *n* niepełnosprawny
**discount** zniżka
**discount card** karta rabatowa
**dish** (meal) danie
**dishcloth** ścierka
**dishwasher** zmywarka
**dishwashing liquid** płyn do zmywania
**display cabinet** gablota
**display case** gablota
**disposable camera** aparat jednorazowy

**disturb** przeszkadzać
**dive** (scuba dive) nurkować; (jump) skakać
**diving equipment** sprzęt do nurkowania
**divorced** rozwiedziony
**dizziness** zawroty głowy
**do** robić
**doctor** lekarz
**doll** lalka
**dollar** dolar
**domestic** (flight) krajowy
**door** drzwi
**double bed** podwójne łóżko
**double room** pokój dwuosobowy
**downtown area** centrum
**dozen** tuzin
**dress** sukienka
**drink** *n* (alcoholic) drink; *v* pić
**drink menu** lista drinków
**drip** ciec
**drive** jechać
**driver** (car) kierowca
**driver's license** prawo jazdy
**drown** tonąć
**drugstore** drogeria
**drunk** pijany
**dry cleaner's** pralnia chemiczna
**dry-clean** czyścić (chemicznie)

dubbed dubbingowany
dummy [BE] smoczek
during podczas
dustbin [BE] śmietnik
duty cło
duvet kołdra

## E

ear ucho
ear drops krople do uszu
earache ból ucha
early *adj* wczesny; *adv*
wcześnie
earring kolczyk
east wschód
easy łatwy
eat jeść
economy class klasa
turystyczna
elastic *adj* elastyczny
electric shaver golarka
elektryczna
electrical outlet gniazdko
elektryczne
electronic elektroniczny
elevator winda
e-mail *n* e-mail; *v* napisać
maila
e-mail address adres e-mail
embassy ambasada
embroidery haft

emerald szmaragd
emergency nagły wypadek
emergency exit wyjście
awaryjne
emergency ward izba przyjęć
empty pusty
enamel emalia
end *n* koniec; *v* kończyć (się)
engaged zaręczony
engine silnik
engineer inżynier
England Anglia
English *adj* angielski; *n* Anglik
enjoy podobać się
enjoyable przyjemny
enlarge (photos) powiększyć
enough dość
entertainment guide program
rozrywek
entrance fee opłata za wstęp
envelope koperta
epilepsy epilepsja
epileptic *n* epileptyk
equipment (sports) sprzęt
era epoka
error błąd
escalator schody ruchome
escape route droga
ewakuacyjna
essential niezbędny
e-ticket bilet elektroniczny
eurocheque euroczek

**European Union** Unia
  Europejska
**evening** wieczór
**evening dress** strój
  wieczorowy
**every** każdy
**examination (medical)**
  badanie
**example** przykład
**except** oprócz
**excess baggage** nadbagaż
**exchange** wymienić
**exchange rate** kurs wymiany
**excursion** wycieczka
**exhausted** wyczerpany
**exit** wyjście
**expensive** drogi
**experienced** zaawansowany
**expiration date** data ważności
**expiry date [BE]** data
  ważności
**exposure (photos)**
  naświetlanie
**express** ekspres
**express mail** priorytet
**extension (phone)**
  wewnętrzny
**extra (additional)** dodatkowy
**extract (tooth)** wyrwać
**eye** oko

**fabric** materiał
**face** twarz
**facial** zabieg oczyszczania
  skóry
**faint** v zemdleć
**fairground** wesołe miasteczko
**fall** n jesień
**family** rodzina
**famous** sławny
**fan (electric)** wentylator
**far** daleko
**farm** gospodarstwo
**far-sighted** dalekowidz
**fast** szybko
**father** ojciec
**faucet** kran
**faulty** wadliwy
**favorite** ulubiony
**fax** faks
**fee** opłata
**feed** nakarmić
**feel** czuć (się)
**female** kobieta
**ferry** prom
**fever** gorączka
**few** parę
**fiancé** narzeczony
**fiancée** narzeczona
**field** pole
**fight (brawl)** bójka

fill out (a form) wypełnić
fill up (car) nalać do pełna
filling (dental) plomba
film (camera, movie) film
filter filtr
find znaleźć
fine (well) dobrze; (penalty) grzywna
finger palec
fire pożar
fire alarm alarm pożarowy
fire brigade [BE] straż pożarna
fire department straż pożarna
fire door drzwi przeciwpożarowe
fire escape schody pożarowe
fire exit wyjście awaryjne
fire extinguisher gaśnica
first class pierwsza klasa
first floor parter
fish store sklep rybny
fit v pasować
fitting room przymierzalnia
fix v naprawić
flame płomień
flashlight latarka
flat (tire) przebity
flavor smak
flea pchła
flea market pchli targ
flight lot

flight number numer lotu
floor (level) piętro
florist kwiaciarnia
flower kwiat
flu grypa
flush (toilet) spuszczać wodę
fly n mucha; v latać
fog mgła
folk art sztuka ludowa
folk music muzyka ludowa
follow (pursue) podążać; (road, sign) jechać zgodnie z
food jedzenie
food poisoning zatrucie pokarmowe
foot stopa
football [BE] piłka nożna
footpath [BE] dróżka
for (time) przez; (duration) na
foreign currency obca waluta
forest las
forget zapominać
fork widelec
form formularz
formal dress strój formalny
fortunately na szczęście
fountain fontanna
foyer (hotel, theater) foyer
fracture złamanie
frame (glasses) oprawka
free (available) wolny; (without charge) bezpłatny

freezer zamrażarka

frequently często

fresh świeży

friend przyjaciel

friendly (person) przyjazny; (place, atmosphere) przyjemny

frightened przerażony

from (place) z; (time) od

front przód

frost mróz

frying pan patelnia

fuel paliwo

full pełny

full board z pełnym wyżywieniem

fun zabawa

funny śmieszny

furniture meble

## G

gallon galon

game gra; (sports) mecz

garage (mechanic) warsztat samochodowy; (parking lot) garaż

garbage śmieci

garbage bag worek na śmieci

garden ogródek

gas (fuel) benzyna

gas station stacja benzynowa

gate (airport) wyjście

gauze gaza

genuine prawdziwy

get (buy) kupić; (find) znaleźć

get back (return) wrócić

get off (bus/train) wysiąść

get to dojechać do

gift prezent

gift shop sklep z upominkami

giftwrap zapakować na prezent

girl dziewczyna

girlfriend dziewczyna

give dać

glass (non-alcoholic) szklanka; (alcoholic) kieliszek

glasses (optical) okulary

glove rękawiczka

go (on foot) iść; (by bus, train) jechać; (by plane) lecieć

go away odejść

goggles (swimming) okularki; (skiing) gogle

gold złoto

golf golf

golf club kij golfowy

golf course pole golfowe

good dobry

good evening dobry wieczór

good morning dzień dobry

good night dobranoc

**goodbye** do widzenia
**gram** gram
**grandfather** dziadek
**grandmother** babcia
**grandparents** dziadkowie
**grass** trawa
**gray** szary
**great** *adj* świetny; *adv* świetnie
**green** zielony
**greengrocer** [BE] warzywniak
**grocery store** sklep spożywczy
**ground (earth)** ziemia
**ground floor** [BE] parter
**groundcloth** podłoga namiotu
**groundsheet** [BE] podłoga namiotu
**group** grupa
**group guide** przewodnik grupowy
**group leader** kierownik grupy
**group ticket** bilet grupowy
**guarantee** gwarancja
**guest** gość
**guesthouse** pensjonat
**guide (tour)** przewodnik
**guidebook** przewodnik
**guided tour** wycieczka z przewodnikiem
**guided walk** wycieczka piesza z przewodnikiem
**guitar** gitara

**gym** siłownia
**gynecologist** ginekolog

## H

**hair** włosy
**hair gel** żel do włosów
**haircut** strzyżenie włosów
**hairdresser** fryzjer
**hairspray** lakier do włosów
**half** pół
**hammer** młotek
**hand** ręka
**hand luggage** [BE] bagaż podręczny
**hand washable** prać ręcznie
**handbag** torebka
**handicapped** niepełnosprawny
**handicrafts** wyroby rękodzielnicze
**handkerchief** chusteczka
**hanger** wieszak
**hangover** *n* kac
**happy** szczęśliwy
**harbor** port
**hard (texture)** twardy; **(difficult)** ciężki
**hat** kapelusz
**have** mieć
**hay fever** katar sienny
**head** *n* głowa; *v* **(go towards)** jechać w kierunku

**head waiter** kierownik sali
**headache** ból głowy
**health** zdrowie
**health food store** sklep ze
  zdrową żywnością
**health insurance**
  ubezpieczenie zdrowotne
**hear** słyszeć
**hearing aid** aparat słuchowy
**heart** serce; **(cards)** kier
**heart attack** zawał serca
**heat** ogrzewanie
**heater** grzejnik
**heating [BE]** ogrzewanie
**heavy** ciężki
**height** wzrost
**helmet** kask
**help** pomoc
**hemorrhoids** hemoroidy
**her** jej
**here** tutaj
**hernia** przepuklina
**herpes** opryszczka
**hers** jej
**high** wysoki
**highchair** wysokie krzesełko
**highlight** v **(hair)** robić
  pasemka; **(stress)** podkreślić
**highway** autostrada
**hiking (general)** turystyka
  piesza; **(trip)** wędrówka
**hill** wzgórze

**him** niego
**hire [BE]** v wynająć
**his** jego
**historic site** miejsce
  historyczne
**hobby (pastime)** hobby
**holiday [BE]** wakacje
**holiday resort** miejscowość
  wypoczynkowa
**home (be/go)** w domu/do
  domu
**honeymoon** miesiąc miodowy
**horse** koń
**horse racing** wyścigi konne
**hospital** szpital
**hot** gorący
**hot spring** gorące źródło
**hotel** hotel
**hour** godzina
**house** dom
**housewife** gospodyni domowa
**hundred** sto
**hungry** głodny
**hurt** boleć
**husband** mąż

## I

**ice-cream parlor** lodziarnia
**icy** oblodzony
**identification** dowód
  tożsamości

**ill** chory
**illegal** nielegalny
**imitation** imitacja
**in (place)** w; **(period of time)** w ciągu
**included** wliczony
**incredible** niewiarygodny
**indicate** wskazywać
**indigestion** niestrawność
**indoor pool** kryty basen
**inexpensive** niedrogi
**infected** zakażony
**infection** infekcja
**inflammation** zapalenie
**informal (dress)** nieformalny
**information (desk, office)** infomacja
**injection** zastrzyk
**injured** ranny
**innocent** niewinny
**insect** insekt
**insect bite** ugryzienie owada
**insect repellent** środek na owady
**insect sting** użądlenie
**inside** w środku
**insist** nalegać
**insomnia** bezsenność
**instead** zamiast
**instruction** instrukcja
**instructor** instruktor
**insulin** insulina

**insurance** ubezpieczenie
**insurance card** polisa ubezpieczeniowa
**insurance certificate [BE]** polisa ubezpieczeniowa
**insurance claim** wniosek o odszkodowanie
**interest (hobby)** zainteresowanie
**interested** zainteresowany
**interesting** interesujący
**international (flight)** międzynarodowy
**International Student Card** Międzynarodowa Karta Studenta
**internet** internet
**internet cafe** kafejka internetowa
**interpreter** tłumacz ustny
**intersection** skrzyżowanie
**into** do
**intolerance** nietolerancja
**invite** zaprosić
**iodine** jodyna
**Ireland** Irlandia
**iron** *n* żelazko; *v* prasować
**itch** swędzieć
**item (object)** przedmiot
**itemized bill** szczegółowy rachunek

## J

**jacket (men's)** marynarka;
  **(women's)** żakiet
**jaw** szczęka
**jazz** jazz
**jeans** dżinsy
**jellyfish** meduza
**jet-ski** skuter wodny
**jeweler** jubiler
**jewelry** biżuteria
**join (a group)** dołączyć się
**joint (body)** staw
**joke** żart
**journalist** dziennikarz
**journey** podróż
**jug (water)** dzbanek
**jumper [BE]** pulower
**junction [BE] (intersection)**
  skrzyżowanie

## K

**keep** zatrzymać
**kerosene** nafta
**kettle** czajnik
**key** klucz
**key card (hotel)** karta
**kiddie pool** brodzik
**kidney** nerka
**kilometer** kilometr
**kind** *adj* uprzejmy; *n* rodzaj

**kiss** *n* pocałunek; *v* całować
**kitchen** kuchnia
**kitchen foil [BE]** folia
  aluminiowa
**knee** kolano
**knickers [BE]** majtki
**knife** nóż
**know** wiedzieć
**kosher** koszerny

## L

**label (sticker)** nalepka;
  **(on bottle)** etykieta
**lace** koronka
**ladder** drabina
**lake** jezioro
**lamp** lampa
**land** *v* lądować
**language course** kurs
  językowy
**large (size)** duży
**last** *adj* ostatni; **(previous)**
  zeszły; *v* trwać
**late (not early)** późny;
  **(delayed)** opóźniony
**later** później
**laundromat** pralnia
  samoobsługowa
**laundry facilities** pralnia
**lawyer** prawnik
**laxative** środek przeczyszczający

lead *n* smycz; *v* prowadzić

leader (ideological) przywódca; (manager) menedżer

leak *n* przeciek; *v* (roof, pipe) przeciekać

learn (language) uczyć się

leather skóra

leave (depart) odjeżdżać; (deposit) zostawić; (on foot) odejść; (depart of plane) odlatywać

left *adj* lewy

left-luggage office [BE] przechowalnia bagażu

leg noga

legal legalny

lend pożyczyć

lens (optical) soczewka; (camera) obiektyw

lense cap nakładka na obiektyw

less mniej

lesson lekcja

let *v* (permit) pozwolić

let go puścić

letter list

library biblioteka

license plate number numer rejestracyjny

life preserver koło ratunkowe

lifeboat łódź ratunkowa

lifeguard ratownik

lifejacket kamizelka ratunkowa

lift [BE] winda

lift pass (skiing) skipass

light *adj* (weight) lekki; (color) jasny; *n* światło

light bulb żarówka

lighter *adj* jaśniejszy; *n* zapalniczka

like *v* lubić

limousine limuzyna

line (subway) linia metra

linen len

lip warga

lipgloss błyszczyk

lipstick szminka

liquor store sklep monopolowy

liter litr

little (small) mały

live mieszkać

liver wątroba

living room salon

lobby (theater) foyer; (hotel) hol

local lokalny

lock *n* (door) zamek; (bike) blokada; *v* zamknąć

log off wylogować się

log on zalogować się

login login

long długi

**long-distance bus** autokar
**long-sighted [BE]** dalekowidz
**loose** luźny
**lorry [BE]** ciężarówka
**lose (item)** zgubić; **(person)** stracić
**lost-and-found** biuro rzeczy znalezionych
**lost-property office [BE]** biuro rzeczy znalezionych
**love** *n* miłość; *v* kochać
**lovely** śliczny
**low** niski
**lower (berth)** dolny
**low-fat** o niskiej zawartości tłuszczu
**luck** szczęście
**luggage** bagaż
**luggage cart** wózek na bagaż
**luggage locker** schowek na bagaż
**luggage trolley [BE]** wózek na bagaż
**lump** guz
**lunch** obiad
**lung** płuco

## M

**machine washable** prać w pralce
**madam** pani
**magazine** czasopismo

**magnificent** wspaniały
**maid** pokojówka
**mail** *n* poczta; *v* wysłać
**mailbox** skrzynka pocztowa
**main** główny
**make** zrobić
**male** mężczyzna
**mallet** młotek drewniany
**manager** menadżer
**manicure** manicure
**many** dużo
**map** mapa
**market (job market)** rynek; **(place to buy)** targ
**married** żonaty
**mascara** tusz do rzęs
**mask (diving)** maska
**mass** msza
**massage** masaż
**match (game)** mecz; **(light)** zapałka
**mattress** materac
**maybe** może
**me** ja
**meal** posiłek
**measles** odra
**measure** zmierzyć
**measurement** miara
**measuring cup** miarka kuchenna
**measuring spoon** łyżka do odmierzania

mechanic mechanik
medication lek
medicine lekarstwo
medium średni
meet (get to know) poznać;
  (appointment) spotkać
meeting place miejsce zbiórki
meeting point [BE] miejsce
  zbiórki
member (association) członek
memorial (war) pomnik
mention wspominać
menu menu
message wiadomość
metal metal
microwave (oven) kuchenka
  mikrofalowa
midday [BE] południe
midnight północ
migraine migrena
million milion
mine mój
mini-bar mini-bar
minute (time) minuta
mirror lustro
miss (lack) brakować; (lost)
  zaginąć
mistake błąd
misunderstanding
  nieporozumienie
mobile home przyczepa
  mieszkalna

mobile phone [BE] telefon
  komórkowy
moisturizer (cream) krem
  nawilżający
monastery klasztor
money pieniądze
money order przekaz
  pieniężny
month miesiąc
monument pomnik
mop mop
moped motorower
more więcej
morning rano
mosque meczet
mosquito bite ukąszenie
  komara
mother matka
motion sickness choroba
  lokomocyjna
motorbike motor
motorboat motorówka
motorcycle motor
motorway [BE] autostrada
mountain góra
mountain bike rower górski
mountain pass przełęcz
  górska
mountain range łańcuch
  górski
moustache wąsy
mouth usta

move ruszać
movie film
movie theater kino
much dużo
mug *n* kubek; *v* napadać
mugging napad
mumps świnka
muscle mięsień
museum muzeum
music muzyka
music store sklep muzyczny
musician muzyk
must *v* musieć
my mój

# N

name imię
napkin serwetka
nappy [BE] pieluszka
narrow wąski
national narodowy
national park park narodowy
nationality obywatelstwo
native tutejszy
nature reserve rezerwat
   przyrody
nature trail szlak przyrodniczy
nausea mdłości
near niedaleko
nearby niedaleko
near-sighted krótkowidz

necessary konieczny
neck (body) szyja
necklace naszyjnik
need *v* potrzebować
nerve nerw
nervous system układ nerwowy
never nigdy
new nowy
newsagent [BE] kiosk
   z gazetami
newspaper gazeta
newsstand kiosk z gazetami
next następny
nice miły
night noc
night club klub nocny
no nie
noisy hałaśliwy
none żaden
nonsense bzdura
non-smoking *adj* dla
   niepalących
noon południe
normal normalny
north północ
nose nos
nothing nic
notify zawiadomić
now teraz
number numer
nurse pielęgniarka
nylon nylon

## O

**occasionally** czasami
**occupied** zajęty
**office (place)** biuro
**off-licence [BE]** sklep
 monopolowy
**often** często
**okay** okay
**old** stary
**old town** stare miasto
**on (day, date)** w
**once** raz
**one** jeden
**one-way** w jedną stonę
**one-way ticket** bilet w jedną
 stronę
**open** *adj* otwarty; *v* otwierać
**opening hours** godziny
 otwarcia
**opera** opera
**opera house** opera
**operation** operacja
**opposite** naprzeciwko
**optician** optyk
**or** albo
**orange (color)** pomarańczowy
**order** *n* zamówienie; *v* zamówić
**our(s)** nasz
**outdoor pool** basen otwarty
**outrageous (price)**
 horrendalny

**outside** na zewnątrz
**oval** owalny
**oven** piekarnik
**overcharge** *v* policzyć za dużo
**overheat** przegrzać się
**overnight** na noc
**owe** być dłużnym
**own** *adj* własny
**owner** właściciel

## P

**p.m.** po południu
**pacifier** smoczek
**pack** pakować
**package** przesyłka
**paddling pool [BE]** brodzik
**padlock** kłódka
**pail (toy)** wiaderko
**pain** ból
**painkiller** środek
 przeciwbólowy
**paint** *v* malować
**painter** malarz
**painting** obraz
**pair** para
**palace** pałac
**panorama** panorama
**pants** spodnie
**pantyhose** rajstopy
**paper napkin** serwetka
 papierowa

**paper towel** ręcznik papierowy
**paracetamol** [BE] paracetamol
**paralysis** paraliż
**parcel** [BE] paczka
**parent** rodzic
**park** *n* park; *v* parkować
**parking garage** parking podziemny
**parking lot** parking
**parking meter** parkometr
**parliament building** budynek parlamentu
**partner** partner
**party (social)** przyjęcie
**passenger** pasażer
**passport** paszport
**passport number** numer paszportu
**password** hasło
**pastry shop** sklep cukierniczy
**patch** załatać
**patient** *n* pacjent
**pavement** [BE] chodnik
**pay** płacić
**pay phone** automat telefoniczny
**payment** zapłata
**peak** szczyt
**pearl** perła
**pedestrian** pieszy
**pedestrian crossing** przejście dla pieszych

**pedestrian zone** strefa zamknięta dla ruchu kołowego
**peg** [BE] spinacz do bielizny
**pen** długopis
**per** za
**perhaps** być może
**period (time)** okres; **(menstrual)** miesiączka
**person** osoba
**petrol** [BE] benzyna
**petrol station** [BE] stacja benzynowa
**pewter** cyna
**pharmacy** apteka
**phone** *n* telefon; *v* dzwonić
**phone card** karta telefoniczna
**photo** zdjęcie
**photocopier** kopiarka
**photograph** zdjęcie
**photographer** fotograf
**phrase** zwrot
**phrase book** rozmówki
**pick up** odebrać
**picnic** piknik
**picnic area** miejsce piknikowe
**piece (item)** sztuka; **(amount)** kawałek
**pill (contraceptive)** pigułka antykoncepcyjna; **(tablet)** tabletka
**pillow** poduszka

pillow case poszewka na poduszkę

pink różowy

pipe (smoking) fajka

pitch (camping) pole namiotowe

pizzeria pizzeria

place miejsce

plan n plan; v planować

plane samolot

plant (greenery) roślina

plaster [BE] plaster

plastic adj plastikowy

plastic bag torebka plastikowa

plastic wrap folia spożywcza

plate talerz

platform peron; [BE] tor

platinum platyna

play n (theater) sztuka; v grać

playground plac zabaw

playing field boisko

pleasant przyjemny

please proszę

plug zatyczka

plunger przepychacz

pneumonia zapalenie płuc

point wskazać

poison trucizna

Poland Polska

police policja

police report raport policyjny

police station komisariat policji

Polish adj polski; n Polak

pollen count stężenie pyłków w powietrzu

polyester poliester

pond staw

pop (music) pop

popular popularny; (well-known) znany

port (harbor) port

porter bagażowy

portion porcja

possible możliwy

post [BE] n (mail) poczta; v wysłać

post office poczta

postage opłata

postcard pocztówka

poster plakat

pot (for cooking) garnek; (for tea) dzbanek

pottery ceramika

pound (sterling) funt

powdery (snow) puszysty

power (electricity) prąd

precipice przepaść

pregnant w ciąży

prescribe przepisać

prescription recepta

present (gift) prezent

press naciskać

**pretty** ładny
**price** cena
**print** *n* sztych; *v* drukować
**prison** więzienie
**produce store** sklep
  spożywczy
**profession** zawód
**program** program
**pronounce** wymawiać
**pub** pub
**public** *n* publiczność; *adj*
  publiczny
**pump (gas station)** pompa
**puncture** przebicie
**pure** czysty
**purple** fioletowy
**purse** torebka
**push-chair [BE]** wózek
  spacerowy
**put** włożyć

## Q

**quality** jakość
**quarter** ćwierć; **(time)** kwadrans
**queue [BE]** *n* kolejka; *v* stać
  w kolejce
**quick** szybki
**quickly** szybko
**quiet** cichy

## R

**race course [BE]** tor
  wyścigowy
**racetrack** tor wyścigowy
**racket (tennis, squash)**
  rakieta
**railway station [BE]** stacja
  kolejowa
**rain** *n* deszcz
**raincoat** płaszcz
  przeciwdeszczowy
**rape** *n* gwałt; *v* zgwałcić
**rapids** progi rzeczne
**rare (unusual)** rzadki
**rash** wysypka
**razor** maszynka do golenia
**razor blade** żyletka
**read** *v* czytać
**ready** gotowy
**real (genuine)** prawdziwy
**rear** tylny
**receipt** paragon
**receive** odebrać
**reception (desk)** recepcja
**receptionist** recepcjonista
**recommend** polecić
**red** czerwony
**reduction (price)** obniżka
**refrigerator** lodówka
**refund** zwrot pieniędzy
**region (area)** region

**registered mail** list polecony
**registration form** formularz rejestracji
**reliable** niezawodny
**religion** religia
**remember** pamiętać
**rent** wynająć
**rental car** wynajęty samochód
**repair** *n* naprawa; *v* naprawić
**repeat** powtórzyć
**replacement** wymiana
**replacement part** część zamienna
**report (crime)** zgłosić
**require** wymagać
**reservation** rezerwacja
**reservations desk** okienko rezerwacji
**reserve** *v* rezerwować
**rest** *v* odpoczywać
**restaurant** restauracja
**restroom** toaleta
**return** wrócić; (surrender) zwrócić
**return ticket [BE]** bilet powrotny
**reverse-charge call [BE]** rozmowa na koszt rozmówcy
**rheumatism** reumatyzm
**rib** żebro
**right (correct)** poprawny; (good) dobry

**right of way** pierwszeństwo przejazdu
**ring** pierścionek
**river** rzeka
**road** droga
**road map** mapa drogowa
**road sign** znak drogowy
**rob** obrabować
**robbery** rabunek
**rock (music)** rock; (land formation) skała
**romantic** romantyczny
**roof** dach
**roof-rack** bagażnik dachowy
**room (hotel)** pokój
**room service** room service
**rope** lina
**round** okrągły
**round-trip ticket** bilet powrotny
**route** trasa
**rubbish [BE]** śmieci
**rude** niegrzeczny
**ruins** ruiny

## S

**safe** *adj* bezpieczny; *n* sejf
**safety** bezpieczeństwo
**safety pin** agrafka
**sand** piasek
**sandal** sandał
**sanitary napkin** podpaska**

sanitary pad [BE] podpaska
satellite TV telewizja satelitarna
satin satyna
saucepan rondel
sauna sauna
say v powiedzieć
scarf szalik
scissors nożyczki
Scotland Szkocja
screwdriver śrubokręt
sea morze
seasickness choroba moska
season ticket bilet okresowy
seat (train) miejsce
seat reservation (train) miejscówka
second class druga klasa
secondhand store sklep z używaną odzieżą
secretary sekretarka
sedative środek uspokajający
see (spot) zobaczyć; (inspect) sprawdzić; (observe, witness) widzieć
self-employed samozatrudniony
self-service (gas station) samoobsługa
sell sprzedawać
send wysłać
senior citizen emeryt

separated w separacji
separately osobno
serious poważny
service (in restaurant) obsługa; (religious) nabożeństwo
sex seks; (gender) płeć
shade odcień
shady cienisty
shallow płytki
shampoo szampon
share v dzielić
sharp ostry
shaving cream krem do golenia
she ona
sheet (bed) prześcieradło
shirt (men's) koszula; (women's) bluzka
shock (electric) porażenie
shoe but
shoe repair naprawa obuwia
shoe store sklep z obuwiem
shop assistant sprzedawca
shopping area centrum handlowe
shopping basket koszyk
shopping cart wózek
shopping centre [BE] centrum handlowe
shopping mall centrum handlowe

shopping trolley [BE] wózek

short *adj* (length) krótki;
(person) niski

shorts (clothing) szorty

short-sighted [BE] krótkowidz

shoulder bark

shovel (toy) łopatka

show *n* (presentation) pokaz;
(theater) sztuka; *v* pokazać

shower prysznic

shrine kapliczka

shut *v* zamykać; *adj* zamknięty

shutter okiennica

side (head) bok

side order dodatek

side street boczna uliczka

sidewalk chodnik

sights atrakcje turystyczne

sightseeing tour wycieczka po
mieście

sign znak

silk jedwab

silver srebro

singer pieśniarz

single sam

single room pokój
jednoosobowy

single ticket bilet w jedną
stronę

sink zlew

sir pan

sister siostra

sit siadać

size rozmiar

skate łyżwa

skewer rożen

ski narta

ski boot but narciarski

ski pole kijek

skin skóra

skirt spódnica

sleep spać

sleeper car [BE] wagon
sypialny

sleeping bag śpiwór

sleeping car wagon sypialny

sleeping pill tabletka
nasenna

sleeve rękaw

slice plasterek

slip *v* poślizgnąć się

slipper pantofel

slow wolny

slowly wolno

small mały

smell pachnieć

smoke palić

smoking (area) dla palących

snack przekąska

snack bar bar

sneaker tenisówka

snorkel fajka do nurkowania

snow śnieg

soap mydło

soccer piłka nożna
sock skarpetka
socket gniazdko
sole (shoes) podeszwa
some jakiś
something coś
sometimes czasami
somewhere gdzieś
son syn
soon niedługo
sore throat ból gardła
sorry przepraszam
soul (music) soul
sour kwaśne
south południe
souvenir pamiątka
souvenir store sklep
  z pamiątkami
spa spa
space miejsce
spare zapasowy
speak mówić
special specjalny
specialist specialista
specimen próbka
spell v przeliterować
spend (time) spędzać;
  (money) wydawać
spicy ostry
sponge gąbka
spoon łyżka
sport sport

sporting goods store sklep
  sportowy
spot (place, site) miejsce
sprained skręcony
spring wiosna
square kwadrat
stadium stadion
staff personel
stain plama
stainless steel stal nierdzewna
stairs schody
stamp (postal) znaczek
standby ticket tani bilet
  okazyjny
start v (begin) zaczynać się;
  (car) zapalić
starter [BE] przekąska
statement (police) zeznanie
stationery store sklep
  papierniczy
statue pomnik
stay n pobyt; v zostać;
  (in a hotel) zatrzymać się
sterilizing solution płyn do
  sterylizacji
still adv wciąż
stockings [BE] pończochy
stolen ukradziony
stomach brzuch
stomachache ból brzucha
stop n (bus, tram) przystanek;
  v zatrzymywać się

store sklep
store guide tablica informacyjna
storm burza
stove kuchenka
strange dziwny
straw (drinking) słomka
stream strumień
strong (powerful) silny
student student
study v studiować
style styl
subtitled z napisami
subway map mapa metra
subway station stacja metra
suggest zasugerować
suit (men's) garnitur; (women's) kostium
suitable stosowny
suitcase walizka
summer lato
sunbathe opalać się
sunburn oparzenie słoneczne
sunglasses okulary słoneczne
sunny słoneczny
sunshade parasol
sunstroke udar słoneczny
suntan lotion krem do opalania
superb znakomity
supermarket supermarket
supervision nadzór

supplement opłata dodatkowa
suppository czopek
sure pewien
surfboard deska do serfowania
surname nazwisko
sweater sweter
sweatshirt bluza
sweet (taste) słodki
swelling opuchlizna
swim pływać
swimming pool basen
swimming trunks kąpielówki
swimsuit kostium kąpielowy
swollen spuchnięty
symptom (illness) objaw
synagogue synagoga

## T

table stolik
take brać; (carry) zanieść; (medicine) brać; (time) trwać
take away [BE] na wynos
talk rozmawiać
tall wysoki
tampon tampon
tan opalenizna
tap [BE] kran
tapestry kilim

taxi taksówka

taxi rank [BE] postój taksówek

taxi stand postój taksówek

teacher nauczyciel

team drużyna

teaspoon łyżeczka do herbaty

teddy bear miś

telephone n telefon; v dzwonić

telephone bill rachunek telefoniczny

telephone booth budka telefoniczna

telephone call rozmowa telefoniczna

telephone number numer telefonu

tell powiedzieć

temperature temperatura

temple świątynia

temporarily tymczasowo

tennis tenis

tennis court kort tenisowy

tent namiot

tent peg kołek

tent pole maszt namiotowy

terminal terminal

terrace taras

terrible okropny

terrific wspaniały

tetanus tężec

text n (phone) sms; (document) tekst

thank v dziękować

thank you dziękuję

that to

theater teatr

theft kradzież

their(s) ich

theme park tematyczny park rozrywki

then (time) wtedy

there tam

thermometer termometr

these ci

they oni

thick gruby

thief złodziej

thigh udo

thin chudy

think myśleć

thirsty spragniony

this (one) ten

those tamci

thousand tysiąc

throat gardło

through przez

thumb kciuk

ticket bilet

ticket office kasa biletowa

tie krawat

tight adv ciasny

tights (clothing) rajstopy

time czas; (exact time) godzina

timetable [BE] rozkład jazdy

tin opener [BE] otwieracz do puszek

tire (car) opona

tired zmęczony

tissue chusteczka

to do

tobacco tytoń

tobacconist sklep tytoniowy

today dzisiaj

toe palec u nogi

toilet [BE] toaleta

toilet paper papier toaletowy

tomorrow jutro

tongue język

tonight dziś wieczorem

too (extreme) za

tooth ząb

toothache ból zęba

toothbrush szczoteczka do zębów

toothpaste pasta do zębów

top (head) góra

torn naderwany

tour wycieczka

tour guide przewodnik wycieczki

tour operator organizator wycieczki

tourist turysta

tourist office biuro informacji turystycznej

tow truck pomoc drogowa

towel ręcznik

tower wieża

town miasto

town center centrum

town hall ratusz

toy zabawka

track tor

traditional tradycyjny

traffic ruch

traffic jam korek

traffic light światła

traffic violation wykroczenie drogowe

trailer przyczepa

train pociąg

train station dworzec kolejowy

trained wykwalifikowany

tram tramwaj

transit (travel) przejazd

translate tłumaczyć

translation tłumaczenie

translator tłumacz

trash (garbage) śmieci

trash can śmietnik

travel n podróż; v podróżować

travel agency biuro podróży

travelers check czek podróżny

travelers cheque [BE] czek podróżny

tray taca

tree drzewo
trim *v* podstrzyc
trip wycieczka
trolley wózek
trousers spodnie
truck ciężarówka
true prawdziwy
try próbować
try on (clothes) przymierzyć
T-shirt t-shirt
tumor nowotwór
tunnel tunel
turn skręcić
turn down zmniejszyć
turn off wyłączyć
turn on włączyć
turn up (volume, heat)
  zwiększyć
TV telewizor
tweezers pinceta
twice dwa razy
twin bed łóżko podwójne
twist *v* (hurt) skręcić
type (sort) rodzaj
typical typowy
tyre [BE] opona

# U

U.K. Wielka Brytania
U.S. Stany Zjednoczone
ugly brzydki

ulcer wrzód
umbrella parasol
uncle wuj
uncomfortable niewygodny
unconscious nieprzytomny
under pod
understand rozumieć
underwear bielizna
undress rozbierać (się)
uneven (ground) nierówny
unfortunately niestety
uniform mundur
unit (phone card) impuls
university uniwersytet
unleaded (gas) bezołowiowa
unlimited mileage bez limitu
  kilometrów
unlock otworzyć
unpleasant niemiły
unscrew odkręcić
urgent pilny

# V

vacation wakacje
vacuum cleaner odkurzacz
vegetarian *adj* wegetariański;
  *n* wegetarianin
visa wiza

## W

**wait** czekać
**wallet** portfel
**water** woda
**week** tydzień
**where** gdzie
**white** biały
**window** okno
**window seat** siedzenie przy
 oknie
**wine list** lista win
**wireless** bezprzewodowy
**work** *v* **(function)** działać;
 **(job)** pracować

## X

X-ray rentgen

# Polish–English Dictionary

## A

**adres domowy** home address
**adres e-mail** e-mail address
**adwokat** lawyer
**agencja biletowa** ticket agency
**aktualny** up-to-date
**alarm przeciwpożarowy** fire alarm
**aleja** boulevard
**ambasada** embassy
**angielski** English
**Anglia** England
**antyki** antiques store
**aparat fotograficzny** camera
**apteka** pharmacy
**artykuły bezcłowe** duty-free goods
**aseptyczny** antiseptic
**astma** asthma
**atrakcja turystyczna** tourist attraction
**autokar** long-distance bus [coach BE]
**autostrada** highway [motorway BE]

## B

**bagaż** baggage
**bagaż podręczny** carry-on [hand luggage BE]
**bagno** marsh
**balkon** balcony (theater)
**balsam po opalaniu** after-sun lotion
**bankomat** ATM
**basen dla dzieci** children's pool
**basen kryty** indoor swimming pool
**basen odkryty** outdoor swimming pool
**benzyna** gas [petrol BE]
**bez cukru** sugar-free
**bez tłuszczu** fat-free
**bezglutenowy** gluten-free
**bezołowiowy** unleaded (gasoline)
**bezprzewodowy** wireless (internet)
**bezzwrotny** non-returnable
**biblioteka** library
**biegać** v run
**biegówki** cross-coutry skis
**bielizna** underwear
**bilet** ticket
**bilet elektroniczny** e-ticket
**bilet grupowy** group ticket
**bilet okresowy** season ticket
**bilet parkingowy** parking ticket

**biuro** office
**biuro obsługi klienta** customer service
**biuro podróży** travel agency
**biuro rzeczy znalezionych** lost-and-found [lost-property office BE]
**biuro turystyczne** tourist office
**biznes** business
**biżuteria** jewelry
**błąd** mistake
**blokada** lock (on a bike)
**błyszczyk** lipgloss
**ból** pain
**budka autobusowa** bus shelter
**bungalow** bungalow
**but** shoe
**butelka** bottle

## C

**cena** price
**centrum biznesu** business district
**centrum handlowe** shopping mall [centre BE]
**centrum miasta** downtown area [town centre BE]
**centrum odnowy biologicznej** spa
**centrum ogrodnicze** garden center

**chemiczna toaleta** chemical toilet
**chodnik** sidewalk [pavement BE]
**ciepły** warm (water)
**ciężarówka** truck
**ciężki** heavy (luggage)
**cło** duty (customs)
**cmentarz** cemetery
**cukiernia** pastry shop
**czasopismo** magazine
**czek** check [cheque BE]
**czek podróżny** travelers check [cheque BE]
**czekać** wait

## D

**dabingowany** dubbed
**dania dnia** menu of the day
**darowizna** donation
**data urodzenia** date of birth
**data ważności** expiration [expiry BE] date
**dawkowanie** dosage
**deklaracja celna** customs declaration
**delikatesy** delicatessen
**deska do windsurfingu** windsurfing board
**deska surfingowa** surfboard
**dieta** diet
**długopis** pen

**do** until
**do wynajęcia** for rent [hire BE]
**do żucia** chewable (tablets)
**dokładna reszta** exact change
**dom mieszkalny** apartment
  building
**dom towarowy** department store
**domowej roboty** homemade
**dostawa** delivery
**dostęp** access
**dowód tożsamości**
  identification
**dozorca** caretaker
**drewno** wood
**droga** road
**drzewo** tree
**drzwi automatyczne** automatic
  doors
**drzwi przeciwpożarowe** fire
  door
**dworzec autobusowy** bus
  station
**dworzec kolejowy** train station
**dzbanek** pot (for tea)
**działać** v work
**działanie uboczne** side effect
**dziecko** child
**dzień** day
**dzień powszedni** weekday
**dzisiaj** today

## E

**e-mail** e-mail
**emeryt** senior citizen
**epilepsja** epilepsy
**epileptyk** epileptic

## F

**fabryka** factory
**fajerwerk** firework
**faks** fax
**festyn** fair
**filharmonia** concert hall
**filiżanka** cup
**folia aluminiowa** aluminum
  [kitchen BE] foil
**formularz** form
**fotelik dziecięcy** car seat
**fryzjer** hairdresser
**funt** pound (sterling)

## G

**gabinet dentystyczny** dental
  office [surgery BE]
**gabinet lekarski** doctor's office
  [surgery BE]
**galeria** gallery
**garnek** pot (for cooking)
**gaśnica** fire extinguisher
**gdzie** where

**giełda** stock exchange
**głęboko** deep
**godzina** hour
**godziny urzędowania** business hours
**godziny wizyt** visiting hours
**góra** mountain
**gorączka** temperature
**gość** guest
**gospodarstwo** farm
**gotować** v boil
**gotówka** cash

## H

**hala targowa** indoor market
**hamulec bezpieczeństwa** emergency brake
**hasło** password

## I

**ile** how many, how much
**imię** name
**informacja** information desk
**informacja dla klientów** customer information
**informacja o lotach** flight information
**informacja o sklepie** store directory [guide BE]
**instruktor** instructor

**internet** internet
**izba przyjęć** emergency ward

## J

**jadalnia** dining room
**jakość** quality
**jaskinia** cave
**jasny** light (color)
**jeden** one
**jedwab** silk
**jedzenie na wynos** to go [takeaway BE] (food)
**jesień** fall [autumn BE]
**jeść** eat
**jezioro** lake
**jeździectwo** horseback riding
**język** tongue (part of body); language
**język obcy** foreign language
**jubiler** jeweler
**jutro** tomorrow

## K

**kafejka internetowa** internet cafe
**kamizelka ratunkowa** life jacket
**kantor** currency exchange office
**kapliczka** shrine
**kapsułka** capsule (medication)
**karetka** ambulance

**karta** key card (hotel)
**karta do telefonu** phone card
**karta kredytowa** credit card
**karta pokładowa** boarding pass (airport)
**karta rabatowa** discount card
**karta win** wine list
**kasa biletowa** ticket office
**kasa ekspresowa** express checkout
**kasjer** cashier
**kask** crash helmet
**katedra** cathedral
**kaucja** deposit
**kawałek** piece
**klieliszek** glass (alcoholic)
**kierownik** manager
**kierunek** direction (map)
**kilometr** kilometer
**kiosk z gazetami** newsstand
**klasa biznes** business class
**klasa turystyczna** economy class
**klif** cliff
**klimatyzacja** air conditioning
**klimatyzator** air conditioner
**klinika** clinic
**kolejka linowa** cable car
**koło ratunkowe** life preserver [belt BE]
**komiks** comic book
**komisariat** police station

**kompresor** air pump (gas station)
**komputer** computer
**koncert** concert
**konkurs** contest
**kontaktować** v contact
**kontrola celna** customs control
**kontroler biletów** ticket inspector
**korek** traffic jam
**kościół** church
**kosmetyki** cosmetics
**koszerny** kosher
**kosztować** v cost
**koszyk** shopping basket
**kradzież** theft
**krajowy** domestic (flight)
**kran** faucet [tap BE]
**krem nawilżający** moisturizer
**krem z blokadą UV** sunscreen
**kropla** drop (medication)
**krwotok** bleeding
**książka telefoniczna** directory
**księgarnia** bookstore
**kucharz** cook, chef
**kuchenka mikrofalowa** microwave
**kuchnia** kitchen
**kurs wymiany** exchange rate
**kuszetka** berth (train)
**kwiaciarnia** florist
**kwiat** flower
**kwota** amount (money)

## L

**lądować** arrive (plane)
**las** forest
**latarnia morska** lighthouse
**lato** summer
**lecieć** v fly
**lekarz** doctor
**lekki** light (weight)
**leżak** deck chair
**linia (lotnicza)** airline
**list polecony** registered letter
**list priorytetowy** express mail
**lista drinków** drink menu
**lokalny** local
**lot** flight
**loteria** lottery
**lotnisko** airport
**lotnisko krajowe** domestic airport
**lotnisko międzynarodowe** international airport
**lubić** v like

## Ł

**łazienka** bathroom
**łopatka** spatula
**łódź ratunkowa** life boat
**łóżeczko dziecięce** crib [child's cot BE]
**łóżko** bed

**łyżka do odmierzania** measuring spoon
**łyżwiarstwo** ice skating
**łyżwy** ice skates

## M

**mały** small (size)
**mapa drogowa** road map
**matka** mother
**mdłości** nausea
**mdły** bland
**meble** furniture
**mgła** fog
**miarka kuchenna** measuring cup
**miejsce** seat (bus, train, plane)
**miejsce na piknik** picnic area
**miejsce przy oknie** window seat
**miejsce przy przejściu** aisle seat
**miejsce urodzenia** place of birth
**miejsce zbiórki** meeting place [point BE]
**miejscówka** reservation (train)
**międzynarodowy** international
**mikrofalówka** mircowave
**miska** bowl
**mleczarnia** dairy
**młodzież** youth
**młyn** windmill
**mniej** less

**moczary** swamp
**mokry** wet
**mop** mop
**morze** sea
**motor** motorcycle
**motorower** moped
**mówić** speak
**msza** mass
**muzeum** museum
**mydło** soap

## N

**na dole** downstairs
**na górze** upstairs
**na zewnątrz** outside
**nadbagaż** excess baggage
**namiot** tent
**napad** mugging
**napisać** write
**napiwek** tip
**naprawa** n repair (car)
**naprawić** v fix (a car)
**narty wodne** water skis
**następny** next
**nawierzchnia** road surface
**nawilżacz** moisturizer
**nazwisko** last name
**nazwisko panieńskie** maiden name
**niedaleko** close
**niepalący** non-smoking

**nierówny** uneven (surface)
**noc** night
**nocleg** accommodation
**nocny dyżur** night duty
**nocny portier** night porter
**normalny** normal
**nowy** new
**numer kierunkowy** country code
**numer lotu** flight number
**numer miejsca** seat number
**numer pierwszej pomocy** emergency number

## O

**objazd** detour [diversion BE]
**obóz** n camp
**obozować** v camp
**od** from (time)
**odbiór bagażu** baggage claim
**oddział** department
**odebrać** receive
**odkurzacz** vacuum cleaner
**odlatywać** leave
**odprawa** check-in (airport)
**odprawa bagażu** baggage check
**odwołany** cancelled
**odzież damska** ladieswear
**odzież męska** menswear
**ognisko** campfire
**ograniczenie prędkości** speed limit

**ogród** garden
**okazja** bargain
**okno** window
**okres** period (of time); menstruation
**okulary** glasses (optical)
**okulary przeciwsłoneczne** sunglasses
**opera** opera
**opis** description
**opłata bankowa** bank charge
**opłata obowiązkowa** minimum charge
**opłata za dzień** day charge
**opłata za usługę** service charge
**opłata za wstęp** admission charge
**opóźniony** delayed
**optyk** optician
**ostry** spicy
**ostrzeżenie** warning
**otwarty** open (shop)

## P

**paczka** package [parcel BE]
**paczka ekspresowa** express mail
**pakować** pack
**palacz** smoker
**paliwo** fuel
**pan** sir

**pani** madam
**panie** ladies (toilet)
**panna** miss
**panowie** gentlemen (toilet)
**papierowy ręcznik** paper towel
**paragon** receipt
**parasol** umbrella [sunshade BE]
**park narodowy** national park
**park publiczny** public park
**parking** parking lot [car park BE]
**parking podziemny** underground garage
**parking wielopoziomowy** parking garage
**parkometr** parking meter
**parkować** v park
**parter** first floor [ground floor BE]; orchestra [stalls BE] (theater)
**pas** lane
**pasażer** passenger
**pasmo górskie** mountain range
**pawilon** pavilion
**pchać** push
**pchli targ** flea market
**peron** platform
**piasek** sand
**pić** v drink
**piekarnia** bakery
**pielęgniarka** nurse
**pieniądze** money
**pierwsza klasa** first class

**pierwsza pomoc** emergency services; first aid
**pierwsze piętro** second floor [first floor BE]
**pieszy** pedestrian
**piętro** floor (level in building)
**pigułka** pill
**pikantny** spicy
**pilny** urgent
**pismo** periodical
**piwnica** basement
**plac** square
**plasterek** slice
**plaża dla nudystów** nudist beach
**plecak** backpack
**plomba** filling (dental)
**płacić** v pay
**płeć** sex (gender)
**płyta kompaktowa** CD
**płytki** adj shallow
**pływać** v swim
**po południu** p.m.
**pociąg Intercity** Intercity train
**pociąg lokalny** local train
**początkujący** beginner
**poczekalnia** waiting room
**poczta** post office
**podarunek** gift
**podjazd** ramp
**podłoga** floor
**podobać się** like

**podpaska** sanitary napkin [pad BE]
**podróż powrotna** round-trip [return trip BE] (ticket)
**poduszka** pillow
**pokład** deck (ship)
**pokoje do wynajęcia** rooms for rent [to let BE]
**pokój** room (hotel)
**pole** field
**pole bitwy** battle site
**pole namiotowe** camping
**polecać** recommend
**policja** police
**policja drogowa** traffic police
**polisa ubezpieczeniowa** insurance card [certificate BE]
**Polska** Poland
**południe** noon (time); south (direction)
**pomiędzy** between
**pomnik** monument
**pomoc drogowa** breakdown services
**poranek** morning
**port** port
**portfel** wallet
**postój taksówek** taxi stand [rank BE]
**pościel** sheets
**potrzebny** required
**potwierdzenie** confirmation

potwierdzić confirm
powiedzieć v say
powtórzyć repeat
poznać meet
pożar fire
północ midnight (time); north (direction)
półwysep peninsula
pracować v work
prać oddzielnie wash separately
prać ręcznie hand wash only
pralnia laundry
pralnia chemiczna dry-cleaner
prasować v iron
prawnik lawyer
prawo jazdy driver's license
priorytet express mail
progi rzeczne rapids
prognoza pogody weather forecast
prom ferry
proszę please
prowizja commission
prysznic shower
prywatny private
przebieralnia fitting room
przecena sale
przechowalnia bagażu baggage office
przeciek leak
przed before
przed południem a.m.

przedstawić introduce (someone)
przedział compartment
przejście path; aisle (plane)
przejście dla pieszych pedestrian crossing
przejście podziemne underpass
przejściówka adapter
przekaz pieniężny money order
przekąska appetizer [starter BE]
przepaść precipice
przepychacz plunger
przesiadać się change [transfer BE] (bus)
przesyłka package
przeszkadzać disturb
przetłumaczyć translate
przewodnik guide (person); guidebook
przyczepa trailer
przyloty arrivals (airport)
przymierzalnia fitting room
przystanek autobusowy bus stop
przystanek na żądanie on-demand stop
ptak bird
punkt widzenia view point
pusty vacant

## R

**rabat** discount
**ratownik** lifeguard
**ratusz** town hall
**recepta** prescription
**recycling** recycling
**ręcznie robione** handmade
**ręcznik** towel
**rejs** cruise
**reklama** advertisment
**rentgen** X-ray
**restauracja** restaurant
**reszta** *n* change (money)
**rezerwacja** reservation
**rezerwuar** reservoir
**robak** bug
**rogatka** toll booth
**rondel** saucepan
**rondo** roundabout
**room service** room service
**rower** bicycle
**rozkład jazdy** schedule
  [timetable BE]
**rozkładane łóżko** cot
**rozmowa na koszt rozmówcy**
  collect call [reverse-charge
  call BE]
**rozumieć** understand
**rura** pipe (water)
**rząd** row (of seats, people)
**rzeka** river

**rzeźnik** butcher

## S

**sąd** courthouse
**sala** hall (large public room)
**sala konferencyjna** conference
  room
**sala zebrań** convention hall
**salon gier** arcade
**sam** alone
**samolot** plane
**sauna** sauna
**schowek na bagaż** luggage
  locker
**schronisko młodzieżowe** youth
  hostel
**ściana** wall
**ścieżka** path
**sekretarka** secretary
**serwetka** napkin
**sieć** network (of computers);
  chain (of stores)
**siedzenie** seat
**siedzenie przy korytarzu** aisle
  seat
**siedzenie przy oknie** window
  seat
**silnik** engine
**siłownia** gym
**skala** scale
**skała** rock

skasować validate (ticket)

skipass ski pass

sklep store

sklep bezcłowy duty-free store

sklep mięsny butcher shop

sklep muzyczny music store

sklep osiedlowy convenience store

sklep papierniczy stationery store

sklep z narzędziami hardware store

sklep z zabawkami toy store

sklep ze zdrową żywnością health food store

skóra leather; skin

skręcić v turn

skrytka bagażowa luggage locker

skrzynka pocztowa mailbox [postbox BE]

skrzyżowanie intersection [junction BE]

skuter wodny jet-ski

ślepy zaułek dead end

śliski slippery

słony salty

śmieci trash [rubbish BE]

śniadanie breakfast

spa spa

śpiący policjant speed bump

spotkanie appointment (business); meeting (friends)

spóźniony late

stacja benzynowa gas [petrol BE] station

stacja kolejowa train [railway BE] station

stadion stadium

stal steel

stanowisko odprawy check-in desk (airport)

Stany Zjednoczone United States

startować take off, depart

statek ship

staw pond

steward flight attendant

strój codzienny casual clothing

stolik table

straż pożarna fire station

strażak firefighter

strój suit, clothing

strój wieczorowy evening dress

strój wizytowy formal dress

strumień stream

studiować v study

suszarka do włosów hairdryer

światła traffic light

światło light

święto państwowe national holiday

świeży fresh

szewc shoe repair [cobbler BE]

szklanka glass (non-alcoholic)

szkoła school

**szlak** trail
**szpital** hospital

## T

**tabletka** tablet
**taksówka** taxi
**talerz** plate
**targ** market
**telefon** phone
**telefon komórkowy** cell phone [mobile phone BE]
**telefon publiczny** pay phone
**telefonistka** operator (phone)
**terminal** terminal
**toaleta** restroom [toilet BE]
**tor** track [platform BE]
**tor wyścigowy** racetrack [race course BE]
**torebka** purse [handbag BE]
**trampolina** diving board
**trasa** route
**trasa autobusowa** bus route
**trawa** grass
**turystyka piesza** hiking
**tutaj** here
**tydzień** week
**tylko** only

## U

**ubezpieczenie** insurance

**ugryzienie** bite
**ulepszony** improved
**ulica** street
**ulica jednokierunkowa** one-way street
**uniwersytet** university
**unowocześniony** modernized
**usługa** service
**uwaga** attention

## W

**w budowie** under construction
**w jedną stronę** one-way (trip)
**wagon** car (train)
**wagon restauracyjny** dining car (train)
**wakacyjny rozkład jazdy** holiday schedule [timetable BE]
**walizka** suitcase
**waluta obca** foreign currency
**warsztat samochodowy** car mechanic [repair garage BE]
**wąwóz** gorge
**wejście** entrance; gate (at the airport)
**wełna** wool
**wentylator** fan (electric)
**wesołe miasteczko** amusement park
**wewnętrzny** extension (phone)
**wiadomość** news

**widelec** fork
**więcej** more
**Wielka Brytania** Great Britain
**wieczór** evening
**wiedza** knowledge
**winda** elevator [lift BE]
**windsurfing** windsurfing
**wiosna** spring
**włączyć** turn on
**własność prywatna** private property
**woda** water
**wolno** slowly
**wolny** free (place)
**wolny pokój** vacancy (accommodation)
**wózek bagażowy** luggage cart [trolley BE]
**wpłata** deposit
**wschód** east
**wskazówka** instruction
**wspinaczka** rock climbing
**wstęp wolny** admission free
**wstęp wzbroniony** no access
**wybrzeże** coast
**wydarzenie** event
**wydrukować** v print
**wyjście** exit; gate (at the airport)
**wyjście bezpieczeństwa** emergency exit
**wyjście przeciwpożarowe** fire exit
**wyjście wzbronione** no exit

**wykręcić** dial
**wyłączyć** turn off
**wylogować się** log off
**wymiana** exchange
**wymiana walut** currency exchange
**wynajem samochodów** car rental [hire BE]
**wypadek** accident
**wypłata** cash withdrawal
**wyprzedaż** clearance
**wyprzedzać** v pass (car)
**wysiąść** get off (bus, train)
**wysłać** send
**wysokie krzesełko** highchair
**występ** show (in front of audience)
**wzbroniony** forbidden
**wzgórze** hill

## Z

**z napisami** subtitled
**zaawansowany** advanced
**zabawka** toy
**zachód** west
**zaczekać** wait
**zadzwonić** call (phone)
**zagraniczny** international (flight); foreign (product)
**zajazd** guest house
**zakaźny** contagious, infectious

**zakupy** shopping
**zalogować się** log on
**zamawiać** *v* order
**zamek** castle (building); lock (door)
**zamknięty** closed (store)
**zamówienie** *n* order
**zamrożony** frozen
**zamykać** *v* lock
**zapakować** wrap
**zapakować na prezent** giftwrap
**zaparcie** constipation
**zapinać** fasten (seat belt)
**zapłacony** paid
**zapominać** forget
**zarezerwować** reserve (tickets)
**zatkany** blocked
**zatłoczony** crowded
**zatoka** bay
**zatrzymać się** stay (at a hotel); stop (not move)
**zebra** pedestrian crossing
**zepsuty** broken
**zgwałcić** *v* rape
**zima** winter
**zimno** *adv* cold
**zimny** *adj* cold
**złoto** gold
**zły** bad
**znaczek** stamp
**znaczek pocztowy** postage stamp

**znaczyć** mean (meaning)
**znak drogowy** road sign
**zniżka** discount
**zwolnić** slow down
**zwrot pieniędzy** refund
**zwrotny** returnable

## Ż

**żelazko** *n* iron